READING, PUBLISHING AND THE FORMATION OF LITERARY TASTE IN ENGLAND, 1880–1914

Reading, Publishing and the Formation of Literary Taste in England, 1880–1914

MARY HAMMOND
Open University, UK

Routledge
Taylor & Francis Group

LONDON AND NEW YORK

First published 2006 by Ashgate Publishing

2 Park Square, Milton Park, Abingdon, Oxfordshire OX14 4RN
52 Vanderbilt Avenue, New York, NY 10017

Routledge is an imprint of the Taylor & Francis Group, an informa business

First issued in paperback 2019

British Library Cataloguing in Publication Data
Hammond, Mary
  Reading, publishing and the formation of literary taste in England, 1880–1914
  1. Books and reading – Great Britain – History – 19th century 2. Books and reading – Great Britain – History – 20th century 3. Publishers and publishing – Great Britain – History – 19th century 4. Publishers and publishing – Great Britain – History – 20th century 5. English literature – 19th century – History and criticism 6. English literature – 20th century – History and criticism 7. Popular culture – Great Britain – History – 19th century 8. Popular culture – Great Britain – History – 20th century 9. Great Britain – Intellectual life – 19th century 10. Great Britain – Intellectual life – 20th century
  I. Title
  028'.0941'09034

Library of Congress Cataloging-in-Publication Data
Reading, publishing, and the formation of literary taste in England, 1880–1914 / Mary Hammond.
        p. cm.—(The nineteenth century series)
    Includes bibliographical references and index.
    ISBN 0-7546-5668-3 (alk. paper)
  1. Books and reading—England—History—19th century. 2. Books and reading—England—History—20th century. 3. Publishers and publishing—England—History—19th century. 4. Publishers and publishing—England—History—20th century. 5. Popular culture—England. 6. Authors and readers—England. 7. England—Intellectual life—19th century. 8. England—Intellectual life—20th century. 9. English literature—19th century—History and criticism. 10. English literature—20th century—History and criticism. I. Title. II. Series: Nineteenth century (Aldershot, England)

    Z1003.5.G7H36 2006
    028'.90942—dc22

                                                                    2005037690

ISBN 978-0-7546-5668-5 (hbk)
ISBN 978-0-367-88792-6 (pbk)

Contents

List of Figures

General Editors' Preface

The aim of the series is to reflect, develop and extend the great burgeoning of interest in the nineteenth century that has been an inevitable feature of recent years, as that former epoch has come more sharply into focus as a locus for our understanding not only of the past but of the contours of our modernity. It centres primarily upon major authors and subjects within Romantic and Victorian literature. It also includes studies of other British writers and issues, where these are matters of current debate: for example, biography and autobiography, journalism, periodical literature, travel writing, book production, gender, non-canonical writing. We are dedicated principally to publishing original monographs and symposia; our policy is to embrace a broad scope in chronology, approach and range of concern, and both to recognize and cut innovatively across such parameters as those suggested by the designations 'Romantic' and 'Victorian'. We welcome new ideas and theories, while valuing traditional scholarship. It is hoped that the world which predates yet so forcibly predicts and engages our own will emerge in parts, in the wider sweep, and in the lively streams of disputation and change that are so manifest an aspect of its intellectual, artistic and social landscape.

Vincent Newey
Joanne Shattock
University of Leicester

Acknowledgements

This project would never have been possible without the encouragement and support of a number of key people. David Glover was unstintingly generous with his time and expertise, and Cora Kaplan, Peter Middleton, Lucy Hartley, Bryan Cheyette, John Spiers and John Stokes all provided invaluable advice at crucial moments. My colleagues at the Open University have been unfailingly enthusiastic and supportive, and fellow members of SHARP provided feedback when I most needed it. Thanks to all those whose comments and advice helped to keep me going, and to make this book far better than it could ever otherwise have been.

I am very grateful to the many librarians and archivists whose patience and professionalism made researching this book a pleasure. In particular, I would like to thank Martin Maw, archivist at Oxford University Press; Roger Sims at the Hall Caine archive in the Manx Museum; the staff of the British Library and the BL Colindale; the librarians at Leeds, Southampton, Winchester and York; the archivists at Tower Hamlets Local History Library and Archive; staff at the W.H. Smith and Sons Archive, the Library Association, the National Railway Museum and the London Metropolitan Museum. I also gratefully acknowledge the support of the Arts and Humanities Research Board, who funded the PhD research on which this book is based, and the British Academy, who awarded me a series of travel grants which enabled me to present key parts of this work at international conferences. My gratitude also goes to the anonymous reader whose suggestions led to important improvements, and to all the staff at Ashgate Publishing for their cheerful professionalism.

Thanks to all those friends and family members who helped me along the way with research, memories, and general moral support, and in particular to Katherine Moy for friendship, fun, and putting me up in London. And finally thanks to my family, Mike, Alex and Sarah, for everything. This book is for you.

Copyright Permissions

and the Corporation of London, London Metropolitan Archives for permission to quote material from their collections in Chapter 2. Copyright material in Chapter 3 is printed by permission of the Secretary to the Delegates of Oxford University Press.

Cover illustration by permission of the British Library.

Figure 2.1: every reasonable attempt has been made to trace the copyright owner of this image, and it is hereby reproduced with full acknowledgement to that anonymous person or persons.

Figures 2.2. and 3.1: reproduced by permission of the John Spiers Collection of Victorian and Edwardian Fiction.

Figures 3.2 and 3.3: reproduced by permission of Oxford University Press and the John Spiers Collection of Victorian and Edwardian Fiction.

Introduction
Modernity and the Reading Public

Two milestones in English publishing history frame the period under consideration in this book.[1] The first took place on 17 May 1881 when, after 11 years of painstaking translation work by a committee made up of experts from the Universities of Oxford and Cambridge, a new Revised Version of the New Testament was released. The interest that it generated was unprecedented. In the words of the contemporary periodical *Leisure Hour*:

> the excitement in the forenoon in Paternoster Row was intense, and the public were literally scrambling for copies. The shilling size was being sold at the Underground bookstalls as rapidly at one-and-sixpence as by the discount booksellers at ninepence … In every omnibus, in every railway compartment, and even while walking along the public thoroughfare, people were to be seen reading the New Testament. It was the universal subject of conversation throughout the land. On the evening of that memorable day the newspapers were full of it. The whole nation seemed to be reading or discussing the revision.[2]

This somewhat hyperbolic account is at least partially supportable by the facts: one million copies were sold from OUP's warehouse in London inside 24 hours,[3] and contemporary reports expected that number to double.[4] Nor was this interest confined to the UK or within the bounds of honourable conduct. Henry Frowde, who had been in overall charge of OUP Bibles and Prayer books since 1874 and largely spearheaded the distribution of the Revised Version, had chartered vessels several months previously to take copies to America and the Colonies. But on board the steamer bound for the States were representatives of the New York firm of Appleton and Co. who had the

---

[1] This study concentrates on book-production, selling, distribution and reading practices in England rather than in Great Britain for the simple reason that legislation (for example on public libraries) was quite different in each corner of the British Isles. Each tended to be supplied by separate companies and experience slightly different social and cultural conditions. Throughout this book, then, where I refer to 'England' or 'English' I am referring to a specific geographical area and its inhabitants and practices rather than adopting the nineteenth-century metonymic usage of the words.

[2] Peter Sutcliffe, *Oxford University Press: An Informal History* (Oxford, 1978), p. 51.

[3] Sutcliffe, p. 51.

[4] *Publishers' Circular*, 1 June 1881, p. 425.

entire book set up and stereotyped during the crossing, and pirated copies on sale in the streets of New York within two days of docking. The spread didn't stop there: on 22 May the *Chicago Times* spent £10,000 having the Gospels, Acts and Epistles to the Romans cabled from New York for unauthorised publication in its pages.[5]

The second publishing sensation occurred almost three decades later with the explosion of another book onto the literary scene. This one started more slowly, but within a few weeks of publication it had become a surprise best seller on both sides of the Atlantic, going through two editions a month at the height of its fame until, like its predecessor, it too: 'was to be seen everywhere; in railway compartment, hotel lounge, and under the arms of busy people hurrying along the streets'.[6] This book was not, however, another Bible. It was a popular novel, *The Rosary* by Florence Barclay: a morally blameless, Evangelical popular novel, but a popular novel nonetheless.[7] Between these two publishing events – so close in time and measure, so far apart in almost every other way – lies a rich landscape of changing literary taste shaped and fought over by governments, philanthropists, educators and clerics; by writers, publishers, agents and distributors, and, of course, by readers of both genders and all classes. This landscape is the subject matter of my book.

Popular success was not a new phenomenon in 1881 when the new Bible appeared (one need only think of Wilkie Collins or Dickens), but success on this kind of scale was unprecedented. It owed a lot to recent social reforms: it is significant that the New Revised Version was published at the start of the first decade in which the first generation of Forster's Board School literates might reasonably be expected to have come of age, established themselves in jobs, and/or settled into a reading habit. In 1881 more people than ever before were able to read, however imperfectly. And the Bible was an important port of call for most of them. Even this late in the century it was still one of the most important books on which many were likely to spend their hard-earned cash.[8] But the 1880s marked what has accurately been called the 'culminating phase of the Victorian Cult of the Bible'.[9] OUP's production of Bibles and Prayer books of all shapes and sizes was to remain a staple of their publishing success, but never again was one of them to engender so much excitement. The publication of the Revised Old Testament five years later, though a success in publishing terms, was a much less spectacular event.[10] In fact, by the time *The*

5   Nicolas Barker, *The Oxford University Press and the Spread of Learning: An Illustrated History 1478–1978* (Oxford, 1978), p. 51.

6   *The Life of Florence Barclay, by One of Her Daughters* (London and New York, 1921), p. 213.

7   Florence Barclay, *The Rosary* (London and New York, 1909).

8   In 'What the Working Classes Read', *Nineteenth Century*, July 1886, p. 116, Edward G. Salmon claims that the Bible is less popular than formerly, but still amongst the most common books to be found in the average home.

9   Barker, p. 51.

10   Sutcliffe, p. 52.

Rosary appeared in 1909, publishing and religiosity had both undergone a series of revolutions.[11]

One of the most important of these was a shift from public worship to private reflection. Even if only implicitly, the new translation held out the promise of answers to a populace increasingly disillusioned with institutionalised religion, and increasingly likely to ask more questions the more widely it read. The book's reviewers picked up on this possibility in a number of ways. G. Vance-Smith began his review in the *Nineteenth Century* by applauding the progressive motives of his fellow translators. They were, he felt, taking important steps to ensure that 'people will no longer look upon the English Bible, chapter headings and italics included, as if it had been dropped from heaven just as it is. ... Perhaps', he added, 'it will be more easy than it was to get a truth of modern science into the heads of ordinary religious people'.[12] But even as he embraced re-interpretation he signalled its dangers, taking issue with a number of the emendations which, he felt, encouraged a blurring of rightful meaning by 'indirectly and quite needlessly importing into the Christian books the conception of certain Pagan mythologies, as to hells of various kinds'.[13] Another reviewer, this time in the *Quarterly Review*, expressed still more clearly his anxieties about tampering with textual truth and historical consensus, suggesting that despite 'the purest intentions and the most laudable industry', the revisers had:

> constructed a Text demonstrably more remote from the Evangelic verity, than any which has yet seen the light ... To attempt, as they have done, to build the Text of the New Testament on a tissue of unproved assertions and the eccentricities of a single codex of bad character is about as hopeful a proceeding as would be the attempt to erect an Eddystone lighthouse on the Goodwin Sands.[14]

Profound insecurities of a particular late nineteenth-century flavour are emerging here. The spectre of revolution hovering over the democratisation of literature had always been invoked in debates around education reform, but by the second half of the nineteenth century the debates were beginning to take a slightly different shape.

---

[11] In his seminal overview of the period Peter Keating confirms that the decline in the production of periodicals 'of a decidedly religious character' from 37 per cent in 1875 to 21 per cent in 1903 demonstrates 'the growing secularisation of British literature'. Peter Keating, *The Haunted Study: A Social History of the English Novel 1875–1914* (London, 1989), p. 34. A useful discussion of the relationship between fictional forms and secularisation is Peter Brooks's, *The Melodramatic Imagination: Balzac, Henry James, Melodrama, and the Mode of Excess* (New Haven and London, 1976), particularly pp. 5–20 where he justifies his claim that 'melodrama becomes the principal mode for uncovering, demonstrating and making operative the essential moral universe in a post-sacred era'.

[12] G. Vance-Smith, 'A Reviser on the New Revision', *Nineteenth Century*, June 1881, p. 936.

[13] Vance-Smith, p. 934.

[14] 'The New Greek Text', *Quarterly Review*, No. 304, Vol. 152, October 1881, p. 368.

Many commentators were beginning to question anew the implications for a newly literate, class-based society of the increasing effectiveness of publishing as a capitalist mode of production, feeling that a free market without adequate controls might have a degenerative social and spiritual, if no longer a dangerously political, effect on the populace. These things were contentious enough when they encouraged the spread of a religious text that no one was certain was sanctifiable. (The Convocation of Canterbury did not accept the New Revised Version until 1899, and even afterwards it continued to be rejected by some churches.)[15] But the developments were viewed in an even dimmer light when they encouraged the spread of lighter kinds of reading whose social and psychological effects were still more unknowable. The criticisms levelled at the New Revised Version are insignificant when compared to the kinds of criticism aroused by a successful popular novel, and by other ephemeral publications.

The statistics were impossible to ignore: novel production rose from an average of 900 new adult and juvenile novels per year between 1875 and 1886 to 1,618 per year by 1914. Newspaper and periodical production experienced a similar growth: the Newspaper Directory lists a total of 1,609 newspapers published in the British Isles in 1875, and 2,504 in 1914. Weekly, monthly and quarterly magazines rose from 643 titles published in 1875 to 2,531 in 1903.[16] But the social effects of these changes in publishing and reading practices were publicly worried over and hotly debated throughout the period. From the eighteenth through the first half of the nineteenth century, when the novel as we now recognise it was in its infancy, the dangers were fairly easily downplayed by means of a critical orthodoxy which constructed fiction as 'bad' and poetry, history and religion as 'good'. James Fordyce's sermons of the 1760s addressed to Young Women set the tone: 'There seem to me to be very few in the style of the Novel, that you can read with safety, and yet fewer that you can read with advantage ... she who can bear to peruse them must in her soul be a prostitute, let her reputation in life be what it will'.[17] Catherine Morland, the heroine of Jane Austen's *Northanger Abbey* (drafted in the 1790s, published 1818) marks an improvement in the novel's fortunes as she receives her education in the right way to read. The novel, Austen declared in her famous preface to this work, is the medium through which 'the most thorough knowledge of human nature, the happiest delineation of its varieties, the liveliest effusions of wit and humour are conveyed to the world in the best chosen language'.[18] The novel's hero, Henry Tilney, also defends novels through his position as both worthy suitor and avid reader of fiction. But while *Northanger Abbey* is part of its creator's belief in the importance and seriousness of the novel as an art form, it does not wholly discredit the notion that reading novels can be an incitement to silliness.

---

[15]   Sutcliffe, p. 52.
[16]   Keating, pp. 32–3.
[17]   James Fordyce, *Sermons to Young Women* (London: 1863), pp. 148–50.
[18]   Jane Austen, Preface to *Northanger Abbey*, ed. by John Davies, with an introduction by Terry Castle (1818; Oxford, 1990) p. 22.

As the contested but inexorable rise of the novel turned into its undeniable dominance in the marketplace, however, the terms of the debate shifted to accommodate it. As Nicola Diane Thompson has shown, from the 1860s on the debate began to reflect increasingly clearly the patriarchal capitalist world in which it circulated, becoming one about 'good' novels (initially canonical, historical and usually male-authored) versus 'bad' novels (initially popular, contemporary and usually female-authored).[19] This development became more complicated as the century wore on; increasingly, the gendering of a particular novel by reviewers was less dependent on the sex of its author or its actual readers than on its popularity or its genre or its perceived literariness. For example, while Thomas Hardy and George Eliot were gendered male by contemporary reviews, Marie Corelli was negatively gendered female, and while Hall Caine may have started out with vigorous masculinity he ended up being consistently feminised. A book's formal properties were also often implicated in this: to an extent, realism implied masculinity, the romance femininity.

But many novels, both 'popular' and 'literary', were hybrids, and no one by the late nineteenth century was feminising the now canonised 'classic' romances of Sir Walter Scott. Thus, a complex set of conditions prevailed in the qualitative categorisation of novels, which meant it was sometimes difficult to know just by looking at a book (or even by reading it) whether it was 'popular' or 'literary', 'bad' or 'good'. As Lyn Pykett has pointed out, 'the gendered discourse on fiction was part of a broadly based nineteenth-century crisis of gender definition ... the unstable, shifting and multivalent nature of the gendered terms of this critical discourse was bound up with a desire to fix gender boundaries and categories at a time of profound anxiety about the nature and fixity of those categories'.[20] This meant a new emphasis on that most slippery of things, cultural 'know-how', a supplementing of the centuries-old policing of literature through religious censorship with a far subtler form of policing through the pages of the critical journals.

Florence Barclay's first novel serves to highlight the complexities of this war between art and the market as it existed by the first decade of the new century. Dubbed 'the Shakespeare of the Servants Hall' by her more literary contemporary John Galsworthy,[21] she claimed a new high ground that refused equally to apologise for the mere fact of popularity, or to recognise that literariness was the only benchmark for worth. This made her a prime target for the purists for years, one of the most famous of whom excused John Galsworthy's tolerance as 'the fascinated envy of the ever-intellectual novelist for the lower organism that exudes vital energy as richly

---

[19] Nicola Diane Thompson, *Reviewing Sex: Gender and the Reception of Victorian Novels* (London, 1996), p. 20.

[20] Lyn Pykett, *The Improper Feminine: the Woman's Sensation Novel and the New Woman Writing* (London and New York, 1992), p. 23.

[21] Q.D. Leavis, *Fiction and the Reading Public* (1932; London, 1965), pp. 62–3.

as a manure heap'.[22] Barclay had not just popularised God. She had been crowned Queen of the bestsellers, and for the serious artist and critic that meant she reigned over a rising tide of 'feminine' trash which daily threatened to engulf the 'masculine' province of Real Literature.

Many critics have suggested that the art/market dichotomy as it emerged in the 1890s was instrumental in the early twentieth century appearance of modernism, a form of aesthetic elitism apparently self-consciously designed on 1890s purist lines to separate itself from the mass market.[23] It seems reasonable, certainly, to view modernism's reactionary politics in the light of preceding ideologies that explicitly linked artistic and social hegemony. But, as others have argued, this dichotomy is something of a false one since many of its participants not only played important roles in each others' lives and works, they also frequently thought of themselves as part of the same literary tradition. It was, as Raymond Williams points out, largely later critics who consigned both realism and popular novels to the 'wide margin of the century' in favour of a more exclusive canon.[24]

At any rate, it is something of a critical commonplace now that modernism, like realism, or the romance, or indeed most literary movements, had very ill-defined and somewhat permeable boundaries, and that consequently the art/market opposition was less a divide than a negotiating table. The examples of these negotiations in practice are legion: Joyce, Woolf and Conrad submitted work to (and had it rejected by) *Titbits*, the popular lowbrow periodical that helped to launch the career of Arnold Bennett. *Dubliners* was seriously considered by the mass-market publisher Mills and Boon. Joyce was fascinated by Marie Corelli, and at one time ran a cinema. Henry James was one of only a handful of people invited to Rudyard Kipling's wedding. Also present was the publisher William Heinemann, whose innovative company published novels by the financially risky Joseph Conrad at one end of the period, and the equally financially risky D.H. Lawrence at the other, with the hugely successful but now largely forgotten best seller Hall Caine somewhere in the middle. James wrote an important critical essay, 'The Rise of the Novel', for the 'Library of Famous Literature', a ragbag of condensed classics published by the *Standard* and aimed at the mass market. Conrad, Bennett and Galsworthy were regular, friendly correspondents for years.

[22]   Leavis, pp. 62–3.
[23]   See, for example, Andreas Huyssen, *After the Great Divide: Modernism, Mass Culture, Postmodernism* (Bloomington, 1986); John Carey, *The Intellectuals and the Masses: Pride and Prejudice among the Literary Intelligentsia, 1880–1939* (New York, 1992); David Trotter, *The English Novel in History 1895–1920* (London, 1993); and R.B. Kershner's essays on Marie Corelli and Modernism. More recently Jonathan Rose has added further evidence to the idea that modernism depended on the mass market against which it defined itself in *The Intellectual Life of the British Working Classes* (New Haven and London, 2001).
[24]   Raymond Williams, 'When Was Modernism?' in *The Politics of Modernism*, ed. Tony Pinkney (London, 1989), p. 35.

These historical relationships, and the recent critical work that has unearthed and analysed their complexity, underpin the arguments in this book. But while acknowledging the closeness and interdependence of both 'literary' and 'popular' authors in terms of their lives and careers, and while equally acknowledging the slipperiness of generic definitions, I want to investigate anew the notion of an art/ market divide. I want to do this, not because I want to justify or denigrate either 'modernism' or 'popular fiction', or to redefine their boundaries, or to reinstate an obsolete critical dichotomy. My premise is simply that I don't think we yet know all we can about how the divide functioned, and how it may function still, in the formation of literary taste and its relationship with social identities. In the nineteenth century, an age populated by the socially mobile as well as by those who championed, feared or despised them, and inclined equally to self-culture and self-doubt, what was a 'good book'? Who decided? Who understood and responded to the qualitative distinctions that were everywhere applied in this period but seldom agreed upon, and how did they respond? Thompson's work on the gendering of criticism and Pykett's acknowledgement that this was an age of gender anxiety in general account for some of the complexity, but by no means all.

In some ways my choice of period seems rather an arbitrary one. The critical division between 'good' and 'bad' continued long after the First World War and in one version or another continues still (encompassing along the way debates about the theatre, film, videos and computer games). There were successful popular novels long before 1880, and successful religious texts that were not novels long afterwards. Nor was the art/market divide an Immaculate Conception of the 1890s. John Ruskin is often cited as being among the first to recognise that some sort of divide was emerging between 'popular' and 'literary' forms, his copious writings about art's place in society seen as sounding prescient warnings about dumbing down. Certainly, as early as 1865 he was writing that 'books are divisible into two classes, the books of the hour, and the books of all time'. He also recognised that readerships were changing, and felt this was for the worse: 'it is simply and sternly impossible for the English public, at this moment, to understand any thoughtful writing – so incapable of thought has it become in its insanity of avarice'.[25] But recent scholarship has convincingly demonstrated that a more likely starting point occurred earlier in the nineteenth century, at least with the Reform Acts of the 1830s through which middle-class Britain demanded parliamentary representation and made concrete its increasing cultural domination. Implicit in those political demands was an argument for the recognition of the rights of all trades and craftsmen, including writers and artists, to be granted higher social status. According to theatre historian Jacky Bratton, it was in this period that the idea of the artist as autonomous, pure, spiritual, and removed from the base considerations of Grub Street first emerged.[26]

25 John Ruskin, 'Sesame and Lilies', *Selected Writings*, ed. Philip Davis (1865; London, 1995), p. 363.
26 Jacky Bratton, *New Readings in Theatre History* (Cambridge, 2003), p. 77.

But the period 1880–1914 covered by this book does represent a kind of zenith in the impact of these debates, actual and ideological. The shape of the material book changed as the three-decker was allowed to die. The circulating libraries released their long-standing stranglehold on the price and circulation of new fiction. Authors and publishers organised themselves into societies. Effective international copyright agreements finally regulated the unauthorised leaking of books across borders. Criticism changed too. Despite his reference above to the incompatibility of thoughtful reflection with modern habits, Ruskin is not representative of the art/market debate as it existed by the 1880s and 1890s. He does not condemn the 'book of the hour'. To him it is 'simply the useful or pleasant talk of some person whom you cannot otherwise converse with, printed for you'.[27] In the periodicals of the later nineteenth century, though, we see an overwhelming construction of a civil war between art (a beleaguered island of good books) and the market (a rising tide of bad ones). By 1881 Thomas Wright was declaring that 'the reading of the higher class of novels is calculated to give, and does give, culture ... the works of the great masters of fiction must refine and elevate – ay, and inform too'. But he made it very clear that he was not referring to 'the modern manufactured novels produced in quantities by the trade ... the three-volume collections of dulness [sic] and drivel which lumber all the libraries'.[28] He also considered whether some readers even knew the difference, and concluded that they did not: 'The extension of elementary education ... if left to its single self, will give us a larger number of the people able to read the police intelligence of the lower types of weekly newspapers, and willing to read little else'.[29]

An article on 'Elementary Education and the Decay of Literature' in the middle-class periodical *Nineteenth Century* in 1894 continued this theme. The author, Joseph Ackland, declared that mass-production was more inclined to the 'pushing' of 'weekly papers of a scrappy character and of very various degrees of merit or demerit' than the distribution of 'useful or pleasant talk'. For him, as for Wright, compulsory elementary education fitted the populace only to purchase and swallow whatever literature was thrown at them, rather than to discern the good from the bad.[30] In 1899 a full-page advertisement for the *Standard's* 'Library of Famous Literature' summed up the debate from the point of view of the publishing trade itself: 'the bookmen of the present day may be divided into roughly two classes. One camp is composed of those who deplore the enormous increase of books, the other camp of those who welcome that increase ... Never before were there so many publications, never before so many to read them ... Some bookmen regard this vast army as a barbarian, a Vandal horde which threatens to trample under foot all that is finest in letters; to others, it is a

---

27   Ruskin, p. 363.
28   Thomas Wright, 'On a Possible Popular Culture', *Contemporary Review*, Vol. 40, July 1881, p. 30.
29   Wright, p. 26.
30   Joseph Ackland, 'Elementary Education and the Decay of Literature', *Nineteenth Century*, Vol. 35, March 1894, p. 421.

splendid gathering of recruits. All agree that it needs discipline and training'.[31] The separation of the unscrupulous publisher from the gullible reader in need of guidance has become a common refrain, often – paradoxically – alongside that of the public as an ill-educated, degenerate herd and the best-selling writer as a conscienceless exploiter of its baser instincts. Clearly, by the period under review here the negative views of mass publishing had begun to outweigh the positive predictions of Ruskin's generation.

These shifting metaphorical fashions provide us with some useful ways of thinking about the art/market divide, the perceived responsibilities of the people who published on both sides of the equation, and what that might mean for the reader. Particularly important for my purposes is the fact that their consistent references are not just to books and readers, but also to the spaces and circumstances created by modern life in which they circulate. It is well documented that the same social and technological forces that enabled the mass-production of literature in the shape of the rotary printing press, cheap paper made of wood pulp and the abolition of the 'taxes on knowledge' also created the modern cultural landscape. They created social change in the shape of a new generation of urban white-collar workers with money to spend on books (these included women as well as men and in 1881 showed an increase of 80 per cent in only 30 years),[32] and political change in the shape of the extension of suffrage, compulsory education and reduced working hours.

But these modernising forces also created spatial change and new outlets for art in the shape of galleries, museums, railway stations and public libraries, and contributed to formal development within literary narratives as well as changes in the physical appearances of books. The huge successes of the Revised New Testament and *The Rosary* were made possible not only by new (and ever-changing) readerships for religious literature. They were made possible also by the fact that new printing techniques had enabled the rapid production of millions of copies in a variety of formats to suit almost every pocket. New technologies then enabled their rapid distribution (albeit sometimes illicitly) throughout the world via steamship, railway or cablegram. New networks of communications (including newspapers and periodicals) ensured that potential customers knew about the work in advance and were able to discuss it afterwards. New social spaces enabled purchasers to read, and be seen to read, their new acquisitions. New markets opened up, encouraging the spread of new forms of literature. Across the period the Bible lost ground to the novel,[33] and the Evangelical novel had fierce competition from its more secular relatives. What a given book 'meant' in culture therefore had new definitions, sometimes many of them, and sometimes simultaneously.

---

[31] 'Infinite Riches in a Little Form', *Bookman*, Vol. 17, October 1899, pp. 9–10.

[32] Altick, p. 83.

[33] As Terry Eagleton puts it: 'If one were asked to provide a single explanation for the growth of English Studies in the late nineteenth century, one could do worse than reply: "the failure of religion"'. *Literary Theory: An Introduction* (Minneapolis, 1983), p. 22.

Throughout the nineteenth century, in fact, it was recognised that there was an intimate relationship between the ways and the formats in which a given work reached its reader, and the way that reader was constructed – or self-constructed – socially and psychologically. In the 1860s, for example, over and above Ruskin's division of books into two basic types, another concern seemed to be over a potential leakage between popular books and bodies. This had disturbing class consequences, as though in certain public spaces and through certain fictional forms class could be carried like a disease from book to reader. The 'sensation novels' that were an integral part of the stock at railway bookstalls were famously described by Henry Mansel as carrying 'the whole nervous system by steam … A commercial atmosphere floats around works of this class, redolent of the manufactory or the shop'.[34] By the 1880s Professor W. Stanley Jevons was casting a more positive light on the potential leakage, describing public libraries as 'an engine for operating upon the poorer portions of the population'.[35] Here he figures books as a rescuing scalpel rather than a drug or a disease, though clearly this was only possible because what the public library stocked was different from what the railway bookstall offered. By the 1890s we frequently see a construction that figures the modern human as some sort of hybrid, a 'child of the newspapers', the spawn of the unnatural mating of man and mass-produced literature.[36]

In what follows I will attempt to analyse the changes that these different metaphors signal and relate them to the relevant cultural debates over their specifics. For the moment, though, the point I want to make is simpler. These very public debates indicate that literature is being seen throughout this period as carrying the sometimes exploitative, incalculable and runaway, but sometimes sweepingly beneficial effects of modernity into the reading subject not only via the text, but also via the new places and the new ways in which it is being read. The public described by the *Leisure Hour* bought 'shilling' Bibles at underground stations at a cost of one-and-six as well as at discount bookshops for ninepence. Both the New Revised Version and *The Rosary* were read on trains and buses and in the city streets as well as in the privacy of the home. Literature was in the public domain in myriad new ways and myriad new places. Each of these – precisely because of the social fluidity that it potentially enabled – was discussed, worried over, legislated and catered for in a unique manner and at a unique rate, and that meant the cultural meanings attached to each of these reading venues were very different. The novel certainly 'gradually acquired a class structure analogous to that of the social world surrounding it',[37] as Lawrence Rainey has suggested. But this was neither a natural nor an organic process. The novel – and most other categories of literature – were often, singly or collectively,

---

34   Henry Mansel, 'Sensation Novels', *Quarterly Review*, Vol. 113 , April 1863, p. 484.
35   Professor W. Stanley Jevons, 'The Rationale of Free Public Libraries', *Contemporary Review*, Vol. 39, March 1881, p. 388.
36   'Infinite Riches in a Little Form', p. 14.
37   Lawrence Rainey, *Institutions of Modernism: Literary Elites and Public Culture* (New Haven and London, 1998), p. 2.

designed and distributed to affirm, control and in some cases even help to create that class structure within readerships, often in the name of 'guidance', more often still through the judicious matching of text (or even *version* of a text) to outlet. And, of course, this attempt at socially specific niche marketing created its share of resistors and subversives, readers against the grain.

Many of the nineteenth-century phenomena described above – such as the libraries, museums and shops of the modern city – have, of course, received detailed critical attention in a range of disciplines.[38] Within literary studies, Rainey himself has provided an invaluable addition to the canon of modernist criticism – and raised some crucial questions about the period's publishing practices – by examining the production and reception contexts of a range of key modernist texts. He suggests that 'to trace the institutional profile of modernism in the social spaces and staging venues where it operated can teach us a great deal about the relations between modernism and popular culture, the fate of aesthetic autonomy, authorial self-construction in advancing modernity, and the troublesome place of literary elites in public culture'.[39] But it is outside the scope of his work to examine the effects on writers, books and readers of the 'social spaces and staging venues' in which popular culture operated. I agree with Rainey that modernism was political from birth in part because it self-selected already politicised arenas. But in examining that politicisation holistically and in detail, in examining the subtle differences between a range of 'social spaces and staging venues', I am able to offer a complementary reading of *fin-de-siècle* publishing practices that draws attention both to the ideologies that regulated book distribution, and to the nuances between 'popular cultures'. Culture that is popular has never been a single, identifiable entity (as witnesses the huge popularity of the Revised New Testament on the one hand and *The Rosary* on the other). I am able to suggest in addition – though perhaps less explicitly – how counter-cultures may have operated in this period, how they came about, and for whom they may have been important.

What I want to do in this book is to cast the high/low, art/market debate back into the social, physical, historical arena that helped to form it. I want to ask what it meant – socially and ideologically – to buy, borrow, read or display a particular book in a particular context. We cannot assume that a particular author or genre meant a particular thing to its readers based either on textual evidence alone, or on textual

---

[38] See, for example, Alistair Black, *A New History of the English Public Library: Social and Intellectual Contexts 1850–1914* (London, 1996); Rachel Bowlby, *Just Looking: Consumer Culture in Dreiser, Gissing and Zola* (London, 1985); Leo Charney and Vanessa Shwartz, eds, *Cinema and the Invention of Modern Life* (Berkeley, 1995); Tony Bennett, *The Birth of the Museum: History, Theory, Politics* (London, 1995); Erika D. Rappaport, *Shopping for Pleasure: Women in the Making of London's West End* (Princeton, NJ, 2000); Judith R. Walkowitz, *City of Dreadful Delight: Narratives of Sexual Danger in Late-Victorian London* (London, 1992); Wolfgang Schivelbusch, *The Railway Journey: Trains and Travel in the Nineteenth Century* (Oxford, 1980).

[39] Rainey, p. 5.

evidence combined with an analysis of an assumed or intended audience. Both these approaches have tended to dominate literary studies. For example, as Jonathan Rose has quite rightly noted, it is often assumed rather simplistically that 'popular culture' somehow reflects the attitudes of 'the masses' and this has often resulted in a critical emphasis on textual analysis as infallible evidence of cultural opinion.[40] But, as I have suggested, a given reader might read across genres and mediums and often also against the marketing grain. Queen Victoria had all of Marie Corelli's novels sent to Balmoral as her holiday reading.[41] Lady Bell's study of iron workers in Middlesborough in 1907 records their favourite author as the middlebrow Mrs Henry Wood.[42] In the late nineteenth and early twentieth centuries a commuter or holidaying family had access to literature at second hand and railway bookstalls as well as bookshops, any one of which might offer a very different selection from that available in their own neighbourhood bookshops or hometown public library. Both 'classic' and 'popular' narratives were frequently performed on stage and, from around 1909 onwards, still more cheaply in fixed-site cinemas which made them available to even wider audiences. These narratives could then be fed back into the written medium via the 'book of the play or film'.[43]

Rose is right to insist on the intertextual and intergeneric nature of the reading experience. However, my version of events differs from his in crucial respects. While 'popular culture' may not reflect the attitudes of the masses, if both 'popular' and 'high' culture are equally available then we need to try to explain why the former attracts more readers than the latter, and if not then we need to ask why not. An analysis of readers' autobiographies cannot quite fill in all the blanks. While it is extremely useful to 'consult the readers themselves and let them explain how they made sense of it all',[44] there are some things that they do not record which publishers and distributors do. Within the struggling autodidact culture that Rose examines there were all sorts of hidden forces at work, forces that determined not only what was available and to whom, but also influenced the selection of one book or edition over another where these were coexistent. A given text might – and often did – appear in several editions simultaneously, each quite different in terms of aesthetics and sometimes textual verity as well as price.

---

[40]   Jonathan Rose, 'Rereading the English Common Reader: A Preface to a History of Audiences', *Journal of the History of Ideas*, Vol. 8, 1992, p. 48.

[41]   Annette R. Federico, *Idol of Suburbia: Marie Corelli and Late-Victorian Literary Culture* (Charlottesville and London, 2000), p. 17.

[42]   Lady Bell, *At the Works: A Study of a Manufacturing Town* (1907; London, 1985), pp. 165–6.

[43]   Throughout the nineteenth century, many publishers took advantage of the extra profits to be had from 'theatrical versions'. In 1921 Hall Caine's sons Derwent and Ralph started the first 'book of the film' imprint with their Readers Library Publishing Company, starting with *The Hunchback of Notre Dame*, then a popular movie. Vivien Allen, *Hall Caine: Portrait of a Victorian Romancer* (Sheffield, 1997), p. 385.

[44]   Jonathan Rose, *The Intellectual Life of the British Working Classes* (London and New Haven, 2001), p. 367.

These forces are important to identify wherever possible. They help us to recognise some of the slippages and tensions between 'low', 'middle' and 'highbrow' reading, and between 'working' and 'lower middle class' readers, for these were by no means set in stone. A person might come from a working-class family, but with a better education than his or her parents (within the reach of many children by the 1880s) join the lower middle classes early in adult life by becoming a clerk or secretary, and perhaps move even higher. These sorts of social manoeuvres were often reflected in reading habits; it was well known at the time that an important part of social aspiration was the cultivation of 'literary taste'.[45] Some of this was about social posturing; a reader might display one book on the shelves at home (or record in an autobiography that his or her life was changed by it) but read another for pleasure when alone. It could also be about relative freedoms within the bourgeois family. A businessman might read a very different type of book when travelling to work on the train, from that which he might bring into a home containing a wife and daughters. A single woman living in 'rooms' in town and taking the Underground to work could spend some of her disposable income on easily available reading material that she wouldn't dare bring home to her parents (either because it was too 'racy' and classified her as 'fast', or – paradoxically but by no means unusually – because it was too 'highbrow' and got her accused of 'putting on airs'.)

These types of complications should serve to remind us that our historical readers were human. And they should warn us against over-simplifying the relationship between reader and text. It's crucial, of course (and immensely gratifying), to learn that the working classes were well able to find and appreciate 'great literature' for themselves. Rose's exhaustive research is invaluable, and I have drawn gratefully on it here. But it's just as crucial to understand how and by whom that 'great literature' was defined since it too is subject to historical forces. We need to remember that while then, as now, book buyers had a range of choices, the manner in which they were exercised was influenced in extremely subtle ideological ways. Some readers toed the great book party line. But some did not. If everyone accepted, aspired and had equal access to the literary canon, there would be no counter-cultures (including radical preferences for the popular), no anti-intellectualism, no need for the culturally disempowered to exercise the power of refusal – which they did in significant numbers. We need to find a way of explaining some of Rose's findings, such as the fact that as late as 1936 large groups of working class readers attending WEA classes did not consider modernist texts relevant to them.[46]

There have been a few valuable attempts to theorise the Victorian publishing industry's practices along these lines to which I am indebted here. Nicholas Feltes' Marxist-structuralist reading of Victorian publishing informs my own view that it is

---

45 Manuals instructing readers how to cultivate this taste abounded in this period, and sold extremely well. One of the best known of these was *Literary Taste and How to Form It* (1911) by Arnold Bennett.

46 Rose, *The Intellectual Life*, pp. 139–40.

best seen 'neither as a uniform whole nor as kinds of individual publishers or individual authors or books, but as a distinctive, determinate set of interlocking practices'.[47] In Feltes's account, the late Victorian publishing industry can be separated into 'list' and 'entrepreneurial' houses – those which either protected their reputations with a view to the long term, or looked for profitable new authors who would realise their surplus value immediately. He invokes discourses of gender and class by situating both within a model of late Victorian publishing as 'a patriarchal/capitalist mode of production' which privileged the work of male writers 'while always concealing that privileging by including George Eliot, or perhaps Jane Austen'.[48] In this mode of production, which gave birth to the notion of the largely male-dominated 'classics' and the series of '100 best books' so beloved of the period's middle-class readers, we might recognise the roots of the gendering of much early twentieth century criticism.

However, it cannot be assumed that 'list' and 'entrepreneurial' publishing was easily distinguishable in every case, or that it always meant what its producers wanted it to mean. Is Oxford University Press's position as a 'list' publisher *par excellence* compromised, for example, by the runaway success of their mass-produced Bible, with its cheap versions specifically designed for the lower-class pocket in order, in Feltes' terminology, to realise their surplus value as quickly as possible? Is the economic superstructure undermined or reinforced by its symbolic realisation or refusal in the marketplace? What is required in order to understand the subtleties of these questions is a model that takes into account specific social positions and their relation to cultural products. For these reasons, though I use Feltes' model to explore publishing as a patriarchal/capitalist mode of production, I deviate from his useful but in the end only partially adequate economic model and turn to the French sociologist Pierre Bourdieu. The pairing is not as contradictory as it might seem. Feltes himself uses Bourdieu's notions of phenomenological knowledge and the objectivist mode in order to explain the dialectical relations within publishing structures, and in return he helps to map out the economic aspects of that structure's interrelations so resolutely ignored by Bourdieu.[49]

For my purposes though, where Bourdieu is most useful is in the scope his model provides for exploring what a given work might have meant to its reader in a given context. In Bourdieu's 1979 work *Distinction: A Social Critique of the Judgement of Taste*, the model of the literary field is prefigured in an analysis of the classification of taste among its consumers. Here we find an invaluable theoretical tool for understanding the impact of an explosion of literacy and print technologies on taste:

47 N.N. Feltes, *Literary Capital and the Late Victorian Novel* (Madison, Wisconsin, 1993), p. 16.
48 Feltes, p. 49.
49 See, for example, John Guillory, 'Bourdieu's Refusal', *Modern Language Quarterly*, 58/4 (1997), pp. 367–98.

A simple upward displacement of the structure of the class distribution of an asset or practice (i.e. a virtually identical increase in the proportion of possessors in each class) has the effect of diminishing its rarity and distinctive value and threatening the distinction of the older possessors. Intellectuals and artists are thus divided between their interest in cultural proselytism, that is, winning a market by widening their audience, which inclines them to favour popularisation, and concern for cultural distinction, the only objective basis of their rarity; and their relationship to everything concerned with the 'democratisation of culture' is marked by a deep ambivalence which may be manifested in a dual discourse on the relations between the institutions of cultural diffusion and the public.[50]

This 'dual discourse' is characteristic of debates around the provision of books and education in the period under review here, and it is particularly marked by the tension between symbolic and economic capital, or art and the market.

Bourdieu's later work extends this model, focussing on what he calls the 'structural relations' between 'social positions that are both occupied and manipulated by social agents which may be isolated individuals, groups or institutions'.[51] This insistence on the field's dynamism, a series of ceaseless, often unacknowledged 'position-takings' between the agents who comprise the field, is still more useful in any discussion of the formation of taste. Changing fashions and the existence of sub-cultures have to be accounted for in ways that move beyond economic or historical determinism, and beyond the influence of individuals, if they are to investigate rather than repeat ideologies. In this model the 'profits' to be had may or may not be financial; they may in fact be – or appear to be – completely contrary to financial imperatives, so much so that such imperatives are rendered invisible.[52] The rise of literary purism in the 1890s emerges through this reading less as an aesthetic than as a social response. Seen as a covert reaction to social forces occasioned by the development of the mass market, a disguising of profit motives through a new privileging of 'Art for Art's Sake', literary purism is freed from the ideology with which it attempted to cloak itself. It may then, perhaps, be investigated more critically, as a social phenomenon rather than a form of spiritualism in which 'Art' figures as a visiting angel (visiting men more often than women, of course, and white middle-class men more often than any others).

Bourdieu's model is of a field that works vertically as well as horizontally, in which participants are always in economic competition even when they appear to be on the same side, and can be on the same economic side even when they appear to be in symbolic competition. For Bourdieu, 'every position – even the dominant one – depends for its very existence, and for the determinations it imposes on its

---

50 Pierre Bourdieu, *Distinction: A Social Critique of the Judgement of Taste* (1979; London, 1992), p. 229.
51 Pierre Bourdieu, *The Field of Cultural Production: Essays on Art and Literature*, ed. Randal Johnson (Cambridge, 1995), p. 29.
52 Bourdieu, *The Field*, p. 30.

occupants, on the other positions constituting the field'.[53] This mutual dependency helps us to examine the invisible but vital forces at work in the relationships between taste, history and society. More important still is the fact that his model 'refuses to consider the field of position-takings in itself and for itself, i.e. independently of the field of positions which it manifests ... it applies relational thinking not only to symbolic systems ... but also to the *social relations* of which these symbolic systems are a more or less transformed expression'.[54] The usefulness of Bourdieu for cultural historians lies primarily here, in its insistence on the necessary consideration of the whole network of relations between the producers, disseminators and consumers of a cultural product. The product – and therefore its cultural meaning – is a 'manifestation of the field as a whole'[55] rather than an autonomous end in itself. In the present study the use of Bourdieu's model enables a consideration of the literary work as a symbolic object that confers meaning beyond the words on the page. It holds out the possibility that an analysis of the relations between agents and cultural products might shed some light on the powerful workings of class-consciousness as they are manifested through taste.

Peter D. McDonald has recently provided an excellent analysis of three important agents in the period's literary field, Conrad, Bennett and Conan Doyle, which demonstrates the subtlety and usefulness of Bourdieu's model of tension between economic and symbolic capital.[56] I deviate from McDonald's readings in several significant respects, however, even as I build on his findings. First, although my concern is, like McDonald's, to map some of the 'position-takings' as they occur between authors, publishers and critics across the period in order to illuminate their shifting but far from arbitrary nature, I am not satisfied with a simple map of intersecting literary careers. McDonald quite rightly points out in his introduction that: 'Each objective position in the structure is best thought of as an integrated network of communication circuits in which writers, publishers, printers, distributors, reviewers, and readers collaborate'.[57] The trouble is he fails to heed his own advice. The relationships between publishers and authors are considered in great depth. But he frequently ignores the important roles played by readers and distributors in the literary field analysed in his three chapters. Bourdieu himself insists that 'ignorance of everything which goes to make up the 'mood of the age' produces a derealisation of works: stripped of everything which attached them to the most concrete debates of their time ... they are impoverished and transformed in the direction of intellectualism or an empty humanism'.[58] Distributors, readers and the ideologies behind reading

---

[53] Bourdieu, *The Field*, p. 30.
[54] Bourdieu, *The Field*, p. 32.
[55] Bourdieu, *The Field*, p. 32.
[56] Peter D. McDonald, *British Literary Culture and Publishing Practice 1880–1914* (Cambridge, 1997).
[57] McDonald, p. 18.
[58] Bourdieu, *The Field*, p. 32.

practices form a crucial part of the 'mood of the age'. Distributors too were subject to symbolic struggle; by no means did they all stock the same things. And to ignore readers, as McDonald does, is highly reductive in terms of class, in that it writes out of the literary field a large number of its most vital social operatives.

Equally, in ignoring the social spaces in which reading and book buying took place, McDonald's version is also stripped of the ideologies of public and private that are so crucial in terms of gender. Again, although he suggests at the beginning of his book that 'we clearly need to look beyond the narrow confines of the literary field into the gendered structures of late-Victorian society as a whole'[59] he fails to carry out this suggestion adequately. The three novelists on whom he chooses to concentrate are male (despite the large numbers of women novelists working in this period). The critics and publishers with whom he demonstrates these authors jostling for position are male (despite the significant presence of women journalists, editors and publishers' readers). Women do occasionally appear in McDonald's account, but only as peripheral commentators on male activities (George Egerton condemning George Newnes' *Strand Magazine*, p. 156, or the Suffragettes burning down his house, p. 150), or as fictional heroines (the statistical analysis of Conan Doyles' female characters, p. 166). The literary field of the 1890s, on this reading, is not only male-dominated but also, apparently, naturally so.

My book considers the relative symbolic positions occupied by male and female novelists. And in so doing it argues that there is a place for textual analysis alongside a Bourdieuan sociological methodology. Not only were the symbolic positions 'male writer' and 'female writer' crucially interdependent, they also had a powerful individual effect on the ways in which literary forms changed and interacted according to these positions within the art/market divide. It is important, I think, to consider how a book might have worked to support or subvert its symbolic positioning at the level of the text. A 'popular bestseller' written by a man was not always the same thing as a 'popular bestseller' written by a woman. Not all 'popular bestsellers' throughout history were trash. Not all 'classic' literary texts throughout history were timeless works of genius. An analysis of some of the texts which bore these labels, alongside an analysis of their cultural significance in their own time, can tell us much about the social specificity of literary taste and the work of narrative in culture. If I seem to be hedging my bets here, it is because I believe that in our enthusiasm to move literary criticism beyond the subjective and book history beyond the empirical, we have sometimes tended to throw the baby out with the bath water.

This book considers, then, what reading choices may have meant in terms of gender and class in England's patriarchal/capitalist society in the late nineteenth and early twentieth centuries. It asks what the production and distribution of literary works, and the selection of one type of book or even imprint of a book over another, might be able to tell us about writing, publishing, distribution, and reading as interlocking

---

[59] McDonald, p. 14.

practices with socially specific meanings, and it investigates how these practices changed across the period. In order to approach these questions holistically, the book is roughly organised in three sections covering the production, distribution and reception of a range of literary texts. In organising it this way I am following Robert Darnton's 1982 model of a 'circuit of communication' which, he argues, enables the book historian to show that 'books do not merely recount history, they make it'.[60] True to the spirit of a circuit it does not, however, privilege one over the other by starting with production and finishing with reception. Instead it considers the sections as three parallel, linked and mutually dependent narratives. The same names tend to crop up throughout, and I have indicated wherever possible how the various persons and institutions interacted in different parts of the literary field. The book's guiding principle is loosely chronological, each section beginning roughly in 1880 and ending with the First World War, though I have attempted also to give an indication of this period's relations to those on either side of it. In early chapters, therefore, I trace developments from as far back as the middle of the century, and in later ones I attempt to link my findings with the period of 'high modernism' after the war.

The first two chapters concentrate on the ways in which two new institutions of cultural diffusion worked, exploring what they and their cultural offerings meant for the nineteenth century reader, and how their presence affected the literary field. Chapter 1 explores the tensions between the Public Library Committee (a new legitimating body founded on Arnoldian principles for the good of the poor), fears around the immorality of 'art', reader demand, and the financial restrictions facing a publicly funded institution. Analysing the records of a spread of English public libraries, I demonstrate that by the First World War this tension had led to the characterisation of the public library as a bastion of middle-class, middlebrow values officially sanctioned as representative of an acceptable watered-down version of 'Englishness'. This, I argue, alienated many of the readers whom it had been intended to serve, though there were subtle but important differences between regions and between branch and central libraries – and therefore between different readerships – that have tended to be overlooked in previous accounts.

Chapter 2 draws on a number of archival sources, including the records of W.H. Smith and Son, to explore the literature available at the railway station, another public arena in which readers were initially thought to be at risk. I attempt to show how the conditions of modernity and the machinations of a Victorian patriarchal capitalist dynasty combined to create a marketplace for literature which, like the library, was by the end of the period considered damagingly censorious for the 'pure' artist. These two spaces were not, however, synonymous: Smith's distributed morality to both, but literature in a subtly differentiated fashion. These differences point to vital clues in the reconstruction of the period's reading practices, taking place as they did in arenas which could be considered more or less public or private, and more or less

60   Robert Darnton, 'What is the History of Books?' (1982), *The Book History Reader*, eds David Finkelstein and Alistair McCleery (London, 2002), p. 22.

'dangerous', depending on one's gender or class. Thanks in part to railway reading, by the end of the nineteenth century a new relationship was emerging between fictional form, gender, class and the modern public sphere. The snappy, easily assimilated soundbite and the swift-moving detective or popular novel had become the railway's most appropriate literary forms. 'Banned unless asked for' had become the common refrain for modern 'literary' fiction at the bookstall. A movement that wanted to eschew the popular and guarantee its place in the history of the avant-garde could do worse than pay attention to these conventions, spurning accessibility, clarity and morality in favour of the elitism of opacity, obscurity, and relative obscenity.

Chapter 3 moves away from the places in which literature was displayed to an exploration of one of the period's producers of the literature that appeared in or was withheld from them. Oxford University Press's reputation for Bibles, prayer books, scholarly works and exam papers, which made them a 'list' publisher *par excellence* and a major objectifier of the literary product, was stretched in 1905 to include a purely entrepreneurial sideline of cheap reprints: the World's Classics. By placing evidence from their own records alongside concurrent debates and publishing practices, I seek to define the period's notion of 'the classic' using Bourdieu's model of the 'pure' legitimising gaze hiding its economic interests, in this case linked to copyright law. The 'classics' series was designed to appeal to the Board School educated reader who, no longer at school, desired to increase his or her literary knowledge and had a small disposable income. But self-help was a social practice deeply imbued with a set of contradictory drives that ensured its perpetual status as loser in the field of 'position-takings'. In terms of cultural capital, the cheap classics series was never going to equal the eighteenth-century gentleman's library on which it was modelled. This meant both a new emphasis on a book's aesthetics and price, and in some quarters and some instances a devaluing of the acknowledged 'classic' work at the level of the text itself.

Tied up with the selection of 'classic' works for re-printing cheaply was the practice of persuading big-name authors to introduce them, thus complicating even further the notion of a 'natural' divide between great art and the best-selling novelist. To give just one example, in 1906 Mrs Humphry Ward's new novel was being dismissed as forgettable library- and railway-bookstall fodder. But only seven years previously she was introducing Smith, Elder and Co.'s new edition of the Bronte novels with an assumption of scholarly authority.[61] Chapters 4 and 5 trace the early careers of four of the period's most popular authors: Hall Caine and Marie Corelli in the 1880s and 1890s (Chapter 4), Arnold Bennett and Florence Barclay through the 1910s (Chapter 5). All of these authors were implicated, in one way or another, in debates about fictional form, gender, race, art, morality, public spaces, religion, new technologies and/or readers. As a whole the section considers how these four authors were marketed and reviewed, and attempts to demonstrate how the period's shifts in gender and class biases were reflected in textual forms and reading practices.

---

[61] *Bookman*, Vol. 15, March 1899, p. 163.

I have deliberately not considered the New Woman novelists in any sustained way here, referring to their relative positions in the field only in passing. I have done this, not because I think the New Woman novelists unworthy of mention, but because they have been impressively discussed elsewhere, and because in a sense they are victims of their own success: the recent critical focus on their work has sidelined other novelists, both the merely popular and the politically engaged (or both), both male and female, whose work informed and illuminated theirs, and on whose positions in the field they depended for much of their political efficacy. I hope that by focussing on these now largely lesser-known novelists, I might enrich previous explorations of the work of New Women writers by elucidating some of the non-canonical writers and writing with which they were surrounded.

Chapter 4 deals with Caine and Corelli as bitterly opposed but intimately related and largely self-constructed publishing phenomena, situating their early careers in terms of a common (if radically unstable) critical dichotomy of the 1880s and 1890s between male/realism/art and female/romance/the popular. This set of oppositions had a powerful influence on the kind of fiction which they each produced, the way it was reviewed and written about, and the different kinds of career paths which were open to them. The chapter also considers the slightly different symbolic position occupied by Hall Caine in his role as dramatist. Dismissed by the literary 'purists' for his popularity and his crass self-publicity, Caine was nonetheless admired and courted by the purists of a different cultural realm, working with Henry Irving in the legitimate theatre and later to be adapted for the screen by Alfred Hitchcock. The ability to manipulate and profit from related but symbolically discrete narrative forms in this way was relatively common, of course, but Caine was an unusually successful example of the practice. A consideration of his less well-known authorial roles thus not only renders his position as 'popular male author' slightly more complicated than some recent analyses have allowed, but also illustrates the potential fruitfulness of an interdisciplinary approach to such successfully interdisciplinary historical subjects.[62]

Chapter 5 continues to trace these male/female publishing ideologies into the twentieth century. It explores the gender and class implications of journalist, critic and best-selling novelist Arnold Bennett's attraction to the perceived 'artistry' of realism, and Florence Barclay's construction of a new 'art-free zone' of domesticated religiosity propelled to bestseller status by a powerful publishing and advertising machine. It suggests, further, how these contrasting positions may have paved the way for the self-consciously elite literary movement from whose ramparts Virginia Woolf could attack Arnold Bennett on formal grounds that disguised a complex set of social prejudices. Like McDonald, I examine Bennett's position from the point of view of his very modern adaptability to a wide range of markets. Unlike McDonald, I suggest that his importance to Woolf and to the other literary purists who dismissed him

---

[62] Caine seldom makes more than a cameo appearance in most literary histories. When he does appear, he is either dismissed as Joseph Conrad's *bête noir* or discussed with an air of amused apology. His plays are seldom mentioned at all, even by theatre historians.

does not lie only in his openly market-driven dexterity. We might well, as McDonald suggests, need to consider the impact of his popular serials on his serious writing. They may indeed have adversely affected his bid for the dominant position. But it is just as important, I think, to consider his serious writing in relation to the gendering and social stratification of forms in the literary field. His use of a masculinist form of realism – a form he clung to long after its heyday in a direct if not entirely conscious response to the Evangelical romances of 'popular lightweights' like Barclay, as well as to the impressionistic work of the New Woman novelist – made him a prime target for an avant-garde feminist. His class-conscious insistence on the role played by history in the creation of a liminal, dispossessed social group was almost bound to draw the criticism of a purist for whom both history and the dispossessed were no longer worthy subjects for Art.

Of course, 'realism' and the 'romance', as well as 'modernism', were – and remain – ambiguous terms, for which there have never been any easily identifiable parameters, and critics still argue over their definitions. The chequered historiography of these terms has often been linked with political agendas; for example, Lyn Pykett suggests that 'realism' in the mid-nineteenth century was often thought to be synonymous with 'women's writing', since its focus on the surface of life – particularly domestic life – was though to be 'peculiarly appropriate for women writers'.[63] But even in the middle of the nineteenth century men as well as women produced 'realism', and once again we run up against the problem of definition both within and between texts: 'realism' was itself mutable, filled with borrowings from other forms such as the Gothic, and the realism of George Eliot was a far cry from the realism of Charles Dickens. The confusion continues and deepens as the nineteenth century wears on. According to Pykett, at the end of the century the addition of 'naturalism', including more social or scientific elements, muddied the waters still further, and could be seen as an attempt to 'empty the detail of its limiting feminine connotations, or alternatively to endow it with value by incorporating it in a masculine discourse of judgement, professionalism, labour, system and science'.[64] Similarly, Sally Ledger has suggested that in the 1880s and 1890s, the 'romance' as produced by popular writers such as Corelli was briefly wrested from the hands of best-selling women by the 'masculine' romance fictions of Haggard, Stevenson and Kipling, through a stylistic return to the action 'romance' drawn from Sir Walter Scott.[65] But Corelli's romances were also often action-driven, at least in part, and both Pykett and Ledger fail to mention the 'romances' written by popular male authors such as Hall Caine, or the fact that Scott's romances were being lucratively published in cheap editions throughout the *fin-de-siècle* and that in a sense, therefore, the 'romance' did not need rescuing at all. In using these terms, then, I do not want to imply an easy or stable equivalence to political models or generic

---

63 Pykett, *The Improper Feminine*, p. 25.
64 Pykett, *The Improper Feminine*, p. 28.
65 Sally Ledger, *The New Woman: Fiction and Feminism at the Fin-de-siècle* (Manchester, 1997), pp. 178–9.

definitions. Instead, I want to suggest how their very instability was used to militate against the woman writer, or the popular writer, or both. And I want to suggest that it was the dynamic structure of the literary field at this period which both encouraged this mutability, and enabled its appropriation for symbolic ends.

I am attempting in this book to consider the relationships between readers, writers, genres, literary works and modern public spaces in a manner that illuminates, rather than elides, their interdependency, and their respective roles in the formation of class-inflected literary tastes. We can never know everything about what a given reader read, where and why s/he bought it, what s/he thought s/he was getting, and what s/he thought of the book once it had been read (or even whether it *was* read). But in building on the groundbreaking work of scholars like Jonathan Rose and Peter McDonald, in demonstrating not only what a reader's choices may have been but also what they may have signified, this study seeks to add to our understanding of those facts we do possess. As our knowledge base has increased, the need for interpretative tools has increased accordingly, and we have begun to supplement the questions 'Where and in what form was this book available?' with 'Why, in what ways, and to whom, did these things matter?' This book is an attempt at some possible answers.

Chapter 1

'The Great Fiction Bore':
Free Libraries and Their Users

Gissing and the Common Reader

On Wednesday afternoon, about three o'clock, Nancy walked alone to the library.
There, looking at books and photographs in the window, stood Lionel Tarrant. He
greeted her as usual, seemed not to remark the hot colour in her cheeks, and stepped
with her into the shop. She had meant to choose a novel, but, with Tarrant looking on,
felt constrained to exhibit her capacity for severe reading. The choice of grave works
was not large, and she found it difficult to command her thoughts even for the perusal
of titles; however, she ultimately discovered a book that promised anything but frivolity,
Helmholtz's 'Lectures on Scientific Subjects', and at this she clutched.

Two loudly dressed women were at the same time searching the shelves. 'I wonder
whether this is a pretty book?' said one to the other, taking down a trio of volumes.

'Oh, it looks as if it might be pretty', returned her friend, examining the cover. They
faced to the person behind the counter.

'Is this a pretty book?' one of them enquired loftily.

'Oh yes, Madam, that's a very pretty book – very pretty.'

Nancy exchanged glances with her companion and smiled. When they were outside
again Tarrant asked:

'Have you found a pretty book?'

She showed him the title of her choice.

'Merciful heavens! You mean to read that? The girls of to-day! What mere man is
worthy of them? But – I must rise to the occasion. We'll have a chapter as we rest.'[1]

George Gissing's 1894 novel *In the Year of Jubilee*, from which the above extract
comes, engages overtly and deliberately with a major late-nineteenth-century debate
about books, readers and reading. Sparked by rapid social change and above all by an
increase in literacy, this debate was intricately bound up with anxieties around gender,
class, citizenship and the public and private spheres. It also profoundly affected the
outcome of the utilitarian impulse that had motivated William Ewart to force the Public
Libraries Act through Parliament in 1850. Initially, the library was a public space
which, in Ewart's own words, 'might be legally founded by the people, supported by
the people, and enjoyed by the people',[2] in order to foster self-improvement for the

---

[1] George Gissing, *In the Year of Jubilee* (1894; New York, 1895), pp. 108–9. All subsequent
references are to this edition and will appear parenthetically in the text.

[2] *Hansard Parliamentary Debates*, 3rd Series, 31 January–25 February 1850, p. 762.

good of the individual – and, by common extrapolation, the nation. But by the time its adoption was widespread the public library had become, more often than not, an architecturally repressive and logistically prohibitive symbol of civic pride patronised overwhelmingly by the lower-middle classes. In fact, it was a space that ended up alienating large sections of the population whom it had been intended to serve.

What I want to do in this chapter, though, is to challenge the familiar notion that there is little of interest to say about English public libraries beyond the fact that their mostly middle-class patrons borrowed mostly fiction, although it is clear from the records that they did. What Gissing's novel points to – and, I suggest, my research in a range of English public libraries bears out – is that a more subtle relationship between books, readers and public spaces existed behind the statistics.[3] I want here to demonstrate the emergence of a public space in England that conflated two conflicting contemporary images. The first is the image of the library as a serious male domain predicated on the principle of social harmony and equality through rational debate. This image had been a crucial factor in the passing of the Libraries Act two years after revolution had shaken Europe, and had largely motivated the spirit of self-help that swept into vogue afterwards. But by the last half of the century a widespread demand for novels necessitated negotiation with a second, equally long-standing but largely incompatible image: that of novel reading as a predominantly feminine and socially 'low' activity. This conflation of class and gender stereotypes within the dangerous social melting pot of the public library, set against the background of a prosperous nation anxious about its infrastructure, meant that the activity of reading took on a new dimension. The complex social dynamic that existed in the nineteenth century, I want to suggest, helped to create a new characterisation of reading as a socially specific form of consumption, an answer to the breakdown (perceived and actual) of class, gender and even national boundaries.

My opening quotation is not just an isolated incidence of the connection between books, taste and class identities. Gissing is not alone in the social construction that he places on reading: the importance of literature as social signifier is everywhere discussed in this period. In 1871 Samuel Smiles declared that 'A man may usually be known by the books he reads, as well as by the company he keeps'.[4] In the 1880 polemic *Woman's Work and Worth*, W.H. Davenport Adams suggested that if it came to a toss-up between the two types of signifier, books were the most reliable; while

---

3   I have looked at records from a spread of English public libraries opened at different times and in areas with different demographics. I chose two industrial towns (Leeds in the North and Southampton in the South), two ecclesiastical/agricultural towns (York in the North and Winchester in the South) and a cluster of libraries in London's East End, an extremely poor, working class, 'social problem' area with a high proportion of Jewish immigrants.

4   Samuel Smiles, *Character: A Book of Noble Characteristics* (1871; London, 1905), p. 289.

'it is said that a man or a woman may be known by the company he or she keeps; a truer index to character is the books they read'[5]. H.G. Wells's vulgar, self-satisfied middle-class character Coote is defined in *Kipps: The Story of a Simple Soul* (1905) by a bookshelf the contents of which, 'no worse an array ... than any you find in any public library', represents 'a compendium of the contemporary British mind'.[6] E.M. Forster was still using the connection as a literary device in 1910. For Margaret Schlegel, the upper-middle-class heroine of *Howards End,* class is innate; 'wide' and 'widening' is the 'gulf that stretches between the natural and the philosophic man', and the lower middle classes are simply 'good chaps who are wrecked trying to cross it'. But it is only through the 'vague aspirations, the mental dishonesty, the familiarity with the outsides of books' displayed by bank clerk Leonard Bast that Margaret feels she recognises him as one of these good men, 'one of the thousands who have lost the life of the body and failed to reach the life of the spirit'.[7] Bast's last conscious thought as he falls dead under a bookcase at the novel's end is that 'Books fell over him in a shower. Nothing had sense' (p. 315). The pouring over himself of what to him have always been – and because of his class can always only be – empty signifiers, solves the novel's ambivalence about middle classness by turning it into a simple split between knowing and not-knowing the value of literature. This depends absolutely on a notion of the 'naturalness' of what we might usefully call the cultural capital invested in books. For Forster, some books are simply 'better', 'higher', more 'valuable' than others, and some people – in his terms the most 'spiritual' – are simply more naturally able than others to appreciate and benefit from them.

Gissing's earlier novel posits a slightly more subtle equation between cultural capital and class identity. Its insistence on the performance of class in the public space points to the physical implications of Bourdieu's notion that class is that which is 'defined as much by its being-perceived as by its being, by its consumption – which need not be conspicuous in order to be symbolic – as by its position in the relation of production'.[8] In Gissing's novel books become the bearers *par excellence* of cultural capital in Bourdieu's sense of the term, the public spaces in which the exchanges of capital take place loaded with social significance. For Gissing, choosing the right book in the right way can make or mar a social career.

We are introduced to Nancy as she gazes out of the window of her house, a nondescript dwelling caught, like everything else about her, between gentility and tastelessness:

---

5   W.H. Davenport Adams, *Woman's Work and Worth* (London, 1880), pp. 140–41.
6   H.G. Wells, *Kipps: The Story of a Simple Soul* (London, 1905), p. 115. All subsequent references are to this edition and will appear parenthetically in the text.
7   E.M. Forster, *Howards End* (1910; London, 1989), pp. 122–3. All subsequent references are to this edition and will appear parenthetically in the text.
8   Pierre Bourdieu, *Distinction: A Social Critique of the Judgement of Taste* (1979; London, 1992), p. 483.

> It is a neighbourhood in decay, a bit of London which does not keep pace with the times. And Nancy hated it. She would have preferred to live even in a poor and grimy street which neighboured the main track of business and pleasure (p. 11).

Thus positioned as outside yet acutely aware of the social scene, Nancy is 'haunted by an uneasy sense of doubtfulness as to her social position' (p. 13). Gissing, typically, lays this liminality directly at the door of the social changes he abhorred: Nancy's father, a self-made small merchant, admits that in giving his daughter an education that he has not the wherewithal to match in lifestyle, he has 'made her neither one thing nor the other' (p. 73). This is uncomfortable enough for Nancy when she is at home alone. But it is through the use of public spaces that expose inherent class inferiority that the novel most frequently separates its heroine from the potentially leveling effects of her education. In the pivotal Jubilee Day scene, for example, 'in spite of her professed disregard for the gathering tumult of popular enthusiasm' (p. 11), the two halves of Nancy's social make-up – the vulgarly abandoned shopgirl and the newly-educated, cultured observer – emerge disturbingly as two sides of the same coin:

> She had escaped to enjoy herself, and the sense of freedom soon overcame her anxieties. No-one observed her solitary state; she was one of millions walking about the streets because it was Jubilee Day, and every movement packed her more tightly among the tramping populace ... Nancy forgot her identity, lost sight of herself as an individual. She did not think and her emotions differed little from those of any shop-girl let loose. The 'culture' to which she laid claim evanesced in this atmosphere of exhalations. Could she have seen her face, its look of vulgar abandonment would have horrified her. (pp. 61–2)

For Gissing, a lower-middle-class woman in the public space is separated from the signifiers of status on which she depends. That means she occupies a void between social stations, in constant danger of slipping, and always in a downward direction. This isolated, fluid, permanently anxious social position is frequently marked by her literary taste, whether genuine (and bad) or aspirational (and disingenuous). In this novel it is signified by Nancy's symbolic and in this case very conspicuous literary consumption. On the table in the living room in the introductory scene lies 'a new volume from the circulating library – something about Evolution – but she had no mind to read it; it would have made her too conscious of the insincerity with which she approached such profound subjects (pp. 11–12). Here in a nutshell is her dilemma. As part of the new middle classes, while she consciously rejects the vulgar popular, she cannot wholly shake its unconscious influence. In historical terms the prominent display of her circulating-library volume on evolution is insincerity essential to the maintenance of her position: the minimum guinea per annum membership of a circulating library itself proclaims her social arrival, and the volume's subject matter implies an innate proclivity for serious scientific reading. But this prominent display also denotes class insecurity, a distrust of what the borrowing of fiction might say about her (just as, on a semantic level, it gives away the social evolution in which she is herself perpetually involved).

The table in her sitting room, the Jubilee day adventure and the library are all, then, public 'spaces' in which Nancy might rehearse her own class superiority, but they are also places in which she is in constant danger of being caught 'slipping'. In the library scene with which I began Nancy's social superior Lionel Tarrant is commenting on her slip when he mocks her selection of Helmholtz. Tarrant does not have to worry about literary taste. His class position is such that he displays what Bourdieu calls 'the familiar relation to culture which authorises the liberties and audacities of those who are linked to it by birth, that is, by nature and essence'.[9] Nancy has no such 'audacity', and in front of Tarrant she simply tries too hard, like Forster's bank clerk Leonard Bast who reads Ruskin to his wife 'to show you the kind of man I am' (p. 66) and H.G. Wells's Kipps who reads the same critic to himself 'with ruthless determination' (p. 117). For Gissing, and for many writers and social commentators like him, serious reading is so beyond the new middle classes that it cannot help but be insincere.[10]

In Nancy's irremediably anxious class position, and in the reading habits that somehow both create and mark it, I think we have a model worthy of interrogation. This fictional characterisation raises the intriguing possibility that a reader might be 'constructed' in this period, not just through personal choice or through the publishing and distribution practices which determine access to that choice (or lack of it), but also through the social functions linked to the public spaces in which books were selected, displayed and read.

The Public Library Movement

The circulating library – probably Mudie's (started 1842) or Smith's (1860) – from which Nancy is likely to have borrowed her volume on evolution was a private company that offered a lending service to paying subscribers. For a minimum of a guinea a year a subscriber could borrow one book at a time, and for a maximum of

---

9   Bourdieu, *Distinction*, pp. 330–31.

10   Given Gissing's consistent use of the book as symbol, it is worth mentioning here that his choice of Helmholtz's theories is highly significant. Hermann von Helmholtz was responsible not only for major advances in ophthalmology, but also for famous and globally influential theories on the phenomena of nature which, he declared, 'are to be reduced to movements of bits of matter with unalterable moving forces that depend only on their spatial relations'. What Nancy has chosen in her panic, in other words, is a theory that (if she ever read it) would merely confirm her own deepest fears about her hidden, inalterable inner forces being uncontrollably activated by the spaces and the other 'bodies' around them. Hermann von Helmholtz, 'Ueber die Erhaltung der Kraft', quoted in Michael Heidelberger, 'Force, Law, and Experiment: The Evolution of Helmholtz's Philosophy of Science', in *Hermann von Helmholtz and the Foundations of Nineteenth-Century Science*, ed. David Cahan (Berkeley, 1993), p. 464.

five guineas a parcel of books could be sent every fortnight for a year, either selected by the subscriber or chosen by the library. The circulating libraries were strongholds of middle-class values, long held but finally made public in an announcement on 31 November 1909 which decreed that the books they distributed ought to be morally improving in tone and that they planned to take a stand against books 'which are regarded as transgressing the dictates of good taste in subject or treatment'.[11] By this agreement the circulating libraries divided new books into three categories: a) satisfactory, which meant suitable for general release; b) doubtful, which meant stocked but not distributed unless asked for; and c) objectionable, which meant banned altogether. Many slightly suggestive or in some way progressive books, including those by George Moore, H.G. Wells, Marie Corelli and Hall Caine, fell foul of these regulations and the Society of Authors protested loudly, but records indicate that circulating library clients approved of them; the turnover of Smith's library increased from £2,410 in the half-year of its opening in 1860 to £114,835 in 1913/14[12] and Mudie dispatched some 5,000 or 6,000 volumes from its London headquarters every day.[13] Mudie might be – and frequently was – accused of peddling worthless fiction to bored ladies and of inhibiting the progress of art, but the middle classes apparently had a strong sense of the books that it was acceptable for them to obtain through this public medium. By selling morality and conservatism, circulating libraries like Mudie's sidestepped the fiction as problem issue, made a substantial profit, and largely controlled the publishing industry for some years. When an author was taken on by Mudie's, he or she had arrived financially. The best-selling author Arnold Bennett wrote with heavy irony in 1909 that according to popular wisdom 'without the patronage of the circulating libraries I should either have to live on sixpence a day or starve'.[14] In the case of the highly adaptable Bennett that was far from true, but many authors were not so fortunate. Still, in spite of their apparently winning formula, the circulating libraries were accused sporadically throughout this period of contaminating middle-class households either physically with disease, or intellectually with socialism, and their policies always represented a balancing act between reader-demand and a highly vocal press.

The public library, designed to make good books available to all, was originally at least partly conceived as an alternative to Mudie's. The full history of the movement

---

[11]   Peter Keating, *The Haunted Study: A Social History of the English Novel 1875–1914* (London, 1989), p. 277.

[12]   Charles Wilson, *First With the News: The History of W.H. Smith 1792–1972* (London, 1985), p. 362.

[13]   Nicholas Hiley, 'Can't You Find Me Something Nasty?: Circulating Libraries and Literary Censorship in Britain from the 1890s to the 1910s', in *Censorship and the Control of Print in England and France 1600–1910*, ed. Michael Harris and Robin Myers (London, 1992), p. 124.

[14]   Arnold Bennett, *Books and Persons: Being Comments on a Past Epoch 1908–11* (London, 1917), p. 88.

is outside the scope of this study, but there are some important historical factors that are worth considering because they contribute to the failure to live up to that promise. For one thing, the Public Library Movement was hardly the result of popular pressure since the Parliament that brought in the Act was not democratically elected; at the time only one person in forty was eligible to vote.[15] The movement therefore has to be seen as in some way engaging with middle-class concerns, which at this time revolved around trade, Chartism, England's future, social control and the public space, particularly in the wake of the 1848 revolutions in Europe. The Commons debates ranged from those which viewed the spread of literacy as dangerous, through those which stressed the need to provide the poor with decent housing, food and jobs rather than improving literature, to those which sided with John Ruskin and Matthew Arnold about the social value of art. All of these conflicting concerns are reflected in the restrictions that marked the bill's passage through parliament: when it finally received Royal Assent on 14 August 1850 and passed into law, it was a pale reflection of Ewart's original premise.

One of the most important and debilitating of these restrictions was financial. Ewart had proposed an unlimited rating power, but ended up being forced to agree to a maximum of a halfpenny in the pound. This meant that the money it was possible to raise from the rates was nowhere near enough to pay for books as well as buildings. Many early public libraries were appallingly under-resourced and forced to rely on donations, usually the passing on of out-dated or highly specialised volumes from private libraries. Winchester, the first public library to open its doors after the passing of the Act, did so (on 10 November 1851) in an inaccessible attic with only 300 books, none of them available for home reading, and even 18 years later was lamenting that its stocks were appallingly low and easily explained Wintonians' lack of interest in their library.[16] A second restriction was that only towns with a population of over 10,000 were empowered to adopt, and even then only if two-thirds of the ratepayers agreed. All of this suspicion, apathy and restraint meant that adoption was extremely slow in the early years.

By 1880, the beginning of the period with which I am concerned here, Andrew Carnegie had begun adding to the momentum with his grants, and the halfpenny rate had been raised to a penny in the pound. But there were still financial obstacles to adoption that many councils felt were insuperable, and even in towns that had decided to adopt the Act, lack of money continued to exercise an influence on stock. For example, the Whitechapel Public Library and Museum, opened in 1892, quickly exceeded its available building funds and, unable to raise a loan to cover the shortfall, was grateful for a generous donation of £6,454 from the wealthy West-end

---

[15]   W.J. Murison, *The Public Library: Its Origins, Purpose and Significance as a Social Institution* (London , 1955), p. 25.

[16]   *A Hundred Years of Library Service* (Winchester, 1952), pp. 4–5. Department of Local Studies, Winchester Public Library.

philanthropist J. Passmore Edwards.[17] Like many late Victorian philanthropists, Edwards explained his gift in terms of a Christian gratitude for his own good fortune which manifested itself in moral obligation: 'I have long felt that the East End has stupendous uncancelled claims on the wealthy and well to do people of the West End of London', he wrote to the Library Committee on 25 February 1892, 'and it affords me unalloyed gratification that I am enabled to wipe out a small portion our moral indebtedness [sic]'.[18] His generosity and sense of duty were not sufficiently gratified by this gift, however. In a letter dated 29 February he explained further that since he thought 'a good start will import into your enterprise moral momentum', he also intended to donate 'a thousand volumes of suitable standard works'.[19] In this period that meant 'serious' reading among history, religion, essays and the classics rather than the lighter kinds of reading more likely to attract readers.

But the libraries clearly had a vested interest in encouraging an increase in borrower numbers, due to the need to justify their existence both to the councils and to the ratepayers who had voted them into office: they regularly congratulate themselves in their Annual Reports when their borrower-numbers rise in a given year, and lament or rationalise when they do not. This indicates that a curious set of conditions prevailed in which a logistical if not strictly financial impulse was at work, demanding attention to consumer needs as well as moral obligations.

One important result of the money shortages was the decision made by many library committees to take out a subscription to either Mudie's or Smith's. This meant they were able to borrow a certain number of new, high-demand but short life-span books each year, thus borrowing alongside them, of course, the censorship and moral narrowness for which these libraries were famous. J.T. Burchett, Winchester's chief librarian from 1886–1914, explained in an interview with the *Hampshire Chronicle* in 1905 that borrower numbers dropped in 1888–89 because the library 'could not get new books and the people had practically read up'.[20] Shortly after his arrival he suggested to the council that they subscribe to Smith's in order to increase their stock and its appeal to borrowers, but the council resisted until as late as 1897 when the princely sum of £12 12s 6d. was authorised to be spent on a subscription, though the council minutes warn portentously that this was meant be used for the provision of 'expensive books which the Committee were unable to purchase', rather than for cheap popular novels.[21]

---

17   Meeting of the Whitechapel Public Library Commissioners held on 2 March 1892 (Minute Books of the Whitechapel Public Library Commissioners, Ref: s.350, East End Local History Archive), p. 186.
18   Meeting of the Whitechapel Public Library Commissioners, 2 March 1892, p. 186.
19   Meeting of the Whitechapel Public Library Commissioners, 2 March 1892, p. 187.
20   'Twenty-One Years In Winchester Free Library', *Hampshire Chronicle*, 1905, n.p.
21   Winchester City Council Sub-Committee Minute Book, Winchester Local Records Office, File W/B5/22/2.

Fiction and the Public Space

Winchester was not, of course, alone in its resistance to novels. The provision of fiction in libraries was part of a much older debate that had exercised many a committee and filled columns of newsprint long before it passed into the House of Commons debates over the Libraries Act. When the Newcastle Literary and Philosophical Society was formed in 1793, for example, its first list of rules prohibited alcohol, women, children and novels,[22] and the war against fiction, at least, went on well into the nineteenth century. Former Society librarian and the first compiler of its history, Robert Spence, was moved to comment in 1897:

> It is amusing but refreshing to recall ... the tremendous fights which have been waged in this grave Society over the admission of novels ... so early as 1803 the Committee had experienced the extreme difficulty of keeping out fiction ... novels which came out in monthly magazines were admitted to our shelves, but when completed and appearing in separate works, they were strictly tabooed...The last fierce battle was fought some thirty years ago [i.e. in the 1860s] ... And in due course, not many years ago, novels were at length freely admitted, and nobody seems a penny the worse, excepting, possibly, those who are so unfortunate as to read them.[23]

This was a fairly typical pattern. In most libraries and literary societies the evangelical impulse which had set out to condemn all fiction in the early part of the nineteenth century had softened by its final third into a grudging acceptance of certain types, themes and forms, largely comprised of light but morally blameless contemporary novels and serious, male-authored classics. This canon was reinforced and in part controlled by Mudie's and Smith's. Even the Newcastle Lit. and Phil, concerned about falling membership, finally had to make the historic decision to subscribe to Mudie's.[24] Nonetheless, the public library movement continued to rehearse many of these old debates, adding to them a new set of potential problems raised by the as yet undetermined role of a publicly funded book-provision service operating in a public space.

The great fear that the working population would be tempted to use the libraries as places in which to pass a rainy hour in idleness or, worse still, the reading of trash worked powerfully against the provision of all popular forms of reading for some years. Reading and vice were inextricably linked: for a time the racing news was blacked out of newspapers in some libraries.[25] But the debates around whether the ban should be lifted in order to encourage the working classes to return indicate that the notion of self-improvement through aesthetics had already, by the 1890s, lost out

---

22 Robert Spence, *The History of the Literary and Philosophical Society of Newcastle-Upon-Tyne, 1793–1896* (London,1897), pp. 30–40.
23 Spence, pp. 178–9.
24 Spence, p. 193.
25 Keating, p. 280.

to a more powerful notion. Arguing against the lifting of the ban in a paper read out at the Library Association's 1893 conference, the librarian R.K. Dent pointed to:

> numbers of rough and ill-behaved fellows who, in spite of all efforts, persisted in disturbing the peace of the reading rooms, and interfering with the comfort of quiet readers at the news stands. Having no taste for reading whatsoever, beyond the latest tips, programmes, and results of races, and having exhausted these, they would beguile the time of waiting for the arrival of other papers by various loutish tricks, until, in spite of every effort, the reading rooms ... were shunned by the better class of ratepayers.[26]

He makes it fairly clear here that the risk of losing this 'better class' clientele is something that is to be avoided at all costs.

The kinds of literature that a library stocked was by this time seen as crucial, then, and not merely in order to serve the spirit of self-help which was the guiding principle of Ewart's Act. The pre-Act enquiries had been lent considerable weight by the evidence given by Samuel Smiles, then Assistant Secretary of the Leeds and Thirsk Railway and an enthusiastic supporter of rate-supported libraries, shortly thereafter to become the widely-read author of the self-help movement's bible, *Self-help: with Illustrations of Conduct and Perseverance* (1859). The book struck such a chord with the public that it sold 20,000 copies in its first year and was still selling well forty years later.[27] In this book Smiles stated that 'the healthy spirit of self-help created amongst working people would more than any other measure serve to raise them as a class, and this, not by pulling down others, but by leveling them up to a higher and still advancing state of religion, intelligence and virtue'.[28] His follow-up volume *Character* (1871) made the connection between self-help, moral virtue and reading still more explicit: 'one should always live in the best company, whether it be of books or men ... good words almost invariably inspire to good works'.[29] Instead of the use of literature as social leveller that Smiles clearly envisioned here, though, what we are seeing by 1893 when Dent made his plea to the Library Association conference is literature as a form of social control, a literature that separates, rather than unites, the populace.

Fiction reading had come by this period to stand in a metonymic relation to a number of social ills, and the debate over its inclusion in public libraries foregrounds the thinking behind them. In an ironic reversal of one of the main impulses behind the

---

26   R.K. Dent, 'The Blacking Out Question', *Library*, Vol. 6, 1894, p. 127.
27   Joan Shelley Rubin has demonstrated that a parallel self-help movement arose at around the same time in America. More concerned with exploring the roots of the American condition *in situ* than with relating it to its important European influences, she does not, however, even mention Smiles's best-selling book, though it sold well on both sides of the Atlantic. *The Making of Middlebrow Culture* (Chapel Hill and London, 1992), pp. 5–6.
28   Samuel Smiles, *Self-help: with Illustrations of Conduct and Perseverance* (1859; London, 1879), p. 294
29   Smiles, *Character*, pp. 289–90.

library movement – that of providing working people with an alternative space to the public house – the reading of 'ephemeral fiction' (as it came to be called) is frequently likened to an addiction to drink. An anti-adoption letter to *The Times* in 1886 may have put the movement itself down to 'masculine women and screaming tee-totallers',[30] but throughout the period and particularly towards its close there are numerous examples of the reversal of this objection. In 1863 in an article on 'Sensation Fiction' (then considered a particularly dangerous form of literature) Henry Mansel describes the 'ephemeral' novel as 'striving to act as the dram or the dose, rather than as the solid food, because the effect is more immediately perceptible'.[31] Smiles himself came to warn against popular fiction: 'how much of our reading is but the indulgence of a sort of intellectual dram-drinking, imparting a grateful excitement for the moment?'[32] In 1908 the Library Association, tired of the debate taking up the greater part of its annual meetings, collected a number of such opinions. It reported that according to the *Yorkshire Daily Observer* 'The fine lady who spends all her waking hours upon the couch in reading the latest novels – consuming upon average one romance per diem – rarely develops into an intellectual athlete, and may sometimes resort to worse stimulants'. The *Daily Telegraph* warned that 'fiction-reading is like dram-drinking. It becomes an inveterate habit'. The *Dundee Advertiser* defended fiction on the grounds that 'it is very probable that if the mental grog-shop is closed to them they will find what they want in the other grog shop'.[33] Fiction reading was thought to encourage theft. It was supposed to soften the mind and make it impervious to better things. It turned young mothers into slatterns. It kept the workman from his job. Debates about fiction reading thus drew upon pre-existing concerns about class, gender and morality, and for some time the library as public space was anxiously viewed as an attempt to transgress the boundaries of any or all of these.

'The Great Fiction Bore' (as the Library Association called it in the 1908 report) had almost petered out by the First World War. But almost all library reports continue throughout the period to express some concern on their first pages over the numbers of fiction books borrowed, congratulating themselves on having reduced the number in a given year, or seeking to rationalise the fact that they seem unable to do so, and they often praise their townspeople when they display a propensity for more serious reading matter. These reports, published annually in local newspapers and covered by *The Times*, made explicit the Public Library movement's disapproval of lightweight reading habits, and encouraged the public to think of their library as a somewhat repressive institution which provided fiction unwillingly but bestowed upon its more serious users a certain legitimisation leading to a sense of self-worth and public-spiritedness.

---

30   *The Times*, 23 December 1886, p. 3.
31   Henry Mansel, 'Sensation Fiction', *Quarterly Review*, Vol. 113, April 1863, p. 485.
32   Smiles, *Self-Help*, pp. 326–7.
33   'The Great Fiction Bore', *Library World*, Vol. 7, 1908, p. 131.

In the end, of course, the need to keep up borrower numbers prevailed, and what borrowers wanted above all else was fiction. None of my case studies deviates significantly from the oft-quoted statistics that place fiction at between 50 and 90 per cent of all categories of borrowing in the period. But a closer look at the borrower records of these libraries reveals a more important dimension to the 'Great Fiction Bore'.[34] By 1913 the borrowing of fiction at Southampton's Central Library stood at 70.78 per cent of total issues after several years of successive decline which the Committee of 1897 had put down to 'the care of the staff in assisting the public to a good choice of books, especially those having an educational value'.[35] At the local branch library in Shirley, however, the picture was slightly different. Here the borrowing of fiction was on average both initially higher than at the Central and steadily increasing throughout the period, until in 1914 it stood at 83.6 per cent – 13 per cent higher than at the Central.[36] Indeed, in the year of Shirley's opening (1896), fiction borrowing from the Central dropped from 74.55 to 69.4 per cent, and given the ensuing pattern it seems likely that this change was due as much to the opening of the Branch Library as to the 'care of the staff'.

The town's demographics are revealing. Borrower occupation records from the whole period show that of users at the Central, students tended to be the highest category with clerks next on the list. These occupations were associated with lower middle to middle-class groups. In Shirley, however, clerks and students were a much smaller category of borrowers, with working-class occupations such as Steward, Chauffeur and Grocers' Assistant figuring more prominently.[37] The ratio of unoccupied women to men is also considerably lower in Shirley, standing at 140 women to 23 men in 1912, while in the Central Library area it is 244 women to 20 men.[38] This could be an indication that the middle-class households utilising the central library, wealthy enough to permit their women to stay in the home, were also those most likely not only to buy rather than borrow such fiction as they read or to get it from a subscription library, but perhaps also to use the free library as a public space in which to engage in different and perhaps more serious kinds of reading. There is further evidence. When the Portswood Branch was opened in 1915 in Southampton's suburbs, an area of urban renewal specifically designed to attract the aspirant middle classes,[39] we find fiction reading on average 12 per cent

---

[34]   Library records represent a very uneven resource; there was for many years no centralising influence that forced them to record the same things. But most libraries took themselves seriously enough to keep records of some sort and it is usually possible to piece together a picture from fragments of other clues.

[35]   *Southampton Library Annual Report*, 1896–97, p. 7.

[36]   *Southampton Library Annual Report*, 1913–14, p. 5.

[37]   *Southampton Library Annual Report*, 1913–14, p. 5.

[38]   *Southampton Library Annual Report*, 1912–13, p. 4.

[39]   Sir Sidney Kimber, *Thirty-Eight Years of Public Life in Southampton* (London and Southampton: published privately, 1949), p. 21.

lower even than the Central, and categories such as History, Art and Science top of the list.[40]

Unfortunately neither Winchester nor York lists borrower statistics, though they do provide catalogues and financial details. In Leeds where we have fuller records, however, fiction represented 75 per cent of total issues in 1872[41] but by 1914 it was down to 46.6 per cent.[42] Leeds does not separate out its issue statistics by branch, but some clues as to how much of each category was borrowed from where are provided by the kinds of periodicals that are stocked in each library, and by its occupation statistics. While the Central stocked predominantly scientific and professional journals such as *Athenaeum*, the *Economist*, the *Lancet* and the *Art Journal*, the branches in the nearby industrial areas of Hunslet and Holbeck tended to stock periodicals devoted at least partially to fiction and lighter kinds of reading such as *All the Year Round*, *Blackwoods* and the *Illustrated London News*. In 1871 the Central's borrowers were predominantly Agents, Collectors, Merchants, Manufacturers, Unoccupied Women, Housewives and Clerks, in keeping with the city centre's profile as an area devoted largely to banking and trading. In Hunslet, however, Mechanics, Artisans, Clerks and Women (employed as well as unemployed) were the heaviest borrowers, and in Holbeck Mechanics far outnumbered other borrowers.[43] Of all these, clerks consulted the reference works most frequently – 6,658 times as compared to only 1,130 consultations by Professional Men. (It is worth noting here that clerks were members of an occupational category often ridiculed for its aspirant petit-bourgeois qualities, as witness Forster's Leonard Bast). By 1891 Pupils, Artisans and Clerks were the heaviest borrowers overall, but Professional Gentlewomen now ran a close fourth, a marker, perhaps, of the town's changing demographic climate in line with its rise in prosperity.

There is, then, a slightly different character to the kinds of reading being done in each case, just as in Southampton, with more serious reading being done at the Central, and by a 'higher' class of reader. Fiction-borrowing as a whole continued to decline in Leeds until 1914–15 when, according to the Annual Report, 'in consequence of the pre-occupation of the public mind with the war and the heavy demands made upon the workers of Leeds in the clothing and other trades for Army work, there has been a tendency to return to the lighter forms of literature'. But also, crucially, during that same year there was a 'considerable issue of books on the various countries of Europe and Asia, affected by military movements, and about War Origins, the Armies and Navies, Aircraft, Imperial Defence, and of works by French and Russian writers'.[44]

The Whitechapel Public Library provides an intriguing comparison. It was situated in London's East End, a region famous in the nineteenth century for its prostitutes, sweatshops and poor immigrants. Library adoption was relatively slow here and

---

40 *Annual Report, Southampton Public Libraries Committee*, 1915–16, p. 7.
41 *Leeds Public Library Annual Reports*, 1870–72, p. 19.
42 *Annual Report of the Leeds Libraries and Arts Committee*, 1914–15, p. 2.
43 *Leeds Public Library Annual Report*, 1870–72, p. 16.
44 *Annual Report of the Leeds Libraries and Arts Committee*, 1914–15, p. 2.

coincided almost exactly with the major period of concern around Jewish immigration sparked by the East European pogroms of the 1880s and 1890s.[45] From the first, Whitechapel signalled its desire to serve the needs of a very specific community. It appointed at least one member of the Jewish community to its Committee, and its reading rooms carried several Jewish newspapers (the *Jewish Chronicle* and *Jewish Times*, and later the Hebrew papers the *Dawn* and the *Intelligentser or Interpreter*).[46] But the selection of books seemed more troublesome. From the beginning, the catalogue contained some works in French, German and Russian, but for several years the Committee rejected offers of Hebrew books, and it was not until 1906 (14 years after its opening) that a special Jewish list was set up. The list demonstrates what at first sight appears to be a curious mixture of the appropriate and the bizarre. It contained, for example, Hebrew, Yiddish, French and German editions of Jewish History, religion and children's books, and novels by Benjamin Disraeli and Israel Zangwill. It also contained English classics and popular novels with Jewish themes such as George Eliot's *Daniel Deronda*, Hall Caine's fictionalised treatise against anti-Semitism *The Scapegoat*, and Eugene Sue's *Wandering Jew*. Of possible Shakespeare inclusions, however, it contains only the two 'Jewish' plays, *The Merchant of Venice* and *Julius Caesar*, although all Shakespeare's other works were available in the main library. The representations of Jewishness in the Shakespeare, at least, were not exactly flattering.

But this selection must, I think, be placed alongside a powerful assimilationist impulse. Aided by pro-immigration lobbyists (among them many of the philanthropists who contributed to the East End public library movement), Jewish immigrants were keen to fit into their adoptive country, and an important part of the way they did so was through their approach to the new language and its literature. Children were taught English in school and encouraged to help their parents to replace Yiddish with English at home.[47] The Girls School (part of the Jews Free School) performed an annual Shakespeare play in English, to great acclaim.[48] It is significant, too, that the Whitechapel Library Jewish List was formed only a year after the controversial 1905 Aliens Act targeted Jewish immigrants with crippling measures designed to keep new immigrants out, and to keep tabs on those already in England. The list's function should properly be seen, therefore, as an encouragement to the formation of an immigrant identity that was strongly Anglo-Jewish, both sensitive to the needs of Jewish immigrants and anxious to defuse the threat of a 'Jewish invasion' that was so powerful in anti-Semitic discourse in this period.

---

[45] For example, Bethnal Green Free Library opened in 1882, Whitechapel in 1892, Poplar in 1894, Stepney and Mile End in 1902.

[46] Minute Books of the Whitechapel Public Library Commissioners, Ref: S.350, East End Local History Archive, pp. 241–2.

[47] Gerry Black, *J.F.S: The History of the Jews Free School in London since 1732* (London, 1998), pp. 126–31.

[48] Black, p. 128.

With this assimilationist project in mind, it is interesting to survey the borrowing records. Fiction was by far the largest part of the library's stock in its early days. In 1893/94 the stock book lists 44,815 volumes of Prose Fiction and 15,390 volumes of 'Juvenile Literature' – usually fiction – as opposed to the next highest category, Literature and Collected Works etc. of which 2,521 were listed.[49] Whitechapel also had one of the most liberal catalogues of new fiction, stocking popular novels that many other public libraries would not touch. Yet Whitechapel has one of the lowest fiction-borrowing rates of any of the libraries I have looked at, declining from 60 per cent to 52 per cent over the period 1893–97.[50] Compared with other libraries in working class areas, this figure represents a significant drop: Shirley Library records, for example, indicate that fiction borrowing in 1897–98 stood 23 per cent higher than Whitechapel at 75.78 per cent. Even in Leeds, fiction borrowing did not fall this low until the eve of the First World War.

These statistics, combined with the other clues, seem to indicate that the higher class or the more aspirational or assimilationist the clientele, the less fiction it borrows. In addition, the patterns suggest that patrons who wanted fiction and were unable either to buy or to borrow it from a circulating library for some reason found it easier or more congenial to obtain it from smaller branch libraries, rather than from the Central.[51] This raises the possibility that during this period reading is becoming a means not just of facilitating self-education, as Ewart and his supporters intended, or of obtaining fiction for free as the movement's critics feared, though both of these functions were obviously being served. For a certain section of the population reading was also a means of creating or cementing affiliation: of class, of taste, of nationality, of political allegiance. And the libraries, particularly the large Central Libraries, were a public space in which these affiliations could be signalled prominently.

Libraries, Reading and the Performance of Gender and Class

Many libraries actively encouraged this development. Despite the financial strictures already mentioned, committees inspired both by Ruskinite notions about the improving nature of art and by bourgeois civic symbolism frequently chose to erect lavish, imposing library buildings in their city centres as soon as they could afford it. Minute books frequently bear witness to council approval for numerous alterations designed to maintain or improve the comfort and grandeur of the accommodation. Running the

---

[49]   Whitechapel Public Library and Museum, 2nd Annual Report of the Commissioners, 26 March 1893–25 March 1895.

[50]   Whitechapel Public Library and Museum 3rd Annual Report of the Commissioners, 26 March 1895–25 March 1897.

[51]   Jonathan Rose confirms that a lighter and freer mood tended to prevail in libraries which served close-knit local rather than heterogeneous urban communities. Rose, *The Intellectual Life of the British Working Classes* (New Haven and London, 2001), p. 84.

library buildings was often, also, expensive, and meant a limited amount of money available for the purchase of books. The effect of this shortage on the Whitechapel library's stock has already been noted. To give a further example, in 1877 Winchester spent £120 on the upkeep of its reading rooms and only £50 on books.[52]

But relating to and using a splendid, imposing and well-policed library was difficult for certain sections of the population. In the early years, as the readership historian Richard Altick has noted, libraries were the haunt of 'public building parasites: vagrants taking shelter from rain and cold, loafers and eccentrics spitting, smoking and discussing the merits and demerits of horses in language unfit for quotation'.[53] 'What shall the librarian do?' lamented the Library Association at its first Annual Meeting in 1889.[54] The answer was to impose a form of social control, not only, as we have seen, by limiting library stock to discourage the undesirable and unredeemable elements thought to be connected to it, but also by instigating severe rules and regulations designed to discourage use of the library as a congenial meeting place, insisting on silence within and prohibiting congregation in doorways or on steps. Persons using the library were expected to be clean, and risked banishment if they were not. This measure was ostensibly designed to protect the books. But it also meant that at a time when few work places provided washing facilities for their employees, calling in to borrow a book on the way home was fraught with risk and embarrassment for those employed in manual jobs. In her 1907 study of the working-class inhabitants of the iron-town of Middlesborough, Lady Bell found that the workingman arrived home in such a condition that 'before looking like a respectable citizen he has to make an elaborate toilet, washing, and changing all his clothes'.[55] The autobiographies of the period's mill and factory workers frequently bear out this assessment. Alice Foley, for example, gives an account of her working-class life in Bolton in 1905 in which she graphically describes the lack of workplace facilities:

> No hot water was available for washing dirty, oily hands, and each Saturday noon after laboriously cleaning clogged, fluffy machinery on hands and knees, we trudged off to the factory lodge seeking to remove excess of grime and grease in its steamy stagnancy before going home for the half-day rest. Old sinks were receptacles for wet tea-leaves and sodden newspapers; no towels were provided and toilets were dark, smelly and inadequate. Of social welfare or refinement there was no hint.[56]

---

[52]   Meeting of the School of Art and Reading Rooms Committee, 28 September 1877, Ref: W/B5/28/1.

[53]   Richard D. Altick, *The English Common Reader: A Social History of the Mass Reading Public 1800–1900* (London, 1957), p. 238.

[54]   *Library*, Vol. I, 1889, p. 410.

[55]   Lady Bell, *At the Works: A Study of a Manufacturing Town* (1907; London, 1985), p. 99.

[56]   Alice Foley, *A Bolton Childhood* (Manchester, 1973), p. 59.

Lady Bell found, in addition, that 'the library is used by many of the better class of workmen, but not much by the very poor', and she goes on to explain the difficulty in terms that are – significantly – ideological as well as practical:

> It is quite possible that some of these are deterred by the mere ceremonies that have to be gone through to take out a book. A woman who lives in a distant part of town, whose outer garment is probably a ragged shawl fastened with a pin, may not like going up an imposing flight of stairs, getting a ticket, giving a name, looking through a catalogue, having the book entered, etc.; whereas many of these would read the book if it were actually put into their hands. Women, at any rate, of all classes know how often our activities are governed by our clothes, and how the fact of being unsuitably clad for a given course of conduct may be enough to prevent us from embarking on it.[57]

Again, Alice Foley bears out Lady Bell's assessment of the difficulty. As she grew up she became her family's chief book-borrower, making a weekly journey to a library that, although a branch, was still some distance away from her home and far from welcoming to girls of her class:

> In those days there was no access to open shelves and the selection of books was quite a business. First came the job of probing through the massive catalogues for author and book number, followed by reference to an in-and-out card index – green in, black out, which often entailed a tedious repetition. After the selection I usually crept upstairs to the reading-room, trying to still the clatter of clogs on stone steps, but on settling down with a picture magazine, up came the irate caretaker, and I was shunted out like an unwanted animal.[58]

What stands out here is that the tedious process of selection and borrowing took place under the eyes, not only of other borrowers, but also of the 'caretaker' or the librarian, who took his or her duties – among them the care of stock and the recommendation of improving literature – very seriously.[59]

There is also evidence that some borrowers were actively discouraged from serious reading – and from writing – because of their class. Jonathan Rose quotes the memoir of Joseph Stamper, a steel worker who was treated with suspicion by a librarian who demanded to know 'Where is the need for study … in a steel foundry?' 'I told him I'd had two books published', the worker recalls. 'It was a false step; I saw his manner harden, accusation swam into his severe eyes. I was an offender against the unwritten law, I had no right to have books published, I was not a member of the book-writing class'.[60] Even after the open-access system was introduced surveillance was a large

---

[57] Bell, p. 163.

[58] Foley, p. 25.

[59] Almost all chief librarians in this period were male, though women increasingly occupied the role of assistant librarian.

[60] Rose, *The Intellectual Life of the British Working Classes*, p. 400.

part of the librarian's role. As the recent library historian Alistair Black has put it: 'the library counter is not just a physical, but also a psychological barrier. It symbolises the power of the library's staff over the user, and it can be positioned in such as way as to enhance, through supervision, that very power'.[61] Black's otherwise excellent history denies the existence of evidence that this supervision led to class selectivity. But it certainly exists, not only in the testimony of those who, like Alice Foley or Joseph Stamper or Lady Bell, either used the library or observed those users, but also in the pages of the reports themselves. While libraries did frequently provide public facilities, for example, they were not intended to take the place of general personal cleanliness, as the 1870 annual report of Leeds Public Library indicates:

> Sometimes we have come in contact with the 'great unwashed' when they have been directed to the lavatory, and duly cautioned that the privilege of borrowing would be cancelled upon a repetition of this offence against the rules of the library ... The stock is new, and comparatively clean, but in a very short time a bloom will grow upon it, in spite of the vigilance used to detect grimy readers, and must be debited to ordinary wear and tear. This is inevitable, and will be so until all classes become more careful in performing their ablutions.[62]

This is a hope which, until the improvement of sanitary facilities in working-class homes and workplaces, was clearly not to be realised, and it indicates that the atmosphere of the library was strongly prohibitive for certain sections of the population.

A related and very public issue was that of disease prevention. Books were generally thought to be potential 'plague carriers' throughout this period. Mudie's were viewed with suspicion for some time for this reason, and articles in the medical journal the *Lancet* recommend both the disinfecting of returned books and that patrons be forced to declare their households free from disease.[63] But public spaces were obviously deemed to be particularly hazardous. Even at the end of the period the novelists Arnold Bennett and Marie Corelli were writing of their distaste for 'filthy' library books. Corelli announced that 'to borrow one's mental fare from Free Libraries is a dirty habit to begin with. It is rather like picking up eatables dropped by someone else in the road, and making one's dinner off another's leavings'.[64] It is possible that her disgust was a result of a combination of rage at her banning by some libraries, and frustration over the loss of income that acceptance by others might mean, since she later adds: '[Free Libraries are] extremely detrimental to the prosperity of authors. A

---

61   Alistair Black, *A New History of the English Public Library: Social and Intellectual Contexts 1850–1914* (London, 1996), p. 244.
62   *Leeds Public Library Annual Reports,* 1870–72, p. 7.
63   Hiley, pp. 126–7.
64   Marie Corelli, 'Free Opinions Freely Expressed', *Publishers' Circular,* Vol. 82, 3 June 1905, p. 621.

popular author would have good reason to rejoice if his works were excluded from Free Libraries inasmuch as his sales would be twice, perhaps three times as large'.[65] But Bennett, who had no such reason, made his disgust yet more explicit, centering it graphically around the site of infection, the home:

> Go into the average good home of the crust, in the quietude 'after tea', and you will see a youthful miss sitting over something by Charlotte M. Yonge or Charles Kingsley. And that something is repulsively foul, greasy, sticky, black. Remember that it reaches from thirty to a hundred such good homes every year. Can you wonder that it should carry deposits of jam, egg, butter, coffee, and personal dirt? You cannot. But you are entitled to wonder why the Municipal Sanitary Inspector does not inspect it and order it to be destroyed.[66]

Library committees held long meetings to debate the problem. By way of a preventative – but also in order to convince users of their safety – notices were prominently displayed in libraries, catalogues and newspapers ordering the burning of infected books and the banning not only of those who were known disease carriers but also of those who cared for them. In York (opened 1892) for example, the Library Regulations contained the paragraph: 'No person who is in a state of intoxication, or uncleanly in person or dress, or who is suffering from an infectious or offensive disease, or who has recently been in attendance upon a person so suffering, shall be admitted or allowed to remain in the Building'.[67] How librarians were expected to know these things is not recorded but the sense of surveillance is, of course, pervasive, and the notion of a book-burning session is an incredibly powerful one. This is particularly true when it is designed to excise, not seditious literature, but traces of people.

Intriguingly, Lady Bell suggests that smaller, less imposing spaces – such, perhaps, as the Branch Libraries provided – might prove more attractive to working-class borrowers. 'The people who, for one reason or another, do not use the Free Library, will sometimes be willing to frequent smaller and less imposing centers of learning',[68] she suggests. It is easy to see how a public space inhabited by familiar types of people if not by friends and neighbors might have been attractive. But the tenor of her discussion indicates that this might be so for reasons of intellectual as well as physical comfort. The embarrassment over 'not knowing' which books to ask for and how is here as important as the embarrassment over clothing and cleanliness:

> A working-class man seeking diversion may be willing to read the things that he finds under his hand, but he may not have purpose and zest enough to take definite steps to

---

65 Corelli, 'Free Opinions', p. 621.

66 Bennett, *Books and Persons*, p. 104.

67 'Report of the Technical Instruction and Public Library Committee', York City Council Minutes, 1892–93, p. 365 (Ref: Y 352, York City Library).

68 Bell, p. 163.

procure anything else, let alone the fact that he may not know what to procure, since he has not the opportunities enjoyed by the better off of compiling lists of books from the literary columns of the newspapers.[69]

Some library catalogues made explicit their expectations in this direction, and positively discouraged the use of public libraries for browsing. Leeds Public Library Catalogue of 1894 includes a section of tips on 'How to Use the Public Library'. Among them, closely echoing Smiles' pronouncement in *Self-help* that 'the most profitable study is that which is conducted with a definite aim and object',[70] is the advice:

> Come to the library with a definite book or subject in mind, rather than with an aimless desire for 'some book – no matter what' ... Read carefully and thoroughly, so as to be able to digest one subject in your mind before passing on to another. Do not form the habit of returning your books every two or three days. Such a practice, if persisted in, will make your reading a morbid habit, rather than a benefit.[71]

This was all very well if one knew what to look for. In Bourdieu's terminology, as in Gissing's, knowing represents cultural capital, and not knowing represents a lack which was made all too embarrassingly public through the process of selection integral to the operations of the public library. Books classify, even before they have been read. The women in Gissing's fictional library who ask whether a book is 'pretty' and thereby proclaim their class inferiority are prime objects of ridicule to Nancy and Tarrant, and clearly – like Nancy herself – represent an immediately recognisable type.

Of course, as many of the examples I've given above indicate, these debates about public reading and novels center in particular on women, fuelled by contemporary discourses which positioned woman's physical and (by extension) spiritual purity as potentially threatened by her increasing access to public spaces and to potentially licentious literature. For a woman, visiting the public library was fraught with danger on a number of levels. Women entering the public sphere were subject to the gazes of untold numbers of men of all classes and, as Kate Flint has suggested, the act of reading publicly was seen not only as an incitement to men to consider the direction of a woman's mental processes, but as an opportunity for advantage to be taken of the relaxed social awareness which absorption in reading might entail.[72] Libraries were, in addition, widely recognised as potential courting grounds, as Nancy and Tarrant indicate.

Physical danger was only part of the problem. Fiction reading had long been thought to encourage mental laxity, even, as we have seen, to develop into a form of addiction akin to drink in its symptomatic abdication of social responsibility.

---

69 Bell, p. 165.
70 Smiles, p. 323.
71 *Leeds Public Libraries: Catalogue of the Central Lending Library 1894*, p. v.
72 Flint, p. 4.

Stories abounded of young women neglecting their families' needs in favour of the temptations of the latest fictional serial, much as earlier in the century the figure of the young mother debilitated by drink was used to raise social consciousness of the issue as a whole. 'Many are the crimes brought about by the disordered imagination of a reader of sensational, and often immoral, rubbish', wrote one correspondent to the *Evening Standard* in 1891, 'whilst many a home is neglected and uncared for owing to the all-absorbed novel-reading wife'.[73] This mental laxity was seen as dangerous for women themselves, of course, but it was also thought to intervene in the self-improvement impulses of men and thus to problematise the public sphere itself. A direct line was posited by many social commentators from the novel to women to the family and thence to the fabric of society. In 1908, according to the Library Association, the *Manchester Guardian* had reported that: 'those who have observed most closely the life of Manchester workmen will tell you that a strong impulse towards serious reading is very common among them, and that to a great extent it is baulked by the difficulty of obtaining space and quiet to read either at home or in a branch library that is mainly engaged in distributing feeble fiction to uncritical young women'.[74]

According to Smiles, indeed, it is not only the presence of biological femininity, but also of gendered types of literature which is a problem; fiction was so tied to notions of women's feebler intellects that it was capable of feminising men. Smiles's Self-help manual is filled with metaphors of this type. To give just one example, for Smiles fiction reading engendered 'the habit of intellectual dissipation', among men, and 'thus engendered, [it] cannot fail, in course of time, to produce a thoroughly emasculating effect both upon their mind and character ... It is the idlest of all idlenesses, and leaves more of impotency than any other'.[75] This impotence had dire consequences. Without his 'spring' and his 'powers of life' the Englishman is able to 'produce no healthy growth either of character or intellect'.[76] And of course, it is character that 'constitutes the true source of national vigour and strength'.[77] On this reading, fiction is capable of weakening the nation itself.

The answer to the problem of a 'feminising' literature that emasculated the nation might seem to be obvious – teach women to read and write more serious 'masculine' books. But the idea of encouraging serious reading among women was itself problematised by medical arguments which constructed women's physiology as intrinsically unsuited to study because it interfered with the energies required by her idealised role as the nation's mother. Jessica, Gissing's satirical representation of a female student in *In the Year of Jubilee*, gives herself a complete breakdown by diverting all her energies into her studies. Her moral courage, her usefulness as a

---

[73] Altick, p. 232.
[74] 'The Great Fiction Bore', p. 131.
[75] Smiles, *Self-help*, p. 325.
[76] Smiles, *Self-help*, p. 334.
[77] Smiles, *Self-help*, p. 1.

friend, her mental and physical health and therefore, we are expected to assume, her prospects for marriage and motherhood decline in direct proportion to the amount of serious reading with which she crams her overloaded brain. Following her partial recovery, she then abandons one sort of fanaticism for another and becomes a zealous Evangelist, repressing once again the sexual and emotional energies that she ought to be channelling into motherhood and becoming a sad, pale creature on the brink of madness. For Gissing, mass literacy's increasing dominance over religion was a simple case of one evil replacing another.

This anxiety about the dangers of educating women came from a much older notion. As Jürgen Habermas's influential work on the public sphere has shown, at least since the eighteenth century, woman's place in the dominant model of citizenship had been to perpetuate the illusion of individual freedom on which the concept of 'natural' man was predicated within the sphere of the bourgeois family. There, male domination was also perceived as 'natural', and the 'natural' woman's freedom was spiritual and conceptual rather than actual. (She was free, that is, to have a good moral influence over men through the illusion of the love-match.)[78] 'Man is the brain, but woman is the heart of humanity;' Smiles writes in *Character*, 'he its judgement, she its feeling; he its strength, she its grace, ornament, and solace … And thus, though man may direct the intellect, woman cultivates the feelings, which mainly determine the character'.[79]

But if woman was to remain the nation's moral and spiritual guiding light she must, it was becoming clear, also partake in some way in the great industrial and intellectual advances of the second half of the nineteenth century through which both citizenship and nationhood itself were being redefined. In order to fulfill her role adequately, the angel in the house needed to know something about the world outside where her father, husband and sons operated, and to be able to educate her daughters in that knowledge. The Empire, with its dependence on patriarchy, was under threat. There was a woman on the throne. Middle-class women had been struggling for intellectual and legal equality at least since Mary Wollstonecraft in the 1790s, and a hundred years later these demands were becoming difficult to ignore. Sex, physiology, and the double standard were no longer wholly taboo, but increasingly topics for public debate.[80] Things were changing. By 1910 *The Times* was still insisting that a woman needed instinct and emotion if she was to fulfill her role, but now she needed her intellect too: 'It is the perfect balance of head and heart that makes, and must make, the power of modern women … for a nation to be truly great, must always have high ideals, and it is the women who mould those ideals'.[81] The increasing acceptance of

---

[78]   Jürgen Habermas, *The Structural Transformation of the Public Sphere: An Inquiry into a Category of Bourgeois Society*, trans. Thomas Burger (Cambridge, MA, 1989).

[79]   Smiles, *Character*, p. 41.

[80]   Lucy Bland, *Banishing the Beast: English Feminism and Sexual Morality 1885–1914* (Harmondsworth, 1995).

[81]   'The Spiritual Influence of Women', *The Times*, 14 May 1910, p. 7.

certain kinds of fiction in public libraries can be seen in part as an effect of these two conflicting ideas – the old and the new – being brought together: the provision of uplifting but not-too-taxing reading that had been passed through rigorous censorship was one way of encouraging women to use their public spaces as 'natural' citizens without turning them into an intellectual threat. And for those who wanted (or wanted to be seen to want) something more serious, there were history, biography, science, and the male-authored canon of classics.

Women readers were clearly seen as important to the success of the movement (though some, like the correspondent to the *Manchester Guardian*, disapproved). Many libraries set aside separate reading rooms for women and supplied them with novels and fashion magazines, and women librarians were increasingly taken on both because they were cheaper to employ and because they were seen to exert a positive influence on rowdy boys and impressionable young girls. Women were encouraged to read aloud to their families, thus combining the demands of pleasure, self-improvement and moral responsibility. M.V. Hughes recalls in her autobiography that, while novels and newspapers were never allowed on Sundays, at other times 'Scott, Dickens, Thackeray, Lamb, George Eliot, Tennyson, Byron, Coleridge, Disraeli … became part of our lives'. While the women in the family were not allowed to visit the theatre or the music hall which, 'mother explained, were not dull, only not very nice', by way of compensation her mother told them stories 'from Shakespeare, Jane Austen, [and] Scott'.[82] From a type of reading that, it had been argued in the early years, it was necessary to ban from libraries altogether, by the 1890s fiction was being increasingly accepted as a healthy and even essential component of their stock. This, we might suggest, was a concession to reader demand. And so it was. But it was crucially mediated through the developments in gender relations that occurred during the 1880s and 90s, rooted as they were in debates around the 'nature' and responsibility of citizenship, and around woman's share in that role. This could not help but have an impact on the gendering of literary form.

Moral Guardianship and the Librarian

Libraries maintained their censoring stranglehold on stock not only through their close links with the circulating libraries, but also through the selection by committee of new novels. It was largely the public librarian who perused publishers' lists, made suggestions to the committee and ultimately fed these selections to the readers via catalogues, newspapers and face-to-face consultations. The role of this self-styled 'guardian of public morals' is crucial to an understanding of the role of public reading in the literary field towards the end of the nineteenth century.

There had been no body of professionals on which to draw when Winchester opened its doors in 1851, and early public librarians were appallingly poorly paid. The Library

---

82   M.V. Hughes, *A London Family 1870–1900* (Oxford, 1946), pp. 16; 44.

Association made the issue a top priority at its first annual meeting in 1878, and found that the country's worst paid librarian received only £20 p.a., and while the highest earner received £120, around £60 p.a. was about the norm,[83] and this at a time when a lower-middle class clerk was likely to receive up to twice that amount. Nonetheless, applications for this new role were so numerous that, as Thomas Greenwood notes, 'the task often becomes bewildering and perplexing. These applications have reached in number as high as 450 for only a third or fourth-rate post'. Nor was there any real sense of what social position the public librarian should occupy. Greenwood adds that these applications are not only numerous but they also:

> invariably include soldiers, sailors, pensioners, clerks, teachers, booksellers, and [representatives] from every class and section of society ... Many of the average applicants for these positions who have had no experience of library work, imagine that the post is an easy way to a respectable position in society, or that it affords an opportunity for private study. Both ideas are erroneous.[84]

The idea that both self-improvement and respectability were thought to be on offer in this role is crucial. Despite the fact that, as Greenwood suggests, neither was a possibility in the early years, librarians were struggling throughout much of this period to attain some form of professional status instead of being seen as lowly public servants. They were encouraged in these efforts by the Library Association (LA) which, formed in the late 1870s, held annual meetings and declared that the professionalisation of librarianship was one of its aims.[85] By the 1880s the LA had introduced summer schools and professional examinations to further this end. The examination questions are illuminating, and provide an indication of exactly how it was thought this professionalisation might be achieved. The examiners insisted not only that a librarian should know sufficient Latin to be able to catalogue books and enough about library science to keep up with new methods, but that he or she should be able to attend to reader enquiries with a list of largely male-authored canonical works in English, both fictional and factual, which (inevitably) included Chaucer, Milton, Matthew Arnold and Shakespeare.[86]

In fact, from the first librarians took their duties as guardians of public morals seriously, and understood that these included above all the censorship of novels, and the acquisition of a full canon of works. Responding to a town councillor who had criticised the public library movement in the Publishers' Circular in 1872, Leeds's

---

[83]   *Transactions and Proceedings of the First Annual Meeting of the Library Association* (Chiswick, 1879), p. 94.

[84]   Thomas Greenwood, *Public Libraries: A History of the Movement and a Manual for the Organisation and Management of Rate-Supported Libraries*, 4th edition, (London, 1891), p. 357.

[85]   *Transactions and Proceedings of the First Annual Meeting of the Library Association*, p. 1.

[86]   *Library Association Yearbook*, 1891, pp. 18–19.

Public Librarian James Yates stressed that 'the class of fiction offered is *not* of the most unsatisfactory kind, especially when compared with the garbage which could be obtained at the small cost of one penny per volume at the libraries existing in each town prior to the adoption of the acts ... fiction is tabooed altogether from ... our ... reference shelves, excepting where it is included in the collective works of some of the earlier writers, and in the better class of serials, such as can be found in the British Museum'.[87] The appeal to a higher authority such as the British Museum is indicative of the responsibility that Yates felt he carried, and to whom.

Obviously, though, the inclusion of new, untried, uncanonical fiction was another matter, and the debate by the turn of the century had become one about exactly how a new work which deserved to be included in the canon might be recognised. In public libraries the only practical solution to this complex problem seemed to be that the increasing volume of fiction being produced continued to undergo censorship by committee. Nick Hiley has suggested that if one was a subscriber to Mudie's even after the 1909 agreement it was always possible to purchase under the counter some banned book or other,[88] but there is no indication that the Mudie-style censorship process also used by the public libraries enabled this here; books deemed unsuitable were generally returned to the publishers. Winchester's Mr. Burchett does indicate in the 1905 interview that when his committee decided to ban Thomas Hardy's *Jude the Obscure* one committee member, who turned out to be the mayor, never returned his inspection copy.[89] This, however, seems to be an example of private opportunism or simple forgetfulness rather than large-scale profiteering, since I have found no other mention anywhere of books going astray before they reach the shelves.

The censorship solution was, however, at best a rather inadequate stop-gap; the precarious nature of the librarian's role, and the isolated conditions in which he or she and the committee often worked, led to some interesting discrepancies between different towns. Winchester's Mr Burchett, for example, failed to understand why his committee had refused to allow him to stock some of the novels of Thomas Hardy, but he was frequently asked for novels by Ouida, Fielding and Smollett which he not only did not stock but felt were 'not fit for the shelves of a public library'.[90] Leeds, however, stocked 31 of Ouida's books and most of Hardy's, including *Tess of the D'Urbervilles*, which Winchester refused along with *Jude*. Hall Caine was banned in some libraries as well as (on occasion) by Mudie's and Smith's, but in Winchester his works are given as among the most popular, running a 'neck and neck race for supremacy'[91] with Marie Corelli, who was banned from Acton Library along with Ouida and Zola. Whitechapel stocked all of Fielding, Hall Caine, Hardy, Corelli, and Ouida, carrying in addition some other contentious books and authors including some

---

87   *Leeds Public Libraries Annual Report*, 1870–72, p. 10.
88   Hiley, p. 144.
89   'Twenty-One Years in Winchester Free Library', *Hampshire Chronicle*, 1905.
90   'Twenty-One Years in Winchester Free Library'.
91   'Twenty-One Years in Winchester Free Library'.

Eugene Sue and most of Grant Allen, with the exception of *The Woman Who Did.*
Two of Corelli's novels, *Wormwood* and *Vendetta*, were also banned from Ealing Free
Library in 1899, despite her protestations that they had been enjoyed and endorsed
by the Queen and the Prince of Wales. This ban led the ever-vocal Corelli to write to
the Library Association in indignation:

> For the preservation of innocence and ignorance in the 'Young Person' it would be
> necessary to exclude Shakespeare, Sterne, Swift, Shelley and Byron from free libraries
> ... For myself I take it as a great compliment that my works should have secured the
> veto of the Ealing Free Library judges. I feel that when Ealing condemns, and critics
> wield the flail, I am on the high road to fame indeed.[92]

The idea that the Public Libraries were, like Mudie's, bastions of anti-aesthetic
conservatism was clearly well established by this time, and it aroused the wrath of
more writers and critics than Corelli. Arnold Bennett, for example, noted in 1909 that 'a
few new novels get into the Library every year. They must, however, be "innocuous",
that is to say, devoid of original ideas. This, of course, is inevitable in an institution
presided over by a committee which has infinitely less personal interest in books than
in politics or the price of coal'.[93]

I am not suggesting that Free Libraries were themselves responsible for the
formation of the patriarchal, conservative nature of the late-nineteenth century literary
canon, though they clearly helped both to engender and to perpetuate it. There is for
one thing, as we have seen, no centralising influence on stock throughout much of this
period, and therefore libraries tended to retain a highly parochial character. What I am
suggesting is that something much more subtle is happening. Public spaces like the Free
Library, emerging out of mid-nineteenth-century philosophies around the importance
of literature to the formation of character and citizenship, made public not just their
failures but the ways in which their successes were linked to middle-class hegemonic
codes. As Stefan Collini has pointed out in his exploration of public moralists like
Smiles: 'although the classic scenes of character-building are essentially private ...
it was also true that [in this period] character was an ascribed quality, possessed and
enjoyed in public view'.[94]

One crucial result of this publicisation was a new linking of reading practices
with cultural capital. For some, when a serious book was sanctioned by a central
public library and selected in its atmosphere of seriousness, self-help and responsible
citizenship, it marked its reader out as a student and a thinker. But for others – including
perhaps those whom the library itself had in one way or another excluded – serious
library reading was a sham, a pose or a waste of time. On the one hand it thus easily

---

[92]   *The Library,* 5, 1899, p. 49.
[93]   Bennett, *Books and Persons,* p. 104.
[94]   Stefan Collini, *Public Moralists: Political Thought and Intellectual Life in Britain
       1850–1930* (Oxford, 1991), p. 106.

spawned anti-intellectualism. On the other it just as easily spawned elitism of the type that enabled representations such as Gissing's Nancy Lord, whose literary tastes, like her name, have no genuine connection to a historically grounded and proven social status and are therefore seen as utterly without value. Another example is provided by H.G. Wells's smug but vulgar Mr Coote who sees himself as 'a Good Influence, a refined and amiable figure' (p. 98), a prime representative, in other words, of the country's lower middle classes. Coote is introduced to us in the act of performing this role in a place which is not only central to the novel's satire, but which, correctly interpreted, can add to our understanding of the social significance, both of the institution, and of the literature which it offered:

> You must figure him as about to enter our story, walking with a curious rectitude of bearing through the evening dusk towards the Public Library, erect, large-headed – he had a great big head, full of the suggestion of a powerful mind well under control ... He was a local house-agent, and a most active and gentlemanly person, a conscious gentleman, equally aware of society and the serious side of life. (p. 98).

To be a 'conscious gentleman' who walked to the library with a sense of self-satisfied moral obligation was not, by 1905, to be thought capable by the literary elite (of which Gissing and Wells both imagined themselves a part) of recognising or appreciating good literature. On the contrary, library visiting pegged any reader who was not a genuine scholar or lightweight fiction-borrower as a laughably strenuous self-improver. So entrenched in critical discourse did the library's construction of its books and its readers become, in fact, that Q.D. Leavis chastised it in 1932 as incapable of even recognising 'good literature' (here, of course, having achieved its apotheosis in a resolutely middle- or highbrow grouping, if not in a modernist canon which we might now wholly recognise):

> The fiction shelves of a public library commonly contain the classics and hardy popular novels of the past, representatives of all the most popular contemporary novelists, and (more rarely) the 'literary' novels of the age, but seldom what is considered by the critical minority to be the significant work in fiction – the novels of D.H. Lawrence, Virginia Woolf, James Joyce, T.F. Powys and E.M. Forster. Apart from the fact that three out of the five are held by the majority to be indecent, a fact suggestive in itself, four out of the five would convey very little, if anything, to the merely literate.[95]

The charge of moral cowardice is an interesting one in the light of the nineteenth-century debates around fiction's effects on public behavior that I have explored here. In its early days, as we have seen, the public library was frequently seen as insufficiently morally conservative in its choice and issue of novels. But the claim that 'significant work in fiction' requires more than basic literacy in order to be

---

[95]   Leavis, p. 5.

comprehensible is equally important. Leavis suggests here that true comprehension requires some invisible cultural awareness intrinsic to 'the critical minority', and that 'significant fiction' is by definition loaded with something beyond mere words, which only these few can understand. The Revised New Testament reviewer's quite progressive concern, noted in my introduction, that the St James' Bible should not be seen as having dropped straight from heaven is reversed here by Leavis's tacit assumption that 'pure', 'real', 'significant' art does just that. During a mere half-century, it seems, art has taken the place of religion in dominating the cultural field, and it has done so by using precisely the same methods, by insisting that it is – and should be – of a special quality interpretable only by those 'in the know'. These are clearly not those working class persons for whom the libraries were founded. Their most noble and natural concern ought, according to E.M. Forster, to be 'the life of the body'. Nor are they those who, like Leonard Bast, exist in modernity's twilight zone between the body and the spirit. For Leavis, Forster, Gissing, and many like them, the 'already knowing' are the already aesthetically spiritual, those who do not need to be taught.

These sorts of beliefs predispose books to function, as Bourdieu would say, 'as markers of class'.[96] And they demonstrate the classic response of the literary field's dominant agents to a challenge from below: a shifting of the goalposts. This shifting, occurring as often as was necessary in the late nineteenth century, both relied upon and helped to create the division of literature into 'good' and 'bad' not only according to its form, but also according to its intended readership and its relative availability. In this period a book's paratexts took on the greatest of significance.

The public library is, of course, only one arena in which we can detect this occurrence. Bourdieu's model of a dynamic, interactive cultural field means it is necessary to consider the relative positions and comparative operations of others if we are to approach an understanding of how it worked. The next two chapters attempt to analyse two such spheres of operation.

---

[96]   Bourdieu, *Distinction*, p. 1.

Chapter 2

Sensation and Sensibility:
W.H. Smith and the Railway Bookstall

An Engine for Social Change

The railway bookstall represented a very different type of public space in which a range of books were both widely available, and anxiously viewed as potential corrupters of women, lower class readers and the mental health of the nation. Some of the same debates about fiction and self-help that we have seen dogging the library movement were rehearsed here. But without the protective armament of the public institution, the librarian and the need to answer to the ratepayer, the debate took a somewhat different turn that gave rise to a different set of solutions and reading practices.

In the case of the railway bookstall, anxieties about the social and political effects of modernity were more explicitly encoded within the model of literature's mechanical effects as described in my introduction. The railway itself, actually and metaphorically, was an engine for social change, and this had tremendous potential for appropriation by both opponents and supporters, both of modernity and of fiction. Smiles himself (an enthusiastic advocate of self-help and libraries as well as a committed professional railway man) declared that '[the steam engine] is indeed, in itself, a monument of the power of self-help in man'.[1] But he was no fan of novels. Yet for many, as I argued in the introduction, there was a direct link between modernity's symbol the steam engine and the psychology of novel reading. Sensation novels 'carried the nervous system by steam'. The public library was 'an engine' for 'operating upon' the masses, for good or ill. For these kinds of critics the link was embodied in the railway bookstall, where two dangers – the shock of modernity and the unknown power of literature – joined forces and lay in wait between yellow covers for the naive or unwary passer-by. In order to explore how this model contributed to the character of railway bookstalls and how that character differed from other marketplaces for fiction, it is necessary to go back to the middle of the century to the height of the debates about the social effects both of modernity's symbol the steam engine, and its partner-in-crime the novel.

On Saturday 9 August 1851, three years after revolution had shaken Europe and a year after the passing of the Public Libraries Act, an article by Samuel Phillips entitled 'The Literature of the Rail' appeared in *The Times*. The article claimed that, like the rise in general literacy and the 1840 re-organisation of the post office, rail

---

[1]   Samuel Smiles, *Self-Help: With Illustrations of Conduct and Perseverance* (1859; London, 1879), p. 30.

travel brought with it a form of intellectual democracy, in this case opening physical paths to knowledge and civilisation by drawing country dwellers to the towns simply by providing them with a method of transport sufficiently cheap:

> The revolution effected in the habits of people by the introduction of railroads is too evident to be insisted upon. It is certain that we are all on the move. Folks travel now, not only because their business urges them abroad, but because the facilities of locomotion are too tempting to suffer them to remain at home. Just as the humble, who never wrote letters under the old postage system, now open the floodgates of their affections once or twice-a-week, indulging in two pennyworth of correspondence and ten shillings' worth of gratification and delight, so do the poorer citizens of the state, who never ventured upon the dearly purchased luxury of the mail coach, greedily avail themselves at this hour of the cheap and manifold enjoyments of the rail ... Nobody shuts himself up in exclusive ignorance at home. People who never quitted their village for the first 40 years of their lives, and whose bodies, souls, limbs, ideas, prejudices and passions have daily revolved in the narrowest of circles, have this year, by means of steam, in the course of a few hours, been brought in presence of the congregated productions of the world, and within reach of civilising influences unknown to monarchs of a former age.[2]

The tone is hopeful, but the notion of a public 'greedy' for travel simply for its own sake carries with it the implication of a recently recognised danger, rendering somewhat ineffectual the mid-nineteenth-century classification of cities by income and class carried out by social historians such as Mayhew, whose 'London Labour and the London Poor' appeared for the first time in collected form this same year. If 'we are all on the move', then we resist such classification; boundaries dissolve in direct proportion to the miles of track laid down, the number of bridges raised and tunnels bored and cuttings dug and residential districts bisected.

The potentially disruptive forces of modernity – and particularly technology – were by this period well recognised and much discussed. By the 1890s they had also come to be theorised by the German sociologist Georg Simmel, for whom the metropolis transformed the psychological experience of the subject:

> The rapid crowding of changing images, the sharp discontinuity in the grasp of a single glance, and the unexpectedness of onrushing impression: these are the psychological conditions which the metropolis creates. With each crossing of the street, with the tempo and multiplicity of economic, occupational and social life, the city sets up a deep contrast with small town and rural life with reference to the sensory foundations of psychic life.[3]

In an earlier essay he had figured this psychic transformation in terms of 'shock', arguing that modern life 'make[s] us more and more sensitive to the shocks and

---

2   Samuel Phillips, 'The Literature of the Rail', *The Times*, 9 August 1851, p. 7.
3   Georg Simmel, 'The Metropolis and Mental Life' (1903), in *The Sociology of Georg Simmel*, ed. Kurt H. Wolff (New York, 1950), p. 410.

disturbances which come to us from the immediate proximity and contact between man and things'.[4] Simmel's theories, despite their grounding in the particular German case, have been influential in many more general explorations of the nineteenth-century European experience of modernity, and I will be returning to some of these. For the moment, though, I want to emphasise that these disruptive experiences had long been an integral part of everyday as well as intellectual discursive practices,[5] and that they frequently centred on representations of the railroad.

There were real as well as theoretical reasons for this notion of disruption. The building of railroads had brought unruly gangs of labourers to many hitherto peaceful areas and the subject was deemed serious enough to warrant investigation by a Select Committee in 1846.[6] In *Dombey and Son* (1846–1848), Charles Dickens (never a fan of the railways and in June 1865 to be involved in a serious railway accident) had used the spreading of the railroad as a timely signal of social as well as physical change, neither of which was positive. At the novel's opening the construction is still under way, and the irony of the description comes from the siting of 'civilisation and improvement' in a hellish, 'unnatural' landscape being torn apart and reconfigured by modernity:

> The first shock of an earthquake had, just at that period, rent the whole neighbourhood to its centre. Traces of its course were visible on every side. Houses were knocked down; streets broken through and stopped ... Here, a chaos of carts, overthrown and jumbled together, lay topsy-turvy at the bottom of a steep unnatural hill; there, confused treasures of iron soaked and rusted in something that had accidentally become a pond ... Boiling water hissed and heaved within dilapidated walls; whence, also, the glare and roar of flames came issuing forth; and mounds of ashes blocked up rights of way, and wholly changed the law and custom of the neighbourhood ... and, from the very core of all this dire disorder [the railway] trailed smoothly away, upon its mighty course of civilisation and improvement.[7]

Later in the novel the railroad, now firmly established, echoes Dombey's thoughts upon the loss of his son, becoming the darkest of social levellers: 'The power that

---

[4]   Simmel, 'Sociological Aesthetics' (1896), in *The Conflict in Modern Culture and Other Essays*, ed. K. Peter Etzkorn (New York, 1968), p. 79.

[5]   Several critics have usefully explored modernity and its relation to social or psychological disruption. See, for example, the essays in Leo Charney and Vanessa R. Schwartz, eds, *Cinema and the Invention of Modern Life* (Berkeley, 1995). Also Lynn Kirby's *Parallel Tracks: The Railroad and Silent Cinema* (Exeter, 1997) which usefully traces concurrent developments and anxieties in North America, tying them in places to the European experience.

[6]   Parliamentary Papers, 8, 1846. Quoted in Kellow Chesney, *The Victorian Underworld* (London, 1970), p. 39.

[7]   Charles Dickens, *Dombey and Son* (1846–48; London, 1985), p. 121. All subsequent references are to this edition and appear parenthetically in the text.

forced itself upon its iron way – its own – defiant of all the paths and roads, piercing through the heart of every obstacle, and dragging living creatures of all classes, ages, and degrees behind it, was a type of the triumphant monster, Death' (p. 354). But the 'Death' represented by the railroad is not intrinsic to it, even for Dickens – at least not at this point in his career; the railroad has merely cut through a socially stratified rock face of recent history and made manifest a pre-existing hell: 'As Mr Dombey looks out of his carriage window, it is never in his thoughts that the monster who has brought him there has let the light of day in on these things, not made or caused them' (p. 355).

The distinction is crucial. It is not, either for Dickens or for Samuel Phillips, that technology merely transforms, but that it also unleashes some slumbering social force and that the outcome of this sudden mobilisation is uncertain. For Dickens, despite the palpable transformation it has effected in urban geography and political opinion, the railroad is a simmering force of still unknown potential:

> Night and day the conquering engines rumbled at their distant work, or, advancing smoothly to their journey's end, and gliding like tame dragons into the allotted corners grooved out to the inch for their reception, stood bubbling and trembling there, making the walls quake, as if they were dilating with the secret knowledge of great powers yet unsuspected in them, and strong purposes not yet achieved (p. 290).

For Phillips, the 'great powers' are more knowable and more concrete – and more controllable – for they centre on intellectual rather than physical potential. Phillips replaces 'strong [and possibly revolutionary] purposes' with reforming zeal: 'men cannot move their bodies and leave their minds behind them. In proportion as we stretch our limbs do we enlarge our thoughts … intellect is emancipated by free intercourse'. Not just bodies but minds are on the move. But the opportunity for intellectual growth afforded by this emancipation must, Phillips adds, be channelled wisely, for it not only provides 'the finest opportunity yet offered to this generation for guiding awakened thought and instructing the eager and susceptible mind' but if mishandled it may 'destroy forever a literary taste that might have been perfectly healthy'.[8]

The 'susceptible mind' might to later commentators such as Simmel be a generic feature of modernity's psychological shocks, but here it is a specifically working-class susceptibility. 'Healthy' taste is, of course, as we have seen, intimately connected in this period in England to responsible citizenship and – by extrapolation – to social control. Literature can and does, Phillips stresses in a familiar contemporary conflation of humanism and social concern, play a crucial role in the formation of public citizens, enabling every man of whatever class to fulfil his potential and, as a useful bonus, making responsible Englishmen out of potential revolutionaries. And, as the very vocal debates around the value of fiction in libraries has shown, in this period it is not enough just to read: in order to be a real citizen, one must read the right things. But

---

8   Phillips, p. 7.

the 'right things' that worked for a public library, it very quickly became apparent, were not the same 'right things' as might work for a railway bookstall.

Self-help books had declined in popularity everywhere by the 1890s due, perhaps, to their inevitable devaluing in the literary field. As William C. Preston expresses it in an article on Smith's bookstalls in *Good Words* in 1895: 'There was a time … when books of the Self-help class were remarkably popular at the bookstalls, but these are now quite out of date'.[9] The rise of literacy and a concomitant increase in the provision of self-help books could not help but devalue self-acquired education, and demand a shift in the stakes in favour of less accessible, institutionalised forms of knowledge. Forster's Leonard Bast is only one – rather late – example among many of the contemporary perception of the self-taught as an inferior and even repulsive type. But at the bookstall there also seemed to be a higher turnover of authors, and ultimately a sense that the stall was not a natural provider of the 'classics'. These certainly appeared in many a popular series in the early days of the railway, as I will show, but by the turn of the century their heyday was over. Preston notes that: 'even the classics are largely displaced by the newer authors', and this applied particularly to the cheap classics series. Henry Frowde, the architect of Oxford University Press's World's Classics series, confirms in a letter to one of his author-advisors: 'Smith's bookstalls dropped the books [i.e. the World's Classics] long before Grant Richards came to grief [in 1904], but the booksellers are purchasing them as largely as ever'.[10] As for new fiction, it had always been in great demand at the bookstall, but from the start it embraced types not generally found in the library. The reasons for this are complex, rooted in the special conditions of rail travel itself, and ultimately to exert a powerful influence, not just on the form which new literature began to take, but on the symbolic value which began to attach to it.

Train Travel and the Reader's Psyche

Important recent work has done much to uncover how train travel may have affected the psyche of the modern subject, and in what manner of reading matter and reading practices those effects appeared. Nicholas Daly has suggested that 'we can see in the sensation genre an attempt to register and accommodate the newly speeded-up world of the railway age … it is through its deployment of nervousness – shown in its characters, elicited in its readers – that the novel seeks to perform this accommodation. To read the sensation novel this way is to suggest that it runs counter to the main tendency of Victorian fiction'.[11] Thrills, danger and excitement were the watchwords

---

9   William C. Preston, 'Messrs W.H. Smith and Son's Bookstalls and Library', *Good Words*, July 1895, p. 476.
10   Letter No. 447, 7 February 1906, Letterbooks of Henry Frowde, Oxford University Press Archives.
11   Nicholas Daly, 'Railway Novels: Sensation Fiction and the Modernisation of the Senses', *English Literary History*, 66 (Summer 1999), p. 464.

in the sensation novel but these were, as we have seen, far from being encouraged as desirable in library novels. Daly is right to read the sensation genre as running 'counter to the main tendency of Victorian fiction'. In fact this counter-current had far-reaching consequences, and Daly sees the advent of the railway as central to a shift in the form of the novel itself. He suggests that the emergence of novelistic suspense, of plots turning on delays, mistiming, missed opportunities and rescues in the nick of time, are made possible by standardised time and the railway timetable: 'the pleasures of fictional suspense ... and the anxieties of clock-watching appear as part of the same historical moment'.[12]

Laura Marcus takes this argument a stage further. Following Benjamin's suggestion that fiction bought at a railway bookstall imbues its purchaser with the knowledge that 'the coins which he offers up to this sacrificial column recommend him to the protection of the boiler god which glows through the night'[13] and is therefore preferable to something brought from home, she adds that this is particularly true of the detective fiction which emerged as a direct descendent of the sensation novel, sharing with it the echoing of train travel in 'the rhythm of the narrative'.[14] For Marcus the detective and sensation novel, like the train itself, feminises the traveller through its inducement of the symptoms of hysteria. If novels in general emasculate men, reading sensation or detective novels on the train is clearly a tripling of the effect.

Both accounts offer important evidence for an understanding of these fictional forms. But they also point towards an unacknowledged problem. If railway reading exacerbated the problems already associated with novels in other arenas, how did the railway bookstall escape the kind of censorship which prevailed in public libraries, and what did that mean in terms of class and gender? If this was a more fluid and less regulated public space than the library, how were the dangers of the 'unhealthy' literature identified by Samuel Phillips actually counteracted? What did a railway novel say about its reader? Both Daly and Marcus draw on the work of Wolfgang Schivelbusch for their models of a psychology of the modern novel, and it is from him, I think, that they have inherited some of their assumptions about the nature of railway reading. It would be useful here to outline Schivelbusch's findings in order to extract both their value and their potential limitations.

Schivelbusch has suggested that nineteenth-century train travel was instrumental in bringing about the alteration in the modern individual's psychical, physical and temporal relationships with the world. It did this through its astonishing and unprecedented velocity, and its effect both on the landscape and on the interactions of a carriage's occupants. Leisurely intercourse with fellow travellers over a period of days was no longer possible in trains as it had been in the days of coaching. Landscape watching at high speed had necessitated a new panoramic sense in which 'the tendency

---

12   Daly, 'Railway Novels', p. 475.
13   Laura Marcus, 'Oedipus Express: Trains, Trauma and Detective Fiction', *New Formations*, Vol. 41 (Autumn 2000), p. 173.
14   Marcus, p. 4.

[is] to see the discrete indiscriminately'.[15] Benjamin, heavily influenced by Simmel and in turn to inform Schivelbusch's work, notes in his essay on Baudelaire that: 'the interpersonal relationships of people in big cities are characterised by a markedly greater emphasis on the use of the eyes than on that of the ears. This can be attributed chiefly to the institution of public conveyances. Before buses, railroads and trams became fully established during the nineteenth century, people were never put in the position of having to stare at one another for minutes or even hours on end without exchanging a word'.[16]

Schivelbusch takes this emphasis on looking in an important direction when he suggests that enforced confinement with strangers in closed compartments and the ever-present fear of accident had encouraged a new, interior consciousness in which 'the traveller's gaze [has moved] into an imaginary surrogate landscape',[17] that of the novel or newspaper. For Schivelbusch, this new interiority that made reading on trains a necessity by the mid-nineteenth century had a class bias:

> A glance at the offerings of the English and French railway bookstalls shows that the reading public is almost exclusively bourgeois. An English survey in 1851 shows that, in contrast to the supply of trashy mass literature in the regular bookstores, the railway bookstalls and lending libraries in London carry highly respectable fiction, non-fiction, travel guides etc ... Reading while travelling is an exclusively bourgeois occupation.[18]

He roots this argument in the prevailing conditions inside the railway carriages themselves. While third- and fourth-class passengers travelled in large communal coaches, second- and first-class carriages were compartmentalised, built on the same lines as the private or mail coach that accommodated a handful of passengers and from which exit was only possible when the coach was stationary. A major result of this structural difference in railway carriage design was the enforced proximity with one or more people (who, due to the shortening of journey times, must remain strangers) that first- and second-class passengers endured in between stops. Nor was there at first any opportunity of communicating either with other compartments or with the driver or guard while the train was in motion. There were obvious drawbacks to this design, intended to make the switch to rail travel easier and more natural for the rich by emulating the conditions to which they were accustomed. Enforced confinement with other passengers who could escape into the crowd at any station carried risks; two much-publicised murders occurred in these kinds of compartments in the 1860s,

---

[15]   Wolfgang Schivelbusch, *The Railway Journey: Trains and Travel in the Nineteenth Century* (Oxford, 1977), p. 64.
[16]   Walter Benjamin, 'Charles Baudelaire: A Lyric Poet in the Era of High Capitalism', quoted in Frisby, *Fragments of Modernity : Theories of Modernity in the Work of Simmel, Kracauer and Benjamin* (Cambridge, 1985), p. 78.
[17]   Schivelbusch, p. 66.
[18]   Schivelbusch, p. 69.

one in France, the other in England, and public anxiety was such that in 1866 a House of Commons Committee was designated the task of finding a solution.[19] This took the form initially of the installation of communication cords which, when pulled, rang a bell on the footplate (and which, incidentally, the passenger had to lean out to operate). This system remained in use on some lines until the 1890s, when both internal communication cords that directly applied the train's brakes and corridor-style carriages came into widespread use.[20]

For Schivelbusch, then, reading in first- and second-class coaches is not merely a means of passing time, it is 'an attempt to replace the conversation which is no longer possible. Fixing one's eyes on a book or a newspaper, one is able to avoid the stare of the person sitting across the aisle'[21] (who may or may not be a murderer, a rapist, or a bore), as well as keep one's mind off the possibility of accident, since 'the traveller who sits reading his newspaper or novel instead of worrying about the ever-present possibility of accident or collision no doubt feels secure'.[22] Reading not only helps to consolidate the inner boundary which Simmel feels is necessary to counteract the 'fear of contact [which] is reinforced by the ease of travel over long distances',[23] but it helps to 'form a new psychic layer that obscures the old fears and lets them lapse into oblivion'.[24]

It also, as Kate Flint has noted, may have been seen as a means of establishing personal space that had a particular resonance for middle-class women.[25] Anne Bowman in *The Common Things of Everyday Life: A Book of Home Wisdom for Mothers and Daughters* (1857), recommends that 'it is not a prudent plan to attempt to look out to view the countryside through which the train is passing while it is in motion: the eyes and the head usually become confused and there is neither benefit nor pleasure from such scanty observation. Reading or improving conversation is the most rational mode of employing the time'.[26] But she also warns: 'all young ladies travelling alone should be cautious in entering into conversation with strange fellow-travellers. Civilities should be politely acknowledged, but, as a general rule, a book is the safest resource for the "unprotected female"'.[27]

The fears of accident might be well worn by mid-century, but they were by no means obsolete. Amongst Bowman's advice to women travellers is the warning:

---

[19] Schivelbusch, pp. 84–8.
[20] Robin Linsley, *Railways in Camera: Archive Photographs of the Great Age of Steam from the Public Record Office 1860–1913* (Stroud, 1996), p. 12.
[21] Schivelbusch, p. 80.
[22] Schivelbusch, p. 153.
[23] Simmel, 'Sociological Aesthetics' (1896), in *The Conflict in Modern Culture and Other Essays*, p. 79.
[24] Schivelbusch, p. 132.
[25] Kate Flint, *The Woman Reader 1837–1914* (Oxford, 1993), p. 105.
[26] Anne Bowman, *The Common Things of Everyday Life: A Book of Home Wisdom for Mothers and Daughters* (London, 1857), p. 162.
[27] Bowman, p. 163.

'in case of an accident, the most prudent conduct is, not to put your head out of the window, not to attempt to jump out, and, if there be time, to draw your legs up on the seat, as the front of the carriage is often driven in, by a concussion, and broken legs are the consequence'.[28] Nor was this mere paranoia. Robin Linsley's pictorial record of nineteenth-century railways, drawn from the archives of the Public Records Office, contains 28 photographs showing serious accidents that resulted in a total of 283 recorded deaths. The two worst of these were the Tay Bridge Disaster of 28 December 1879 in which 78 lives were lost, and the Armagh disaster of 12 June 1889 that killed 80 people, most of them children, but Linsley's list is by no means comprehensive: fatalities and injuries were a fairly regular occurrence. In the 1880s both *Tit-Bits* and its rival paper *Answers* turned the public's fear into a marketing ploy, offering their readers a bizarre insurance policy under the terms of which a rail passenger was covered against accident if s/he happened to be carrying the latest copy of the paper at the time – a concrete example, we might say, of Schivelbusch's contention that reading 'protects' against accident. In the single year of 1890, by which time the railways were well into their decline, *The Times* records 56 fatalities on the rails in Britain, including murders and suicides.[29] Mishaps continued to be common enough into the early 1900s for W. Gothard of Barnsley to issue a series of 'accident postcards' featuring photographs of the wreckage and some of the dead, with dramatic captions. As Lynn Kirby has shown, accidents were still more numerous on the still-expanding American railways; according to one British observer, 'in 1901 ... 4,135 people other than passengers were killed and 3,995 wounded'.[30] British audiences were well aware of these sorts of statistics since they too appeared in *The Times*.

So familiar were the dangers to a reading public that they appeared in numerous novels, though fictional handling of the railway's dangers took a number of forms across the decades, ranging from injury to sexual scandal. The plot of Mrs Wood's sensation novel *East Lynne* turns on the disfigurement and social transmogrification of Lady Isabel Vane during a horrific railway accident which thoroughly punishes her for an illicit affair by killing her illegitimate child.[31] George du Maurier viewed the social mixing which railway travel made possible in a more positive light in his 1894 popular sensation *Trilby*, using it to display not only optimism over the sight which the Great Western station afforded of people 'following the sun', but the goodness of his hero Little Billee. Despite being miserable over the loss of the heroine Trilby and (as an upper-middle-class reader) well equipped with an eclectic range of reading matter from the *Origin of Species* through *Silas Marner* to *Punch*, Billee beguiles his time instead by making himself 'useful and pleasant to his fellow-travellers in many ways – so many that long before they had reached their respective journeys' ends they had almost grown to love him as an old friend ... and they wondered at the

---

28   Bowman, p. 162.
29   *The Times Index* for 1890.
30   Kirby, p. 30.
31   Mrs Henry Wood, *East Lynne* (1861; London, 1994).

happiness that must be his at merely being alive, and told him more of their troubles in six hours than they told many a friend in a year'.[32] Nonetheless, recent dangers are signalled in this text. The character sketch raises and indeed relies upon the ghost of the reverse possibility: that of interaction with travelling companions who might not be so congenial, and with whom confinement over a period of six hours might be unpleasant or downright dangerous.

Such negative representations were, in fact, far more common, and as Lynn Kirby points out, as a consequence numerous early films 'made use of the train as a ready-made site of crime, disaster, and romance – in a word, drama'.[33] Kirby is referring to American films, but many of these appeared in British picture houses, and British audiences easily picked up the references to a connection between train travel, danger and sex. Indeed, as Figure 2.1 shows, there were British counterparts to this model which explicitly figure reading as an integral part of this relationship; in this image from the British film, *The Kiss in the Tunnel* (George Albert Smith, 1899), a couple chastely reading on a train (he a newspaper, she a novel) take advantage of the sudden darkness of a tunnel in which to steal a kiss.

Reading might 'protect' the traveller against unwanted advances, but the dangers of and sexual opportunities provided by train travel were commonly assumed to be just beneath the surface and readily available to those who felt the urge. Such representations draw on a well-established literary tradition, as we have seen, and it was not confined to the popular. Ford Madox Ford utilises the danger of women being accosted in railway carriages as a plot device in his 1915 novel *The Good Soldier*,[34] and here the complex nature of this particular danger is illustrated by the extent to which this convoluted modernist narrative's theme depends upon it. Edward Ashburnham's fatal complexity is revealed by the incident in which, on finding himself in a railway carriage with a pretty, weeping nursemaid of 19 and being himself 'quite democratic', he forgets the 'difference in their station' (p. 101) and, meaning to offer 'comfort', kisses her. But the nursemaid has not forgotten the 'difference in their station'. The democratising properties of the railroad are, for her, a mere increasing of their dangers. She is alone with a gentleman, the kind of man against whom she has been warned all her life. She screams and pulls the communication cord, setting in motion the train of events that is to lead to Ashburnham's downfall. In this novel it is the railway itself that has made possible the crucial thematic blurring of seeming and being, innocence and guilt, private outrage and public scandal. The liberties which Ashburnham, 'a normal man and very much of a sentimentalist' (p. 102) takes with a nursemaid in a public/private place indicate his complete failure to understand the dangerous blurring of boundaries that comprises the modern world. The self-doubting narrator admits after relating the railway incident that he is unable to get to the heart

32 George du Maurier, *Trilby* (1894; London, 1994), pp. 199–201.
33 Kirby, p. 1.
34 Ford Madox Ford, *The Good Soldier* (1915; London, 1995), p. 101. All subsequent references are to this edition and appear parenthetically in the text.

Figure 2.1   Still from *The Kiss in the Tunnel* (UK, Dir. G.A. Smith, 1899)

of Edward Ashburnham, unable to penetrate beyond the 'outline of Edward's life [which] was an outline perfectly normal of the life of a hard-working, sentimental and efficient professional man' (p. 102). The conditions of modernity make it impossible any longer to 'give an all-round impression of any man' (p. 101), and it is significant that it is the railroad which Ford decided upon to demonstrate the difficulty of accurate identification. Here, modernism's interrogation of the subject relies heavily upon pre-existing discourses of modernity and its effect on social identities.

Due to the large numbers of people involved, rail travel not only represented the possibility of death, injury or scandal, it also increased the chances of bearing witness to one of these events. This is, in fact, what happened to Dickens. Though he was himself uninjured in the 1865 crash, the trauma of the experience remained with him for the rest of his life, turning his dislike of the railways in more sinister fictional directions such as his 1866 Christmas story 'The Signalman' in which the ghost of one railway employee not only predicts but actually causes the death of another. This popular story of cyclical mayhem and self-fulfilling prophecy gives some indication of the level of anxiety that attended train travel in mid-century and the ambivalence, however unconscious, with which it was still being viewed.

In the third- and fourth-class coaches, Schivelbusch suggests, things were very different. The crowded conditions and open nature of the design made interaction easier as well as safer, and these travellers were in addition new to public transport and therefore 'unencumbered by memories of previous forms of travel',[35] and probably also better able to take one another's minds off the possibility of accident. But this notion of a class split between a happy, crowded lower-class carriage full of talkative non-readers, and an anxiety-ridden upper- and middle-class carriage full of silently reading potential victims is problematised both by Phillips's observations and by his subsequent research. He is concerned (somewhat predictably given the prevailing notions about society's highest risk groups) at the sight of 'two young ladies and a boy' in a first-class carriage 'amusing themselves and alarming us by a devotion to a trashy French novel, most cruelly and sacrilegiously misplaced'. It is perhaps worth noting again here the seamless application of theological terminology to literature. But Phillips main concern is for the unformed tastes of those other social and cultural 'women and children', the newly mobile masses. They have 'hungry minds that sought refreshment on their feverish way' and, on close inspection of 'every railway terminus in the metropolis', are being provided for with 'poison in [the] literary refreshment rooms, and stuff whose deleterious effects 20 doctors would not be sufficient to eradicate'.[36] Literature, for Phillips as for many of his contemporaries, including both supporters and opponents of the public library movement, has the power to corrupt as well as to heal the body politic, down to its lowest organs.

This article, it should be noted, appeared in the same year as Schivelbusch's unsourced 'English survey' and it is, of course, possible that they are one and the

---

[35]   Schivelbusch, p. 69.
[36]   Phillips, p. 7.

same, but there is a vital discrepancy in the two accounts. Phillips did not in fact find 'highly respectable non-fiction, fiction, travel-guides etc'. at the majority of London's bookstalls. What he found, on the contrary, was that:

> with few exceptions, unmitigated rubbish encumbered the bookshelves of almost every bookstall we visited and indicated only too clearly that the hand of ignorance had been indiscriminately busy in piling up the worthless mass ... Here and there crouched some old friends, who looked very strange indeed in the midst of such questionable society – like well-dressed gentlemen compelled to take part in the general doings of the Rag-fair.[37]

Here the books themselves are categorised by social class, and the lower kind are by far the most numerous; an indication that the railway was not yet being seen in any systematic way either as a travelling schoolroom, or as an opportunity for public displays of taste. Indeed, the writer remarks that the reverse was probably generally true at this period and the railways provided an opportunity for private vice to be indulged in anonymously, for 'persons who apparently would be ashamed to be found reading certain works at home have asked for publications of the worst character at railway bookstalls'.[38] Preston's 1895 article confirms that this idea, however apocryphal, was well established by the end of the century: 'Some people sought for and found on railway stalls books that [which] they would have been ashamed to inquire for from tradesmen with a character to lose'.[39]

While Schivelbusch sees class distinctions among readers as being determined by technology – conditions inside the railway carriages – then, Phillips indicates that technology is responsible for eroding any social distinctions among readers. If anyone can travel almost anywhere, almost anyone can read almost anything, which is purchasable at almost any bookstall. The psychology of reading, like Schivelbusch's psychology of train travel, is changing the nation's mental landscape, and for the worse. I do not want to dismiss Schivelbusch's important study. But the addition of Phillips' account with its nuances of anxiety has to be seen as challenging Schivelbusch's technological determinism, for it indicates that the provision of literature at bookstalls was seen as a cross-spectrum social problem that required a specific policy by way of a solution. And where there is policy there is regulation, control, and (usually) reaction, all of which – as we have seen in the example of the public library – have great significance for the degree of cultural capital that might come to be invested in books.

Phillips' disgust at the offerings of the South London bookstalls is palpable. But once he ventured further north the picture changed dramatically. At Euston, the terminus of the London and North Western Railway, there finally appeared the

---

[37] Phillips, p. 7.
[38] Philips, p. 7.
[39] Preston, p. 474.

'schoolmaster' for whom he had been searching in the belief that he was sorely needed by the whole of travelling society. Here there were none of the trashy novels, French or otherwise, found at most other stalls. A conversation with the bookseller produced quite different results: when asked for 'something highly coloured', the bookseller produced Krugler's *Handbook of Painting*. When pressed for a volume 'more intimately connected with life and the world', he produced *Kosmos*. When these were refused and the writer requested 'something less universal [as] befits the London traveller', the bookseller handed him Prescott's *Mexico, Modern Travel* and Murray's *Handbook of France*. A request for something for the masses was met with *Logic for the Million*, and for 'books of a more chatty character' with Coleridge's *Table Talk*. 'We could not get rubbish whatever price we may offer to pay for it', the author asserts with satisfaction. 'There were no Eugene Sues for love or money – no cheap translations of any kind – no bribes to ignorance or unholy temptations to folly.'[40] A new era in railway reading is announced by this deliberate refusal on the part of the bookstall clerk to acknowledge the long-established underworld of bookselling (here figured, through the use of a popular but salacious French author, as a form of prostitution) in favour of a literary taste rooted in moral purity and self-help.

Phillips praises highly but does not name the proprietor of this bookstall in Euston station, though he makes what now seems an astonishing list of claims for it when he urges railway directors to emulate it in 'elevating the character of our humbler fellow countrymen ... adding to the happiness of the individual and conducing to the permanent good of society'. In fact the proprietor was W.H. Smith and Son, and the stall the dawn of an empire.[41] This was the first of hundreds of Smith's bookstalls to spring up nationwide and provide customers with a unique library service as well as travel guides, newspapers and books carefully – and at times contentiously – chosen for their wholesomeness. For more than half a century – and in some cases beyond – Smith's exercised a virtual monopoly over the bookstall trade that was of enormous importance to their distribution business. It was not achieved, though, through a straightforward distributor-consumer relationship of supply and demand. This, it should by now be apparent, would have been all but impossible anyway given contemporary debates about the relative merits of – and bourgeois responsibilities towards – different forms of literature.

---

40   Phillips, p. 7.
41   It is worth noting here that Phillips (1814–54) was not only a *Times* staff writer, but also a friend of William Henry Smith II. However, according to the *DNB* he had a reputation for outspoken conservatism in his articles and reviews; he could, for example, 'see nothing in *Uncle Tom's Cabin* but a violation of the rights of property'. The *DNB* also suggests that it was this article 'The Literature of the Rail' which prompted Murrays to introduce their series 'Reading for the Rail' and Longmans to introduce 'The Traveller's Library'. It seems likely, therefore, that Phillips was speaking to and for the conservative *Times* reader and the boosting of his friend's business was a beneficent side-effect.

In order to mark himself and his business out from his dubious forebears at the bookstall, Smith needed something else; something that would answer the consumer's needs while allaying bourgeois fears. As it turned out, W.H. Smith II had what was needed in vast measure. The empire was achieved, in the end, through a combination of astute business sense and a subtle reading of the contemporary middle-class mood, which, as Phillips suggests above, valued 'character' almost above all else. 'Money is power after its sort', wrote Samuel Smiles, 'but intelligence, public spirit and moral virtue are power too, and far nobler ones'.[42] These are the constituents of 'character', a list of qualities belonging to a belief system that sets itself up in opposition to the economic world. It was 'character' that was meant to smooth over social iniquities and (almost incidentally) provide the backbone for sound economic growth, for as Smiles goes on to insist: 'the worth and strength of a state depend far less upon the form of its institutions than upon the character of its men'.[43] Crucial also is the sense that 'character' is truly democratic, that with application it can be moulded from a man from almost any social sphere. Smiles' list of worthies in *Self-help* includes many from humble beginnings, and Phillips specifically mentions 'our humbler countrymen' as railway travellers. A man of character could, in effect, be trusted to do what was right and to positively influence those beneath him. 'Men of genius stand to society in the relation of its intellect, as men of character of its conscience;' wrote Smiles in his best-selling follow-up to *Self-help*, called – significantly – simply *Character*, 'and while the former are admired, the latter are followed'.[44]

This wrapping of the economic motive in a cloak of public spiritedness exercised a powerful influence on the shaping of railway reading habits. It could not help, in the end, but be classified as 'middlebrow' and conservative in relation to 'art'. But the policy was part of a wider field in which the need to sell certain types of literature co-existed with discourses which sought to discredit their sale. This means that the character of railway bookstalls did not, as Schivelbusch suggests, somehow spring up fully formed overnight or indicate that reading on trains was a 'bourgeois occupation' by nature. What it indicates, on the contrary, is that bookstalls were a response to the fluidity of social relations brought about by the railway and the democratisation of culture, and that it is as a fluid but unique response that their social significance should be viewed. Only then is it possible to explain the difference in character between the literature sold at stalls and that stocked in the public library (where conservatism also ruled), and explore its importance both to the subsequent changes in form noted by Marcus and Daly, and to the other positions in the literary field.

---

[42] Smiles, *Self-Help*, p. 312.
[43] Smiles, *Self-Help*, p. 2.
[44] Samuel Smiles, *Character* (1871; London, 1905), p. 2.

Circulation and Censorship: Policing the Literature of the Rail

It is difficult to pinpoint the precise policy with which W.H. Smith II, concerned to carve his own niche in a distribution business still largely controlled by his father, set out to achieve his bookstall monopoly.[45] But the bookstalls seem to have sprung up as adjuncts to the newspaper distribution network which, begun in the days of coaching, recognised under William Henry II the advantages to speed and efficiency offered by the steam age. William Henry's contacts with the powerful railway managers such as Captain Mark Huish of the LNWR almost certainly helped him to establish the first stalls. As Charles Wilson has pointed out, he was well aware that in 1850 alone 'more than 60 million passengers travelled over 40 million miles over 6,635 miles of track', and that 'all had to pass through two or more stations for each journey made'.[46] Clearly, even with a literacy rate estimated at only 61 per cent of the population, this represented a vast potential market.[47]

The first bookstall franchise was awarded to Smith's in 1848 by the LNWR. They set up their first stall at Euston station, replacing the current tenant who, despite having been given the right to sell papers there in 1846, lost the court case in which he alleged unfair family connections between Smith's and Captain Huish. He thereby became the first of many such casualties – mostly ex-railway employees and their widows – in the next two decades of expansion. Exactly to whom Smith's initially thought they were selling remains unclear, but a flier for their advertising business dating from around the same period provides some clues. The advertising department, run side by side with the bookstalls, was covered by the same kinds of contracts and subject largely to the same rules. Smith's rented space on the station concourses which they sublet to clients and filled with posters designed, produced and framed in their own workshop near the Strand. The poster business was for a long time one of their most lucrative assets. As Wilson puts it:

> inside and outside the carriages, in waiting room and booking hall, and on station walls or on hoardings erected along the approaches to railway stations, advertisements multiplied like mushrooms: wide-eyed, fascinated or unimpressed, travellers gazed at W.H. Smith's panels and posters which, decade by decade, celebrated the claims, merits or powers of Rowntree's Cocoa, Reckitt's Blue, Masawattee Tea, Pears or Sunlight Soap, Bovril, cures for anaemia, coughs, constipation, indigestion.[48]

The flier sent out to attract business in the early exploratory days of this impressive empire reads as follows:

---

45   Charles Wilson, *First With the News: The History of W.H. Smith 1792–1972* (London, 1985), pp. 97–8.
46   Wilson, p. 98.
47   Alan J. Lee, *The Origins of the Popular Press 1855–1914* (London, 1976), p. 33.
48   Wilson, p. 92.

The importance of this novel system of Advertising cannot be too highly estimated when it is remembered that Railway Travellers include within their number every individual of rank, property and influence in the three kingdoms ... It must be borne in mind, that these immense numbers – the possessors of the aggregate wealth of the country – are concentrated day by day, at the Railway Stations; and the circumstances of every journey are such, that either on departure or arrival or in course of transit, every passenger must of necessity become acquainted with the announcements which will present themselves to his notice. It may be safely asserted that no other mode of Advertising presents so favourable a means of reaching that class which the Advertiser desires most to attract.[49]

For Smith's, then, the major customers (or, more accurately in this case, the perceived customers of their clients) were people (and especially men) of rank and wealth – the upper and middle classes – and it seems reasonable to assume that they stocked their bookstalls accordingly. At this stage, they were apparently less concerned than Samuel Phillips with the possibility that 'the readers of this circulating library are much too large and indiscriminate, the hours at their disposal by far too many, to permit indifference or neglect ... The Universities are exclusive, but the 'rail' knows no distinction of rank, religion, or caste'.[50] Their burgeoning empire depended on continued good relations with the railway companies, run almost exclusively by middle-class entrepreneurs who had been criticised for the offensive nature of bookstalls and were being forced to take seriously new notions about public duty. Most contracts throughout the period contain a clause forbidding the sale or display of material 'of an indecent, immoral or seditious character or relating to medicines for complaints or ailments of an indecent or indelicate nature'.[51] In sweeping away the motley assortment of original stallholders, the railways wanted to be sure that they were getting something better – and less contentious – in return, and Smith's seem to have won the franchise as much on this premise as on financial terms.

But Smith's bookstall policy is also a complex part of the modern ideological landscape. The mood of self-help that saw the rise of public libraries, museums, parks and art galleries was also on course to produce a rash of periodicals and books aimed at the upwardly mobile. Reading was being established in this period as a means of securing social standing. The railways, with their emphasis on swift, dispersed looking at posters, headlines and titles rather than at faces, and on the ability to judge one's fellow companions at a glance without engaging them in conversation, lent themselves to the display of reading matter which might both proclaim and protect. By the end of the period the habit of silent curiosity about another passenger's reading matter had become commonplace enough to lend itself to humour. In a speech delivered to

[49]   Advertising flier, *c.*1850, WHS 244/1–3.
[50]   Phillips, p. 7.
[51]   For an indication of the endurance of this rule, see, for example, WHS Rail Contract Ref: 410/835, 14 June 1860, WHS Archives and WHS contract with the Metropolitan Railway, 1908, Ref: 1297 Met 10 264, London Metropolitan Archives.

the Edinburgh and District Branch of the Newsagents, Booksellers and Stationers' National Union on 2 March 1914, novelist Jeffrey Farnol described a variety of types of readers. For him the 'selfish' reader was one who while on a train held his book at 'such an impossible angle that he had known it take him three-quarters of an hour before he discovered the title'.[52]

Clearly, in the early days of their monopoly, Smith's was pursuing a shrewd marketing policy as well as performing what they saw as a public service when they insisted on stocking only the 'inoffensive' literature which was a part of middle-class consensus. And after a few difficult years in which returns were relatively small as customers adjusted, Smith's bookstalls entered a phase of expansion and prosperity that remained almost unbroken until 1905. Henry James's reflections on the railway bookstall at the height of its success attest to the soothing, unifying sense of hope that Smith's stock gave to the disparate social types that made up the travelling public:

> If the English are immensely distinct from other people, they are also, socially ... extremely distinct from each other. You may see them all together, with the rich colouring of their differences, in the fine flare of one of Mr W.H. Smith's bookstalls – a feature not to be omitted in any enumeration of the charms of Paddington and Euston. It is a focus of warmth and light in the vast smoky cavern, it gives the idea that literature is a thing of splendour, of a dazzling essence, of a gas-lit red and gold. A glamour hangs over the glittering booth, and a tantalising air of clever new things.[53]

In 1905 (the year, not coincidentally, when everything changed for Smith's), a series of articles appeared in *The Times* that provide a useful retrospective on the bookstall boom decades. The articles are unsigned, but it seems certain that they were written if not by, then at the very least with the full cooperation of, C.H. St John Hornby, who had entered the business in 1893 and set about transforming it 'from the railway and printing departments to its relations with Fleet Street'.[54] Hornby's reflections on the early bookstall years are revealing:

> One of the first great achievements of the late W.H. Smith was the establishment of Railway Bookstalls ... Up to that time, such provision as the railways offered to the reading public had been placed in the hands of crippled *employees*, or widows of *employees*, and of other persons chosen without the least regard to their fitness for the business. They usually offered a heterogeneous collection of gingerbeer bottles, tarts, soiled newspapers, and improper literature. The character of the books kept here became a cause of public scandal; for the stalls supplied novels which no bookseller would dare to expose for sale ... He [W.H. Smith] established well-equipped stalls at the stations, with clean newspapers, placed on sale at the earliest possible moment, and an abundance of good books, the whole being in charge of a trained bookseller

---

[52]   *Publishers' Circular*, Vol. 100, 14 March 1914, p. 329.
[53]   Henry James, 'Essay on London', *Century Magazine*, December 1888, pp. 235–6.
[54]   Wilson, pp. 205–213.

of intelligence and politeness … Thus the nature of the business necessitated from the first a certain discretion as to the character of the books sold, and the enormous and rapid growth of the bookstall system soon gave the firm a powerful influence over general literature. This influence, it is admitted, has always been exercised in the best interests of the general public. Neither trashy nor immoral books have been admitted to the stalls but prudery has never been a guiding principle … In early days especially Messrs W.H. Smith and Son were of enormous assistance in helping young and struggling authors of talent.[55]

The notion that the business managed simultaneously to supply public demand, guard public interests and somehow also serve the future of Art must be considered with a certain amount of caution in light of the evidence. In the same year (1905) Smith's lost their two main bookstall contracts (with the GW and the L & NW Railways) due to impossible rent raises and falling profits. In just ten weeks they accomplished a move from the bookstalls to newly acquired shops situated as close to the railway stations as possible. Nervous about the effect of the move on business, Hornby timed his series of articles to revise Smith's history and bring its recent decision in line with long-held policy, presenting an unbroken line of 'concern for the welfare of the public':

> They were first on the road before railways existed … They have succeeded in living up to this rule for nearly a century and they propose to signalise their devotion to it at the dawn of 1906 by establishing in the towns along the London and North Western and the Great Western Railways 150 new shops which will render an even more rapid, convenient and efficient service in distributing newspapers and books than has ever been obtainable before.

Add to this Hornby's claim for his posters for cocoa and constipation remedies that 'it is no exaggeration to say that the compelling art and literature printed on them will deeply affect the future of this nation',[56] and we have some indication of the level of hyperbole engaged in by Hornby in this most anxious of years. The truth was rather different, though the claim that Smith's exercised a powerful influence on literature was accurate enough.

So concerned were Smith's to be seen as the purveyors of highly moral, inoffensive literature that when they were challenged in court in 1888 over the possibility that they had sold a libellous book (*Great Musical Composers*, published by Messrs Walter Scott, and deemed to contain a libellous reference to a spiritualist named Mrs Weldon), they backed down to the tune of £200 and ordered the immediate withdrawal of all copies of the book.[57] This in spite of the fact that Mrs Weldon famously made

---

55 'The World's Greatest Newsagents: No. 1', *The Times*, 21 December 1905, p. 7.
56 'The World's Greatest Newsagents: No. 3', *The Times*, 28 December 1905, p. 5.
57 Letters and Memos between W.H. Smith and Son book departments and solicitors, re *Mrs Weldon v W.H. Smith and Son* libel action, 1888. Ref: WHS 123/1–6.

a career out of libel cases in the 1880s (she had 17 on the go in 1884 alone)[58] and lost several of them spectacularly enough to be imprisoned. Such was her profile with the popular press, in fact, that as Judith Walkowitz has noted, 'headlines of the half-penny newspapers constantly broadcasted "Mrs Weldon again"'.[59] Whatever advantage they might have gained by publicity in which they were seen to be a voice of masculine reason holding sway against a woman who was frequently characterised as a dangerously unstable campaigner for women's rights, Smith's evidently felt that it would serve their purposes better and far more safely if they addressed the issue as one of public protection.

In 1892 Smith's also publicly defended their withdrawal of the paper *Science Siftings* which, having published an exposé of a well-known businessman, drew the threat of legal action, not against themselves, but against their distributor. *Science Siftings* offered Smith's an indemnity, but this was refused. *The Star*, which published this story under the headline 'The Freedom of the Press is an Idle Boast While the Fear of Publishers can be Worked on', claimed that 'the libel laws give enough protection, in all conscience, if the aggrieved person pursue the real publishers of the paper, but if Messrs Smith, even with a proffered indemnity, decline to circulate papers directly anyone puts pressure on them, the consequences may be far-reaching beyond all calculation'. Smith's did not agree. 'Matter which was alleged to be libellous by a third party could not be sold by the firm', they responded. 'Messrs Smith would not knowingly be the means of distributing any publication alleged to contain libellous matter'. Even when this is the exposure of a swindle, demanded the paper? 'The solution of the problem', Smith's retorted with finality, 'would lie in an alteration of the libel laws so that the innocent vendor should not be held responsible, but only the actual publisher'.[60]

This stance is echoed in a number of similar libel cases in the period, most notably one in August 1893 which Smith's won on the grounds that they would protect the public whenever they could, but they could not possibly read or be held responsible for the contents of every newspaper they sent out. Ignorance of libellous matters was clearly a fair defence; and for Smith's proof enough that not only could sound business sense be convincingly and lucratively wrapped up in concern for the public good, but that they had come to be trusted for their dedication to that public, and that it was now one of the staples of their success. As Smiles expresses it in *Character*, 'a man is already of consequence in the world when it is known that he can be relied on – that when he says he knows a thing, he does know it – that when he says he will do a thing, he can and does do it. Thus reliableness becomes a passport to the general esteem and confidence of mankind'.[61]

---

58   Judith R. Walkowitz, *City of Dreadful Delight: Narratives of Sexual Danger in Late-Victorian London* (London, 1994), p. 185.
59   Walkowitz, p. 171.
60   'The Freedom of the Press is an Idle Boast While the Fears of Publishers Can be Worked on', *The Star*, 22 October 1892, no page number. Copy in WHS Cuttings Book.
61   Smiles, *Character*, p. 8.

As with any operation within a cultural field, though, this situation could not last. Just as in the public library, towards the end of the nineteenth century an increasing number of charges of anti-aesthetic censorship rang the changes, marking both the decline of the cult of character, and the elbowing out of Smith's from their self-styled position as a key distributor of the 'best' new literature through an exposure of their inherent conservatism. On 19 May 1887, the *Evening News* published a review of George Moore's *Parnell and His Island*:

> Mr George Moore is certainly the ablest representative of the realistic school of living English writers ... Therefore we recommend *Parnell and His Island* to our readers ... as readers of Fielding and Sterne, we do not pretend to be shocked when reading a modern author who certainly never sins in this particular as deeply as did some of our classics ... and therefore we regret exceedingly to hear that the book has been boycotted by Messrs Smith and Son. It is not allowed, we understand, to be exposed for sale at their railway bookstalls. This is not as it should be. Messrs Smith and Son enjoy a practical monopoly of a very important portion of the book-selling trade, a monopoly gained, no doubt, by their enterprise, industry, and tact; and, therefore, a monopoly which is certainly advantageous, on the whole, to the reading public. But still power has its responsibilities, and Messrs Smith and Son should not boycott a book lightly, or on inadequate grounds.[62]

The reviewer was backed up by several more powerful figures including Hall Caine (whose own position as a best-selling author consistently pushing at the boundaries of acceptability was vital to his position in the field, as I will demonstrate in Chapter 4). But Smith's refused to cooperate. In 1883 they had received a complaint from two women readers about Moore's *A Modern Lover*, and in 1894 they had refused to distribute *Esther Waters*. Moore was blacklisted. He was not alone; many other authors including Compton Mackenzie and Hall Caine himself found in Smith's a formidably conservative opponent.

In 1909, as we have seen, the circulating libraries including Smith's and Mudie's formed an association and asked publishers to forewarn them of potentially offensive books. Despite objections by representatives of the Society of Authors, again including Hall Caine along with Edmund Gosse and Maurice Hewlett, and the debate being, as Peter Keating has put it, argued out 'in every periodical and newspaper of the day',[63] the circulating libraries got their wish. But their power was waning, in part due to the increasing patronage of public libraries, which as we have seen, were by no means consistent in their responses to 'offensive' books. The attitude of the Library Association on the issue was to prove crucial. Reporting on the Public Morals Conference of 1910, the LA insisted: 'there is no possible means of limiting literature by police regulations, Acts of Parliament, or Vigilance Societies. Every case must

---

[62] *Evening News*, 19 May 1887, no page number. Copy in WHS cuttings book.
[63] Peter Keating, *The Haunted Study: A Social History of the English Novel 1875–1914* (London, 1989) p. 278.

be taken by itself, and on its own merits or demerits'.[64] In the end, the circulating libraries including Smith's were unable to suppress three important novels that year: *The Woman Thou Gavest Me* by Hall Caine, *The Devil's Garden* by W.B. Maxwell and *Sinister Street* by Compton Mackenzie. All three became best sellers.

Smith's conservatism, so lucrative in the decades of the novel's rapid expansion during the great age of 'character' in the 1860s and 1870s, was beginning to lose them their dominant position as 'art' settled into its role as the rising new religion of the 1890s. In the twentieth century under Hornby the company began to change its attitudes towards the Press and the censorship of novels, but despite Hornby's attempts to unify the company's history, it was clearly a far from even progression from the first stall at Euston through the loss of the major contracts almost 60 years later.

This chequered half-century of Smith's bookstall monopoly demonstrates once again the volatility of the literary field in the second half of the nineteenth century, its restless shifting of goalposts in response to increasing challenges from below. From its initial concern to attract the customer of 'wealth and influence', Smith's had moved firmly into the role of moral guardian, protecting 'the public' from a barrage of unsuitable publications. Thus far Smith's appears to share its role with the public librarian. But here the histories crucially diverge. The railway traveller represented quite a different public from that which the public libraries hoped to attract, and no matter what Smith's claimed, it was provided for with quite different literature.

'Something Hot and Strong': Bookstalls, Protection and Escapism

The major difference between the railway station and the public library, of course, is that one represents private enterprise and the other public spending. But there are other crucial discrepancies that revolve around the very different construction of the railway as public space and the railway journey as dangerous. The reader who was meant to visit the public library in a mood of leisurely seriousness, in order to select self-improving literature based on the recommendations of literary columns and librarians, was not the same reader who visited the railway bookstall. They might be the same person. But their reasons for selecting and reading in each place were not the same at all. At a Smith's stall recommendations and advice were always available – and indeed bookstall managers were trained to respond to queries to the extent that several, like Winchester's Mr Burchett, a bookstall manager on the L & SWR for 23 years, went on to become librarians. But the railway public was by its very nature seen as vast, transient, foreign (rather than local), and by the 1880s recognised to be in a state of nervous tension and desirous of mental escape and self-protection. Self-improvement ran a distant third, as witness the 1895 survey, which found that both self-help books and 'classics' were declining in popularity at the stalls.

---

[64] *Library World*, 8 (1910–11), p. 49.

A further example of the difference and how it was negotiated is provided by the fact that Smith's had always stocked much of the sensation fiction which represented enormous potential profits, despite considerable opposition from numerous critics who saw it as emasculating, mentally damaging, and the 'opiate' of the newest and most courted consumers – women. For Smith's this kind of novel hovered behind the line, its sale justified with a paternal shaking of the head at the folly of women. 'Ladies', Samuel Phillips learned from the Euston bookseller in 1851, 'are not great purchasers of good books at the station ... their ordinary request is for the last cheap novel published in the Parlour or Popular library. If they do by chance purchase a really serious book, it is invariably a religious one'.[65] The combination of piety and thrill seeking put forward here as the preferred literary diet of the woman traveller serves not only to nullify Smith's sale of potentially contentious literature by placing it alongside the ultimate in respectability, but also to suggest a praiseworthy paternalism on their part. Smith's here becomes the generous but gently guiding father, good-naturedly tolerating feminine weakness but advising religion as its antidote. With one stroke they safeguard both their market and their reputation by situating them within the bourgeois family framework. This is a different kind of tactic from the emphasising of a male-dominated canon of classics and of serious reading among biography, history and science that we saw occurring in the public library. At the bookstall there is greater lenience, an acknowledgement that the space itself requires a different form of control, at once more personal and more hands-off.

Despite Schivelbusch's claim that 'a railroad journey appears not different from a visit to the theater or the library',[66] then, railway travel in fact represented a very different form of experience, and it began at the station. The correspondence between Smith's and the management of the Metropolitan Railway over the situating of bookstalls on Baker Street station in 1908 offers some useful insights into the extent to which this difference was recognised. Writing to the Secretary of the Metropolitan following his inspection of the plans and proposed sites, the Superintendent gave his reasons for turning down some of them: 'Whilst fully recognising the desirability of meeting Messrs Smith's and Sons desires wherever possible, it is apparent that in some cases they have asked for sites from the point of view of their business without due regard to our limited spaces and heavy traffic, and that applies in any of the instances where I have had to report adversely'.[67] The correspondence continued throughout the latter part of 1908 and several drawings were submitted. Smith's obviously wanted the largest possible retail space for the £650 per annum which they were being charged, and to draw the largest possible crowds to their stalls, but the Metropolitan was concerned above all to keep people moving. The answer, contained in the final plan, was to provide oval rather than the more usual rectangular bookstalls on central

---

[65] Phillips, p. 7.
[66] Schivelbusch, pp. 45–6.
[67] Correspondence between the London Metropolitan and W.H. Smith and Son, 1908, London Metropolitan Archive. Ref: 1297/Met 10/264.

platform areas so that display surfaces might be maximised but crowds might flow easily around them.[68] Unlike the library, the railway station was clearly seen as a place of bustle and activity in which the leisurely perusal of reading matter was undesirable. This had been perceived as a problem earlier in the century. As Henry Mansel notes in his now famous article on sensation fiction:

> the exigencies of railway travelling do not allow much time for examining the merits of a book before purchasing it, and keepers of bookstalls, as well as of refreshment rooms, find an advantage in offering their customers something hot and strong, something that may catch the eye of the hurried passenger and promise temporary excitement to relieve the dullness of the journey.[69]

This danger of a lack of attention had originally been answered in large part by Smith's claims that they were performing the selection on the traveller's behalf. As Stefan Collini suggests: 'to be known as a man of character was to possess the moral collateral which would reassure potential business associates or employers'[70] and presumably, also, customers. But by the turn of the century things were changing again. Speed, short bursts of attention and the benefits of something to read which was disposable, fun and relatively harmless were becoming accepted as part of the travelling experience. There was an increasing sense that while railway reading wasn't art, it was entertainment, and of a kind that signalled its reader was 'not at home'. This shift in the perception of literature's function – forming throughout the latter half of the century, becoming concrete towards its close – was to have a profound impact, not only on its form, furthering and facilitating its diversification, but also on its social significance.

Smith's had responded early on to the particular qualities possessed by the railway. The bulky three-volume novel, for so long kept in a position of dominance by Mudie's and themselves, was unsuitable for carrying on railway journeys and stocking at bookstalls where space was extremely limited. The circulating libraries responded to market changes in the 1890s and by 1897 the three-decker was all but dead, but prior to this Smith's had recognised not only that the railways represented a unique circulating library opportunity and begun to offer travellers the chance to borrow single-volume library books at the station of their departure and return them at a different stall upon arrival, but that small cheap reprints were an equally lucrative alternative for those who preferred to buy. Routledge, Murray's and Longmans all issued a Railway Library of cheap reprints of classical and informative works, and in the 1860s Smith's entered into a discreet arrangement with Chapman and Hall whereby they purchased the copyrights of a number of successful authors and

---

68 Bookstall design for Baker Street Station, 1908, London Metropolitan Archive. Ref: 1297/Met 10/862.
69 Henry Mansel, 'Sensation Novels', *Quarterly Review*, April 1863, p. 485.
70 Collini, p. 106.

novels, and Chapman and Hall did the publishing under the title 'The Select Library of Fiction'. Among the authors were Charles Lever, Ouida, Charles Reade, Hawley Smart, Edmund Yates and R.D. Blackmore, an interesting and crucially eclectic mix of the conservative and the contentious. R.D. Blackmore was the popular author of historical novels, Charles Lever the author of swashbuckling tales of Ireland and army life. In his day Reade was not only considered to be a major serious novelist to rival Dickens, Fielding and Thackeray, but as Nicola Diane Thompson has suggested, he was particularly associated with a predominantly male readership.[71] By contrast, Ouida was assumed to appeal predominantly to women, and although it will be remembered that her novels were banned by several public libraries, the contention surrounding her work was apparently insufficient to induce Smith's to ban it. Popularity, a wide appeal across class and gender lines, and saleability were apparently the guiding principles here; a fact which, coupled with Smith's boycott of certain high-publicity 'literary' books, somewhat undermines Hornby's claims either that the 'public interest' was being universally served regardless of profit, or that 'struggling authors of talent' might find an ally in Smith's.

Constantly harassed over the spaces that were available to them, Smith's had to maximise profits in other ways, and despite their much-proclaimed reputation for the 'decent and inoffensive' they very clearly permitted books at their stalls that they were not inclined to circulate via their home lending library. In 1894 they were questioned by the *Pall Mall Gazette* (which, it will be remembered, they refused to stock and with which they therefore had a fairly acrimonious relationship) as to the reasons for their withholding of Moore's *Esther Waters* from their library. Smith's representative replied that 'our subscribers rely upon us to give them such books as they can carry into their homes ... We are merely caterers, and we have to spread our table with fare which will please, and which will not displease, our customers'. He added, however, that they had withheld the book from the library first and then the stalls only for the sake of consistency and public opinion: 'If we refused it in the library where our profit is small and placed it on the stalls where our profit is large, people would naturally impute motives and say what prigs we were'.[72]

That there was a difference between a book bought at a stall to read on the train and one bought or borrowed to take home remained a commonplace throughout the period. As late as 1921 Florence Barclay's daughter was explaining the success of her mother's 1909 novel *The Rosary* in exactly these terms: 'people bought her books instead of merely borrowing ... A man may read the history of some vile character and his viler doings with a very human thrill of interest as he travels up to business in the train. But he changes the book at Smith's without regret, and hopes his wife and daughter won't come across it. As for having it permanently about the house

[71] Nicola Diane Thompson, *Reviewing Sex: Gender and the Reception of Victorian Novels* (London, 1996), p. 27.
[72] 'Mr George Moore's New Novel', *Publishers' Circular*, 5 May 1894, p. 464.

– God forbid!'[73] It is difficult to be certain how widespread the practice of the sneaky anonymous reading of 'vile' books on the train really was, or indeed how 'vile' the books really were. In this case 'vile' probably meant only mildly risqué, or possibly in some way relatively 'literary', since this author is the daughter and granddaughter of parsons and her motive is the booming of her mother's Evangelical popular novel. But it is certainly true that the members of certain classes were permitted to purchase banned books at Smith's. The 1894 *Pall Mall Gazette* interview concludes with the Smith's representative's statement: 'If anybody likes to order the book from us we gladly supply it, because in that case it is fair to presume that the person ordering it knows what he or she is asking for'.[74] As in the public library, 'knowing' what to ask for signals the difference between the moral majority and what Leavis calls the 'critical minority'. Unlike in the public library though, at a Smith's bookstall the critical minority could usually get what they wanted.

This policy was strengthened by the division of Smith's stalls, not just into regions (of which there were around eight nationwide), but also into classes. Preston explains: 'They are all graded according to a rough scale of their importance; and to each bookstall according to its grade, are new publications distributed. A guinea book of travels, for instance, goes only to those classes i and ii; a popular novel, when reduced to six shillings, goes down as far as class v; the yet smaller stalls hardly rise above 2-shilling literature'.[75] An expensive new work of 'literature' was guaranteed, then, to reach only those who frequented the more important large stalls in the city centres, and/or those who knew what to ask for. Publishers seem to have been aware of this fact, and to distribute and market their products accordingly. In 1907, for example, Henry Frowde of Oxford University Press informed one of his authors: 'Your sonnet sequence is now on sale at all the bookshops at Oxford and at the Railway Bookstalls at Oxford, Paddington, Euston, Reading, Slough etc.', a list which indicates the assumption of a largely urban readership for new poetry.[76] A country or suburban dweller was removed from the cultural metropolis not only geographically but also ideologically, and this was so not just because different value systems and hierarchies of taste naturally prevailed, but because publishers and distributors like Smith's were actually helping to create them.

This did not mean, though, that any stall was likely to be on a par with the public library; even the fiction generally available to the uninformed majority was of a particular character found nowhere else. Smith's arrangement with Chapman and Hall was finally cancelled in the 1880s, by which time there were sufficient cheap one-volume 'yellowbacks' from other publishers. As Richard Altick has put it: 'for one or two

---

[73]   *The Life of Florence Barclay*, by One of Her Daughters (London and New York, 1921), pp. 243–4.
[74]   'Mr George Moore's New Novel', p. 465.
[75]   Preston, p. 477.
[76]   Letter No. 705 to Theodore Watts-Dunton, 26 June 1907. Letterbooks of Henry Frowde, OUP archives.

shillings a volume, the scores of 'libraries' that sprang up offered a tremendous selection to suit every taste but the crudest and the most cultivated'.[77] These 'yellowbacks' were bright, garish, often plastered with advertisements, generally thought of as disposable, and designed accordingly, with cheap bindings and thin paper (see Figure 2.2).

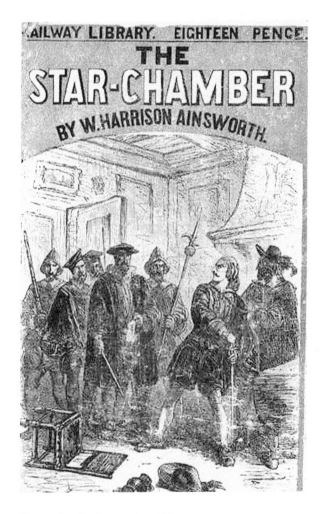

Figure 2.2   Example of a Routledge, Warne and Routledge's Railway Library book, *The Star Chamber*, by W. Harrison Ainsworth (1861). In its original the book is brightly coloured and eye-catching in red, black and yellow

---

[77]   Altick, p. 299.

They encompassed a wide range of works from cheap reprints of selected 'classics' to new novels, although, as I will argue in the next few chapters, the former had a better fate in store for them once their railway days were over, and the latter began to break new ground in other ways.

The conditions of the rail were not only responsible for changes in the physical size of books and periodicals; they also had an effect on subject matter and linguistic form. Nicholas Daly has argued convincingly that sensation fiction was as much a result of the physical conditions of train travel as the economic and social conditions that surrounded it, and Laura Marcus has demonstrated that the detective novel was its natural successor. The shifts in perception that sociologists such as Simmel identified as the inevitable consequences of modernity were also, according to Schivelbusch, particularly affected by railway travel as a special case. For him, 'to adapt to the conditions of rail travel, a process of deconcentration, or dispersal of attention, takes place in reading as well as in the traveller's perception of the landscape outside', and French surveys that indicate a fall in the sale of novels and a rise in newspapers attest to that possibility.[78] In Britain, too, the railways and the technology that they heralded were concurrent with a huge rise in the number of newspapers and periodicals published.

Some of the most popular newspapers signalled an extremely close affiliation with the travelling public. *Tit-Bits* and its rival *Answers* both, as we have seen, were so confident – or desirous – of securing their places amongst essential items in the traveller's kit that their presence there was offered as an insurance policy against railway accidents. They also, in common with many other periodicals, adopted a fragmentary form that, in the case of *Tit-Bits*, is implicit in the title and thus even becomes a major selling point. *Tit-Bits* offered extracts from novels, articles, stories and gossip seldom more than a page in length. This was ideally suited to the fragmentary attention span of the urban dweller and especially the train traveller. And the format worked: in 1899, according to its creator, *Tit-Bits* had a weekly circulation of around half a million.[79] Even self-help for the traveller took a particular form; insistent and pointed, geared towards short bursts and fast results and expendability, it was the antithesis of the philosophy expounded by the public libraries. H.G. Wells's Kipps, who is nonplussed by conventional education, experiences 'something in the nature of a conversion' and is 'stimulated … to the pitch of inquiring about the local Science and Art classes' by the reading of an article on Technical Education in a morning paper left behind by a commercial traveller which 'was written with penetrating vehemence'.[80] He is guided through a course of reading by his new bourgeois acquaintance Coote, who asserts that 'nothing enlarges the mind … like Travel and Books. And they're both so easy nowadays, and so cheap!' (p. 115).

---

[78]   Schivelbusch, pp. 71–2.
[79]   'Interview with Sir George Newnes, Bart.', *Bookman*, Vol. 90, May 1899, pp. 38–40.
[80]   H.G. Wells, *Kipps: the Story of a Simple Soul* (London, 1905), p. 44. All subsequent references are to this edition and will appear parenthetically in the text.

Men were not the only targets. Erika Diane Rappaport has suggested that, by the 1880s, the editors of women's magazines also 'presumed that they were selling to a commuting, suburban, and provincial readership' and that thanks largely to the expansion of the railways 'newspaper and periodical publishers had … changed the form and content of their product for rapid, superficial reading consistent with a less domestic lifestyle'.[81] A glance at the pages of *Woman* in the 1890s bears out her assessment. Under the editorship of Arnold Bennett the magazine contains a colourful mixture of articles and illustrations, none of them too long or too detailed. The issue of *Woman* from the week of 3 January 1894, for example, contains articles on how to brighten up one's lodgings (that apocryphal bugbear of the single girl in town), women who work (with anything from sculpture to machinery), how to give a children's supper party, and reviews of all the latest London plays, operas and ballets as well as the latest books. The fictional serial is short and fast paced, the adverts eye-catching and the tone chatty. This is a magazine for readers who get out amongst friends, work for a living and travel from home in order to do so, as well as for those who stay at home with children.

The market in this period resembles our own far more than it resembled the market of a mere 50 years earlier. It was swamped by specialist, niche-targeting magazines cheap enough for each member of a household of whatever class to purchase his or her own. To name but a few of the publications stocked by Smith's – *Woman*, *Temple Bar*, *The Rural World*, *Bouquet* novelettes, *Cassell's Family Magazine*, *Sketchy Bits*, the *Contemporary Review*, the *Edinburgh Journal*, *Tit-Bits*, *Answers*, the *Englishwoman's Journal*, and a range of dailies – is to recognise the importance of this niche marketing. These titles range from the juvenile and comic, through the lightly romantic and accessibly informative, to the critical and political, and they are designed for audiences from children to men, women and whole families. Even in the 1880s the success of a general publication such as *Cassell's Family Magazine* had been dependent on its understanding of the consumer needs of the average travelling family. The *Cassell's* of 1880, for example, includes a range of articles to suit the whole family on subjects as diverse as gardening, politics, meteorology, railway engineering, children's poetry, 'Chit-chat on Dress by our Paris Correspondent', travel, new advances in science, catering for Christmas parties, how to manage a small dairy and 'The Annual Holiday and how to Benefit from it', not to mention song sheets, illustrations, and a fictional serial.[82] Travelling abroad was also a hugely popular pastime in this period and holiday destinations in Britain equally well frequented, and literature on – and for – both was widely and cheaply available.

There is by this time a widespread understanding that the train traveller, by definition, is either preoccupied and in a hurry, or on holiday. Both have become integral features of the modern urban landscape. Both require escape or short bursts

---

[81] Erika Diane Rappaport, *Shopping for Pleasure: Women in the Making of London's West End* (Princeton, NJ, 2000), p. 122.

[82] *Cassell's Family Magazine*, Vol. 53, 1880.

of information, rather than long hours of concentration on 'good' literature or self-improvement. Schivelbusch has shown that conceptions of time and space were altered by train travel, not only experientially through the annihilation of 'the traditional time-space continuum which characterised the old technology',[83] but institutionally, through the standardising of time to the railway clock (which, although it didn't happen across the country until the 1880s, Dickens had described in the 1840s as so profound in effect that is was 'as if the sun itself had given in' (p. 290)).

The effect on passengers was also recognised early on. Even in 1866, a medical congress held in Paris had recognised that 'today we no longer think about anything but the impatiently awaited and soon-reached destination'.[84] Train travel, particularly for the working or lower-middle classes who made up the bulk of the excursion trade, was seldom romanticised into a luxury like the steamliner trade. V.E. Hughes notes in her autobiography that: '"excursion trains" … meant all that was horrible: long and unearthly hours, packed carriages, queer company, continual shuntings aside and waiting for regular trains to go by, and worst of all the contempt of decent travellers'.[85] Locomotives and some carriages are written about in the period in terms of their beauty, certainly – as witness the success of the Orient Express – and at exhibitions held in Paris at 11-yearly intervals until 1900, medals were awarded for the best new locomotive design.[86] But there is a distinct class bias to these sorts of descriptions of luxury. The Orient Express, for example, was prohibitively expensive for most travellers and for these, speed, comfort and convenience were the more usual hallmarks of railway excellence. 'Since 1899', H.G. Archer lamented in a comparative article on British and French express trains in the middle-class *Pall Mall Magazine* in 1902, 'our railways have dropped behind in the race for speed; and although they still offer the public the most generous – where quantity and superiority of accommodation are concerned – train services in the world … the fastest long, mid, and short distance express trains are no longer to be found in their timetables'.[87] The typical railway traveller wanted to be taken out of awareness of his or her journey, to have time and distance eroded by easy mental preoccupation as well as by technology, to dwell on the destination or prepare for the day's work. A magazine such as *Tit-Bits* with its emphasis on diversity, something for everybody but not too much for anybody, was firmly in the traveller's line.

Apparently not in the traveller's line was a paper such as the weekly *Passenger's Companion* which, started in 1912 with the intention of providing 'that great army of passengers who travel to and fro in every direction' with useful travel information and a romantic sense that the journey was all, lasted only until 1914.[88] In addition

83 Schivelbusch, p. 71.
84 Schivelbusch, p. 71.
85 Hughes, p. 23.
86 Vic Mitchell, *Ashford: From Steam to Eurostar* (Midhurst, 1996), p. 19.
87 H.G. Archer, 'Fast Trains: British and French Express Trains', *Pall Mall Magazine*, Vol. 28, September 1902, p. 97.
88 *Passenger's Companion*, 27 April 1912, p. 1.

to train timetables and descriptions of holiday destinations, it carried articles such as 'On Either Side: Through the Land of History and Romance' and 'The Countryside Through the Window', evidently trying to separate the traveller from his or her newspaper. As one of its contributors declared:

> There is an extraordinary characteristic of travellers as a class that I have never been able to understand, and that is their excessive devotion to light literature. Watch a dozen or so trains start, and although you will see plenty of folk who appear indifferent to the fate of their heavy luggage, and some who will even take the porter's announcement that there is not a single corner seat left, with perfect equanimity, you will scarcely see an individual who can contemplate the prospect of even a short journey minus the reading matter with unshaken nerve. One and all they dive for the bookstall, and if they arrive too late to make a judicial selection, will take anything it pleases the clerk in charge to hand them. So equipped, they will go on their way rejoicing, and to see the manner in which they bury their heads in the printed page the instant the train starts, one would imagine that it was a fatal thing to so much as glance out of the window ... Not for them is the pageant of the seasons unfolded on the broad bosom of the landscape ... Mundane affairs as discussed by Grub Street are their chosen portion, and I am sure that they profit by the discussing, but they cannot know what they miss.[89]

The 'great army of passengers' evidently did not agree, for they did not buy the paper in sufficient numbers to keep it afloat, and they continued to buy *Tit-Bits* and other light publications in their thousands. For them, what the railway provided was a chance to read; what reading provided was a chance not to think about the railway. Tapping into these intertwined psychological desires was a profitable masterstroke on the part of W.H. Smith II. And what purchasing one's travel reading at a Smith's bookstall encouraged was a sense of belonging to a consensus by engaging in an essential (monetary) exchange of 'decent' character and, perhaps, making an offering to the 'gods' of the railway. A bookstall purchase provided both protection and escape in equal measure.

Adapting, defending, or disguising, Smith' marketing policies hung for half a century on to a consumer whose character had changed so radically that whereas at the beginning of the period he was a potential revolutionary, by the end she was a potential voter. Through their careful conservatism and its inextricable link with 'character', in the early days of their monopoly Smith's not only catered to, but also helped to formulate the perceptions of the railway reader. Their thousands of posters plastering every conceivable surface of the railway answered and encouraged the development of a new, swift, dispersed form of looking. Their brightly lit bookstalls drew a disparate collection of travellers into a sense of unity under the banner of 'light' literature, injecting a potentially dangerous – and endangered – heterogeneous urban crowd with the tranquillity of harmless escapism. By the time they had begun to let go of their monopoly and move into permanent shops, they had helped to create a

---

[89]   *Passenger's Companion*, 6 July 1912, p. 6.

sense that nineteenth-century railway reading was essentially harmless, an English institution, so much so that it had already, at the beginning of the new century, come to be viewed with nostalgia, at least by Smith's themselves. As the Bournemouth bookstall manager expressed it in a letter to Smith's in-house newspaper, the *Newsbasket*, 'it is very encouraging during the busy season to hear the remarks passed by visitors (who come from towns chiefly served by the GWR and the L & NWR lines) on the general appearance of the stall in comparison to those owned by other contractors. "What a pleasure to see one of Smith's stalls again!" "Really, it's like old times again." "How much nicer and cleaner this stall appears!" "Good old Smith's! Still going strong, I see".'[90]

This kind of fond nostalgia might well have been a commonplace, but in reality it didn't hide the lasting sense that railway reading, like the airport bookstall purchase of our own time, had come to be viewed as something transient, unchallenging, and even a little seedy, something to be read on holiday, on the beach, or on any occasion on which it was fine or expedient to signal its reader's desire and right to escape. It is, perhaps, obvious by now that this kind of reading was bound to be inferior to the library book in terms of cultural capital. 'That the books and periodicals exposed for sale at these stalls should always have commended themselves to the taste and judgement of every observer was not to be expected', Preston admits. 'The very nature of the bookstall business makes it inevitable that the sales should be mostly in the lighter class of literature. Even the most intelligent and studious readers will not be likely to provide themselves at the beginning of a railway journey with literature that will lay any tax upon the intellectual powers. Moreover, the sales of books as distinguished from magazines and sixpenny editions, are almost exclusively made to the wealthy section of railway travellers, and consequently consist mostly of the later society novels.'[91]

W.H. Smith's self-advertisement was as a respectable purveyor of 'good' literature across the board. But what has emerged from a close look at the history of railway bookstalls and public libraries – just two of the possible marketplaces for fiction with which they were involved – is that even within this one empire of dissemination there existed a subtle but distinct policy of differentiation. This somewhat complicates Nicholas Feltes's notion of a standardising of reading practices through the emergence in the 1880s and 1890s of publishing and bookselling as 'patriarchal capitalist modes of production'.[92] The conditions under which each of these public places emerged and were organised and understood indicates, on the contrary, that by the First World War they were thought of as related but distinct, areas which were at once sites of danger in need of policing, and sites of very specific reading practices which required different types of material in order to be successful. In *Distinction*, Bourdieu suggests that:

---

90   *Newsbasket*, February 1908, p. 20.
91   Preston, pp. 476–7.
92   N.N. Feltes, *Literary Capital and the Late Victorian Novel* (Madison, WI, 1993), p. 49.

the denial of lower, coarse, vulgar, venal, servile – in a word, natural enjoyment, which constitutes the sacred sphere of culture, implies an affirmation of the superiority of those who can be satisfied with the sublimated, refined, disinterested, gratuitous, distinguished pleasures forever closed to the profane. That is why art and cultural consumption are predisposed, consciously and deliberately or not, to fulfil a social function of legitimating difference.[93]

The railway bookstall fulfilled precisely this role of the provider of the low, the natural, and the profane, and of legitimating difference. It became a position in the field against which others could be defined, whether they were concerned with genre, audience or form.

Bamforth and Co.'s version of the film *The Kiss in the Tunnel* (also 1899) provides further proof that the link between railway literature and transgressive behaviour is already firmly established by this time. In this version, different from G.A. Smith's in several crucial details, when the train enters the tunnel the man puts down his paper and sits next to the woman. For a moment she attempts to concentrate still harder on her magazine. But the next moment, as though the reading matter itself has increased the titillation created by the train, they are locked in an embrace. The railway creates social and sexual tension. Railway reading, paradoxically, seems to both mollify and help to create this tension, superficially disguising and diverting it while at a deeper level compounding it. So entrenched in popular consciousness had this notion become that by the First World War Florence Barclay's saintly dedication to her writing task could be signalled by the fact that she wrote *The Rosary*'s most passionate scene while 'sitting in the corner of a third-class railway compartment, travelling from London to Hertford'.[94] Given the prevailing notions about what train travel did to the libido, it is tempting to surmise that the novel's climactic scene came about because of, rather than in spite of, the place in which Barclay wrote it, but the passage was evidently designed to persuade the reader of a sense of moral superiority in the author that enabled her to rise above the situation. Indeed, the purity and impact of the novel's message is signalled in this biography by the fact that it reached people everywhere, even 'in railway compartments'[95] (rescuing from himself, no doubt, the man who usually read the 'history of some vile character and his viler doings as he travels up to business in the train').[96]

Inevitably, the linking of short, accessible, market-led literature with modernity's crude but conservative newly literate, newly mobile masses helped to create the essential characteristics of the next dominant position. 'Literary Art' – to be taken seriously – needed to avoid both the cheap, seedy, watered-down thrills of the bookstall, and the sanctimony of those – like Florence Barclay – who despised them.

---

[93]   Bourdieu, *Distinction*, p. 7.
[94]   *The Life of Florence L. Barclay*, p. 209.
[95]   *The Life of Florence L. Barclay*, p. 213.
[96]   *The Life of Florence L. Barclay*, p. 243.

Chapter 3

'People Read So Much Now and Reflect So Little': Oxford University Press and the Classics Series

Creating a Classic

The fragmentary attention span of the traveller, the nervous condition in which s/he was thought to be traveling, the time constraints imposed by the journey itself, and the sense of the railway station as a fluid and comparatively unregulated public space, combine to make the bookstall purchase a very different proposition with a very different set of cultural meanings from the library loan. A deeply entrenched sense of concentration and clear direction as requirements for the 'right' way of reading – integral to the operations of the public library – meant literature and reading habits that could not conform occupied a distinctly subordinate position in the field. But what of the book selected with the principles of direction and concentration in mind, bought rather than borrowed, and designed to be kept and displayed in the home? Like the library book it carried the potential for the conferring of cultural capital, but unlike the library book it cost money and what it proclaimed was permanent.

By the 1880s, as we have seen, it had already become a trope that reading matter played an important role in social self-construction. Gissing was one for whom the idea had become a truism: as John Carey has pointed out, his characters are habitually introduced either through their physiognomy or their bookcases, and these are in many cases linked: 'Shelves which contain poetry, literature, history and no natural science belong to sensitive, imaginative, intelligent characters. Shelves which contain politics, social science, technology and modern thought of virtually any description brand their owners indelibly as at best semi-educated and at worst cruel, coarse and dishonest'.[1] The trope endured into the twentieth century. In the same year that E.M. Forster's Leonard Bast was desperately trying to impress the Schlegel sisters with his knowledge of 'the husks of books' by Ruskin, Carlyle, George Borrow, R.L. Stevenson, E.V. Lucas, Richard Jefferies and Thoreau,[2] another fictional reader, Arnold Bennett's Edwin Clayhanger, was spending 17 hard-earned shillings on calf-bound volumes of Aristotle, Byron and Voltaire. A wealthy neighbour had opened his eyes to the fact

---

[1]   John Carey, *The Intellectuals and the Masses*, p. 94.
[2]   E.M. Forster, *Howards End*, p. 150.

that 'a book might be more than reading matter, might be a bibelot, a curious jewel to satisfy the lust of the eye and of the hand'. These calf-bound, snowy-paged volumes are like 'the gleam of nuggets' once he gets them home and compares them to their only rivals, the 'half dozen garishly bound Middle School prizes, machine-tooled, and to be mistaken for treasures only at a distance of several yards'.[3] Books classify. And in this period they embroil their readers and their producers in a complex struggle for cultural hegemony engaged in with renewed ferocity and vigor.

The cheap classic series was an important manifestation of the lower-middle classes' drive toward self-education and self-fashioning. It was also part of a corresponding drive on the part of publishers to realise the economic potential of this vast new market. As I demonstrated in the last chapter, Smith's had early on perfected the art of producing cheap reprints of single-volume non-copyright books for sale on their stalls. Even when they withdrew from their publishing arrangement with Chapman and Hall and ceased to produce these themselves, the practice remained a lucrative staple of many an enterprising publishing house. Routledge's Railway Library was one of the most successful and enduring of these. Their brightly-coloured pocket-sized reprints, jammed with small print and adverts and sporting a dramatic illustration on the front cover (see Figure 2.2), for decades enlivened the bookstalls and labelled them as cheap and cheerful, if – in spite of all Smith's could do – slightly shady. Despite its genesis in the railway library of the 1860s, however, the classic library series, though also cheap and reliant upon non-copyright single-volume works, very quickly came to stand for something quite unrelated to travel and transience, and took on a very different set of cultural meanings. These meanings are rooted in self-help, the rise of the suburban bourgeoisie, and a subtle shift in the position of the publisher in the literary field designed at once to accommodate and profit by the changes, and to distance them from the true intellectual.

By the 1880s and 1890s the lurid sensationalism and cheapness of the railway reprint of a particular novel had become, in the hands of the right publisher, a sober, edifying and plain little book with a quite different emphasis. It was often as cheap or cheaper, but it had a slightly different cultural value. This phenomenon, representing as it does both the zenith of mass publishing and a contradictory desire for cultural distinction, became one of publishing's most contested terrains. Gissing's 'cruel, coarse and dishonest' middle classes might find in a classics series the poetry, literature and history which would make them appear more 'intelligent' and 'imaginative'. But almost all of Leonard Bast's favorite authors were represented there, and Edwin Clayhanger's despised machine-tooled prize books were almost certainly drawn from its ranks.

Richard Altick has traced the cheap reprint back to the eighteenth century, when a historic decision by the House of Lords in 1774 upheld the 1709 copyright Act (which gave the copyright holder exclusive rights to a book for only 21 years) in the face of the widespread practice of ignoring it. Previous to this date, the copyright holder had

---

3   Arnold Bennett, *Clayhanger* (1910; London, 1976), pp. 160; 203.

usually applied for and obtained a restraining injunction preventing other publishers from reprinting a work even after it had legally entered the public domain. This meant, as Altick has noted, that copyright was perpetual in practice if not in law, and that 'the copyright holder could charge as much as the market could stand'.[4] After the 1774 ruling, however, everything changed and publishers were quick to take advantage of a suddenly free market. Cheap reprints began with John Bell's Poets of Great Britain Complete from Chaucer to Churchill (109 volumes, 1776–1792) at 1s 6d per volume, and continued for the next two centuries and beyond. They gained added impetus not only from the new Board School generation but also from Mundella's Code of 1883. Under the terms of this code school inspectors had to listen to pupils read aloud from set works such as *Robinson Crusoe*, *Lamb's Tales*, Scott and Macaulay,[5] thus setting the seal of institutional approval on a particular range of works. Even Talfourd's Act of 1842 which had extended the copyright period to an author's lifetime plus seven years, or 42 years, whichever was longer, had made little dent in the trend. Out of the schoolroom libraries of classics also proliferated, such that 'of the Chandos Classics alone over 3,500,000 volumes (according to the publisher) were sold between 1868 and 1884, and in five years Kent's Miniature Library of the Poets had a sale of a quarter-million'.[6]

Useful as they are, though, what these statistics don't tell us is who decided what constituted a 'classic' or a series of 'classics', how it was marketed and to whom, and what that meant to the reader. He or she could, after all, also buy cheap reprints of non-copyright 'classics' individually from the station bookstall or borrow them from the library. But increasingly, in the latter half of the nineteenth century, the cultural value of a particular book had less to do with what it contained than it did with who published it, in what format and for which market. This can be illustrated by tracing the publishing history of eminently reprintable works such as Henry Fielding's *Tom Jones* (1749). Continuing an almost unbroken tradition of popularity, the novel appeared in Routledge's Railway Library in 1867, price 2s, in their usual style of cover of bright green and red over yellow, in this instance sporting a picture of two men scuffling by a plunging horse by way of a promise of the excitement and drama to be found within. The 14-page introduction to this volume gives a brief history of Fielding's life and works and stresses that they 'partake of the natural defects that pertain to things human but they are, for all that, healthy, noble and elevating'. This is an important pronouncement given contemporary ambivalence about railway bookstall fare in general and Fielding's immorality in particular (he was, it will be remembered, banned from Winchester Public Library in 1905 along with Ouida and Smollett, who was also represented in Routledge's Railway Library). Four years previously, Henry Mansel had described the typical railway novel in his famous article in the *Quarterly Review*:

---

[4] Altick, pp. 53–4.
[5] Altick, p. 160.
[6] Altick, p. 243.

> the picture, like the book, is generally of the sensation kind, announcing some exciting scene to follow. A pale young lady in a white dress, with a dagger in her hand, evidently prepared for some desperate deed; or a couple of ruffians engaged in a deadly struggle; or a Red Indian in his war-paint; or, if the plot turns on smooth instead of violent villainy, a priest persuading a dying man to sign a paper, or a disappointed heir burning a will; or a treacherous lover telling his flattering tale to some deluded maid or wife.

There were obvious reasons – or perceived reasons – for this type of marketing, as I showed in the previous chapter; Mansel goes on to point out that:

> the exigencies of railway travelling do not allow much time for examining the merits of a book before purchasing it, and keepers of bookstalls, as well as of refreshment rooms, find an advantage in offering their customers something hot and strong, something that may catch the eye of the hurried passenger and promise temporary excitement to relieve the dullness of a journey.[7]

Mansel was describing sensation fiction, but he could be forgiven for assuming from its cover that the Fielding was one of their number. The covers in which Routledge wrapped its non-copyright railway reprints of 'classics' not only failed to differentiate them from more contentious contemporary offerings, but also actually seemed to encourage the mistake. Figure 3.1 shows another Routledge edition of *Tom Jones*, this time in their shilling Large Format series, the front cover illustration of which foregrounds the story's romance (or perhaps represents the 'treacherous lover telling his flattering tale'). These sorts of decisions about cover design cannot be put down to a general devaluing of Fielding: according to the *English Catalogue of Books*, *Tom Jones* was reprinted steadily throughout the period in formats as diverse as the de luxe Dent 10s version in four volumes (1898); the Routledge 5s library version (1886); (Macmillan's Library of English Classics' 3s 6d version (1900); a version in Caxton's Novels in monthly parts, price 6d each (1894–95); and a Cassell's National Library edition at 6d or 3d. Many of his other novels also enjoyed consistent reprinting. Despite Winchester Library Committee's ruling, there were plenty who, like the well-known critic Andrew Lang, believed that Fielding's works were among those which represented the 'novel of life' and were 'literature' destined to be 'permanent'.[8]

The same treatment was meted out to far less contentious 'classics'. Also among Routledge's Railway Library titles (which numbered 1,300 by 1898)[9] were the works of Marryat who, without the lurid railway covers, was a staple in many a cheap 'classic' library of a quite different character. These ranged from Bell's Reading Books for Schools and Parochial Libraries (1880s, price 1s) through Ward, Lock's Select Library of Fiction (1880s), to Macmillan's Prize Library (1898–1900, price 2s 6d or 3s 6d).

---

7   Henry Mansel, 'Sensation Novels', *Quarterly Review*, No. 226, Vol. 113, April 1863, p. 485.
8   Andrew Lang, 'Current Fiction', *Publishers' Circular*, 12 May 1894, p. 512.
9   Altick, pp. 298–9.

Figure 3.1   **Front cover of Henry Fielding's *Tom Jones* in Routledge's Large Format shilling series (demy 8vo, issued 1881, 1889 and 1896)**

By 1886 Marryat was being recommended alongside Shakespeare and Dickens by a regular contributor to the quality periodicals on such topics; Edward G. Salmon felt that Marryat was one of the 'masterpieces of the English language' that should be drummed into the working classes.[10]

The 'classics' series might, then, already have a long history by the 1880s and 1890s when Altick has estimated that upward of 80 or 90 cheap series of English Classics were being produced. But by this time it bore very little resemblance to the railway reprint that had spawned it. Cheapness – due to the copyright laws – was an

---

[10]   Edward G. Salmon, 'What the Working Classes Read', *Nineteenth Century*, Vol. 20, July 1886, p. 116.

obvious factor in deciding which authors should be represented in either, but actual cheapness existed by the turn of the century in a tense, complex relationship with the cultural value implied by a book's aesthetics. Marryat or Fielding in a 'Railway Library' was a very different cultural object from Marryat or Fielding in a 'classics' series. To give a further example, the 6d *Aesop's Fables* which in 1886 appeared in Routledge's 'World Library' (as distinct from their 'Railway Library', though judging by its preface probably also sold at bookstalls) is very small, brown, unattractive and covered in adverts for everything from 'Judson's Indestructible Marking Ink' to 'Keating's Worm Tablets' and 'Stone Solvent'. It contains an introduction to the series by its editor, the Rev. H.R. Haweis, MA, which declares at great length the laudable intentions of the series:

> to place within everyone's reach what everyone ought to know: to circulate the works of great writers, or portions of books which should be familiar in our mouths as household words … To give such variety that everyone who takes in the series for a year, at a cost of a few shillings will have on his shelf 52 volumes, differing in all but this – that the world will not willingly let any one of them die. To make the price of each volume so low that none need borrow it, everyone being tempted to buy it, and nobody to steal it.

It also makes its perceived audience very clear. They are the masses created or brought together by modernity: by technology, cities and education. This justificatory preface, though long, is worth reproducing as it effectively sums up a widespread contemporary view of the need for cheap classics, and the reasons for this need:

> As I looked down the other day, from the upper deck of a large Atlantic steamer, at the crowd of steerage passengers, and marked how most of them were huddled together hour after hour doing nothing, others crowding round the bar where the beer was being doled out, and just a few reading some greasy tract or newspaper, I thought O, for a stock of cheap books such as will be issued in Routledge's World Library! … When I think of the long, gossiping, yawning, gambling hours of grooms, valets, coachmen, and cabmen; the railway stations, conveniently provided with bookstalls, and crowded morning and evening with workmen's trains … the brief, but not always well-spent leisure of Factory hands in the north – the armies of commercial and uncommercial travellers with spare half-hours … again the vision of 'Routledge's World Library' rises before me, and I say, 'This, if not a complete cure for indolence and vice, may at least prove a powerful counter-charm.'

The notion of literature as a cure for vice is a familiar one, but it here sits a little oddly with the book's aesthetics. At 6d (3d in paper) the book was cheap enough to be disposable and looked it, and its advertisements, rooting it so firmly in the moment of its production, indicate that – far from being a problem – its transience was to be expected.

Despite this editor's hopes for a certain shelf-life, by the beginning of the new century the cheaper reprint tended to be thought of as a disposable form: 'the place of the yellowback has been taken to some extent by the sixpenny novel', wrote a bookseller's assistant in 1905. 'This paper-covered reading matter is bought because it can be parted with once it is read.'[11] Indeed, in advertising their new Sixpenny Classics Series, Nelson's stressed their durability as compared with earlier reprints at a comparable price: 'The sixpenny books hitherto published in paper covers are of no use for library purposes. They are thrown away after reading. 'Nelson's Classics', at the same price, are better printed, are bound in cloth, are handier in size, and will form a handsome addition to any library'.[12] The Routledge *Aesop* does contain a four-page introduction, a feature that was later to take on great significance, but it here seems designed merely to outline Aesop's life and place his work historically for the uninitiated. It concentrates on the more sensational details of Aesop's life such as his slavery and execution and makes no attempt to cite its sources. Routledge's World Library, in short, seems to occupy a position midway between their 'Railway Library' and the later, more sophisticated cheap classic.

J.M. Dent's 'Everyman's Library for Young People' (started 1905) produced a very different volume of *Aesop's Fables* in 1913, price 1s, which serves to illustrate the changes which cheap reprints had undergone in the intervening decades. The Everyman's *Aesop* is small, sober in style and without advertisements, and despite its relatively low price it is decidedly keepable, with clear type and substantial hard covers. It contains a lengthy and scholarly introduction, which imparts a tone of solemn reflection on great works, weaving the Fables into a detailed biography of Aesop taken (we are reliably informed) from Sir Roger L'Estrange's seventeenth-century *Life.* This introduction goes to Indian history for the origin of the beast fable. It cites the translation used (Thomas James's of 1848 rather than Caxton's of 1485) and thanks the revisers of the new versions of 'certain Indian, Russian and other fables', which, along with English and Welsh tales, follow those of Aesop.

Dent's memoirs provide an informative backdrop to the origins of his idea. 'In 1904 and 1905', he writes, ' an idea, long cherished, took definite shape, and I began to set about developing it in earnest. I had felt that in England we had no library of classical literature like the French "Bibliothèque Nationale", or the great "Réclam" collection produced in Leipzig, of which you could buy a volume for a few pence ... I knew that there were promiscuous collections of popular reprints, some very well done as far as they went, as for instance the Chandos Classics, Macmillan's Globe Series, Morley's Library, but none covered the great field of English Literature, let alone that of the whole world'.[13] These memoirs, and the books' own textual production values, indicate that the Everyman's classic is not simply trying to introduce a passing reader to a passing interest or keep him or her out of the grog shop or away from newspapers. It is trying to educate. It places itself critically, historically and generically

---

[11] 'From Yellowback to Sixpenny Re-Print', *Publishers' Circular*, 24 June 1905, p. 695.

[12] *Publishers' Circular*, 11 March 1905, p. 283.

[13] J.M. Dent, *The House of Dent 1888–1938: Being the Memoirs of J.M. Dent with Additional Chapters Covering the Last 16 Years by Hugh R. Dent* (London, 1938), p. 123.

and it assumes an air of scholarly seriousness that invites the reader to be interested not just in the work, but also in its context. It is, in other words, part of a series that offers itself as operating like a formal course of education.

There are many variations between these two extremes and certain publishers adopted or hung onto one style rather than another. For example, the Chandos Classics Series (1868–89) admired by Dent was substantial, scholarly and well presented from the beginning, designed more for prize giving than for throwing away.[14] By contrast, as late as 1909 Nelson's were producing flimsy, badly bound and poorly printed editions on very thin paper without introductions or (despite the claims of the 1905 advert) any real concessions to durability. But the general trend was unmistakably towards the production of series that would please, inform, educate, work together and last. There are crucial differences in the appearance of the 'classic' across the period and these cannot be accounted for simply in terms of a given publisher's aesthetics. What they show, on the contrary, is the development of a style of cheap publishing that actively sought to disassociate itself from the cheap, shoddy, disposable railway-style reprint of the middle of the century. So marked – and so successful – had the distinction become by the end of the century that, as I demonstrated in the last chapter, W.H. Smith's dropped all but the cheapest 'classics' series from their bookstalls altogether.

That there was a need for a cheap literature that was not geared towards the transient, lurid and eye-catching was well recognised throughout the period. Henry Mansel was still warning of the dangers of the bookstall purchase in 1864, despite almost 20 years of Smith's monopoly: 'we have ourselves seen an English translation of one of the worst of those French novels devoted to the worship of Baal-Peor and the recommendation of adultery, lying for sale at a London railway stall, and offered as a respectable book to unsuspecting ladies'.[15] In by now familiar terms of a gendered readership in which women are the yardstick, Mansel makes plain once again the dangers of open access to books in the heterogeneous public space. Even twenty years after this, Matthew Arnold (whose philosophy had lent such impetus to the fiction debate in Public Libraries) was not convinced that the bookstall had improved, and he couched his objections in terms which were inextricably entwined with class and aesthetics:

> A cheap literature, hideous and ignoble of aspect, like the tawdry novels which flare in the book-shelves of our railway stations, and which seem designed, as so much else that is produced for the use of our middle-class seems designed, for people with a low standard of life, is not what is wanted. A sense of beauty and fitness ought to be satisfied in the form and aspect of the books we read, as well as by their contents.[16]

---

14 The British Library's copy of the Chandos Classics *Robinson Crusoe* (1878) bears an inscription on its flyleaf to the effect that it was presented to one Albert Deacon at St Anne's Sunday School Bible Class on 20 January 1887.

15 Mansel, 'Sensation Fiction', p. 486.

16 Matthew Arnold, 'Copyright', *Fortnightly Review*, Vol. 27, March 1880, p. 328.

For Arnold, a badly designed book is as indicative of a particular class readership as a badly written one. As an inspector of schools from 1851 to 1886, Arnold was well-placed to advocate the adoption of his aesthetic philosophy, and it is his influence once again which seems to have proved one of the decisive factors in the new breed of 'classic'. As Altick has noted, the 'classic' series from the 1890s onward was far more inclined to be of good quality. Beginning with Dent's Temple Shakespeare (1894–96), 'once again, after many decades of indifference to physical attractiveness, publishers began to make the classics available to the common reader in a cheap form that was dainty yet sturdy, convenient to the pocket, and printed on good paper in readable type'. [17] But, Arnold notwithstanding, what this durable, attractive library of books ought to contain was an equally important and far more contentious issue.

N.N. Feltes has suggested that a new definition of the classic series was formed by the appearance of Sir John Lubbock (Lord Avebury)'s list of '100 good books'. This had been recommended to students during a lecture at the F.D. Maurice Working Men's College in 1886 and turned into '100 Best Books' by the *Pall Mall Gazette*, which published the list and invited various public figures to comment on it.[18] As Altick has shown, this was not the first time that a collection of books was conceived of as a series (many series pre-date Lubbock's list)[19] but it was the first time that a finite number had been posited. Publishers picked up on this notion of a quantifiable list despite public debate over what it ought to contain, but as Feltes goes on to suggest, 'the significance of the number was not arithmetical but ideological, signifying ... attainable knowledge. Indeed, each term of the formula contributed to its distinctiveness, which has as its ultimate reference Matthew Arnold's idea of "culture"'.[20] The attractions of Arnold's idea wrapped in a convenient and affordable package are obvious, though for Feltes it deviates from Arnoldian philosophy at the level of production:

> The phrase as a whole combines those aspirations for a 'list' in which a publisher might take pride with the purposes of an enterprising publisher ... The prescription of a hundred 'best' books thus completes the fetishization of 'the classic'. No longer the 'undulating and diverse' relation to knowledge which Matthew Arnold prescribed, the 'hundred best books' has an attainable completeness, a finality of its own, existing precisely as a fetish which may be owned.[21]

The influence which Lubbock's list exerted on the notion of a 'classic series' is difficult to overstate. Despite the objections of several public figures (including Ruskin), publishers and writers deferred to it for years, even while they deviated from

---

[17] Altick, pp. 315–16.

[18] Feltes, *Literary Capital*, p. 41.

[19] The John Spiers Collection of Victorian and Edwardian Fiction (1850–1918), perhaps the most comprehensive collection of its type that we have, contains upwards of 800 different 'series' or 'libraries' many of which predate Lubbock's list.

[20] Feltes, *Literary Capital*, p. 44.

[21] Feltes, *Literary Capital*, p. 46.

or added to its prescription. In 1886, for example, Routledge sent review copies of the first of their 'World Library' series not only to the Queen, the Prince of Wales, Gladstone and the Chairman of the London School Board but also to Lubbock. When challenged about his borrowings for his play *Salomé* in 1893, Oscar Wilde replied 'Of course I plagiarise. It is the privilege of the appreciative man. I never read Flaubert's *Tentation de St Antoine* without signing my name at the end of it. All the best Hundred Books bear my signature in this manner'.[22] In Wells's 1905 novel *Kipps: The Story of a Simple Soul*, the vulgar, self-made, middle-class character Coote has a bookshelf that satirically confirms his social status: it contains not only Samuel Smiles's *Self-Help* but also the One Hundred Best Books.[23] As late as 1907, Oxford University Press's warehouse publication *The Periodical* was referring to it, proudly announcing that 32 of Lord Avebury's list were represented in the World's Classics series. It added by way of a further incentive that 'many of the other volumes in Lord Avebury's list are included in other cheap series issued by the Oxford University Press, but with the above-mentioned volumes alone there is a nucleus of the ideal library'. And, in a neat hedging of bets, it concluded with a statement that many of the works cited by those who disagreed with Lord Avebury were also represented in World's Classics.[24]

As Feltes has suggested, it is the *notion* of a number, rather than any number in itself, which seems to have caught on. By the end of the period that cheap staple, the non-copyright reprint, is no longer solely responsible for dictating the contents of the 'library'. Until the 1880s the cheap series had been the product of a system of trawling a seemingly bottomless temporal ocean and coughing up the catch onto the bookstalls, pausing only to weed out its most poisonous elements. But what we are seeing now is a subtle upgrading, a notion that there is indeed such a thing as the 'ideal library', a finite number of 'classics' or 'best books' worth collecting and without which no course of self-instruction can be complete. Feltes' suggestion that the value of this 'library' to the publisher is that it combines the distinction of a 'list' with the profit of an 'enterprise' is lent weight by the fact that in real terms the 'library' is complete only when a publisher says so. Lubbock numbered the best books at a hundred. Dent started Everyman with the conviction that there were a thousand, and as we have seen, felt strongly that they should cover not just 'that great field of English Literature' but also 'that of the whole world'.[25] To facilitate the economic potential still further, a book is a 'classic' almost wholly because a particular publisher says it is. Indeed, in the scramble to make their own series more appealing than those of their competitors, publishers frequently advertised both 'standard' classic components and some more off the beaten track. Some of these (like Trollope, re-introduced by World's Classics) survived, while many others (like the poetry of Marie Corelli's father Charles Mackay, included in the Chandos Classics) did not.

---

22   Richard Ellman, *Oscar Wilde* (London, 1987), p. 355.
23   Wells, *Kipps*, p. 115.
24   *The Periodical*, May 1907, pp. 125–6.
25   J.M. Dent, p. 124.

By the turn of the century, then, a curious and complex set of conditions prevailed in the publication of 'classics'. A 'classic', to achieve its full effect, had to be more than a literary work; it must also be part of a series that both completed and supported it, and bound and marketed in the right way. Feltes's suggestion that this marked the emergence of a new style of publishing and bookselling – which he designates 'patriarchal capitalist' – is persuasive. But his account lacks an adequate exploration of the effect of these shifts on the consumer, who has, after all, a certain amount of choice of both material and marketplace and whose decision is influenced in extremely subtle ideological ways. As I have shown, to buy a 'classic' in a colourful cover from a railway bookstall with the intention of throwing it away or passing it on after reading was to purchase only part of the edifying experience which 'good literature' was supposed to impart. That this increasingly powerful notion had an integral class dimension is, of course, pretty much inevitable.

A New Direction for Oxford University Press

This complex set of ideological practices, this blurring of 'list' and 'enterprising' modes of publishing which destabilised pre-existing cultural demarcations, can be highlighted by a small but significant publishing event of 1905. In that year, 'list' publisher Oxford University Press took over the World's Classics series from bankrupt 'enterprising' publisher Grant Richards. Richards, like many an entrepreneur of the 1890s, had always had more vision and enthusiasm than financial stability. Arnold Bennett wrote to him in 1902 (admittedly somewhat sycophantically, since Richards had published his work *Fame and Fortune* after it had been turned down by Methuen) 'It is impossible for me to disguise my admiration of you as an enterprising publisher. You are the one publisher in London that I know of, and I know a few, who has the courage of his convictions'.[26] This was not all fabrication. It was Richards who had had the courage to publish the poems of Lord Alfred Douglas in 1899, while the budding author briefly shared the European exile of his infamous disgraced lover Oscar Wilde. This was no small act of bravery during the years of moral backlash following the Wilde trials. Richards also took on Joyce's *Dubliners* when few others would consider it (though he backed out at the last minute). Vera Brittain later devoted a whole paragraph of her memoirs to her gratitude to Richards for taking a chance and publishing her first novel.[27] The courage of his convictions Richards may have had, but when he was brought before a bankruptcy hearing in April 1905 the *Publishers' Circular* reported that he owed £55,134 1s 2d and had borrowed £8,000 on the World's Classics series alone. That it was, however, a lucrative part of his business and not responsible for his downfall is shown by the fact that his profit for 1901, the year

---

[26]   Arnold Bennett, *Letters of Arnold Bennett, Vol. II. 1889–1915* (London, 1968), p. 168.
[27]   Vera Brittain, *Testament of Youth: An Autobiographical Study of the Years 1900–1925* (1933; London, 1999), p. 600.

it was introduced, was £596, 1s, while that for 1902 showed a significant increase, standing at an impressive £6,119 18s 8d.[28]

Oxford University Press was in an interesting position at the time. Their Bibles, Prayerbooks, examination papers, dictionaries and scholarly works had been insufficient to shield them during the recession of the 1890s. They had determined then, under the guidance of Philip Lylleton Gell (Secretary to the Delegates from 1894–98) to apply 'what Gell always capitalised as Commercial Standards to the publishing department'.[29] This move was only partially successful. It was only as a result of the combined efforts of Charles Cannan (Gell's successor 1898–1919), Sir Walter Raleigh (literary advisor to OUP, 1905–21) and Henry Frowde (the manager of its London business and, it will be remembered, distribution mastermind behind the 1881 New Revised Version) that OUP was to refloat its finances. Raleigh had written to Cannan on his appointment that 'If I could find a gold-mine for them [i.e. the Delegates] I would … I shall not be at ease until I have introduced them to some enterprise that is both virtuous and profitable'.[30] The take-over of a classics series, especially in the early part of the twentieth century when 'classics' had shaken off the taint of the bookstall, established themselves in clusters and made respectability a defining feature, was tailor-made to fit both criteria. Lending the Press's image of 'massive and unshakeable respectability'[31] founded upon its reputation for divinity and scholarship to a mass-market enterprise was to cement OUP's position as an irreproachable disseminator of learning.

Since it entailed a new editorial direction and depended on a close watch being kept on competitors, the development of this series was remarkably well documented. It has also enjoyed the protection of an old publishing firm with solid foundations and thus avoided the fate of many a publisher's archive by remaining intact. It would be unwise to take this series as wholly representative, and I have indicated wherever relevant how others may have differed. But some of its operations were highly typical, it was far more successful than most of its rivals, and it represents an important watershed in the synthesis between established, scholarly, 'list' publishing and mass-market enterprise. A close look at its development might therefore serve to highlight the typical manner in which a 'classic' was to be selected, defined and marketed in this period, and for whom.

The man most closely connected with the series was Henry Frowde. He had been forewarned of Richards's impending bankruptcy as early as November 1904, as

---

28   What seems to have happened is that Richards's illness during 1904 caused a loss of confidence among his creditors, who called in their notes at an unfortunate time and refused him the grace period necessary for both his health and his fortunes to make a full recovery. Undaunted, Richards had recommenced trading under his wife's name by August that same year. 'Mr Grant Richards' Affairs', *Publishers' Circular*, 22 April 1905, p. 434.

29   Peter Sutcliffe, *The Oxford University Press: An Informal History* (Oxford, 1978), p. 80.

30   Sutcliffe, p. 128.

31   Sutcliffe, p. 110.

Richards owed royalties on the World's Classics reprint of OUP's edition of Chaucer. Frowde had evidently already expressed an interest in the series, since he told Cannan that the receiver had promised to furnish him with 'the first information regarding the sale of the World's Classics and other works'.[32] By August of the following year, after Richards's bankruptcy had been made public, Frowde was writing to Henry Moring, the main purchaser of the estate, for particulars of the three series in which he was interested, and showing signs of impatience to get his hands on the largest of them. To his formal, typewritten instructions to Moring to send him details of the works is added in a hurried, handwritten postscript: 'Please let me have your reply as quickly as you can, but if the World's Classics figures are ready send them on to me at once so that I may let you know whether I can increase my offer'.[33] Reluctant to let what he saw as an excellent opportunity escape him, Frowde fired off several more anxious reminders and was to experience several more delays due to the complex web of liens, copyrights and printers' agreements in which the series was embroiled, before he finally bought it for £4,000. By October he was instructing the printers to bind the next batch of volumes (12,000 in cloth and 2,000 in leather) with the words 'Henry Frowde' on the frontispiece instead of 'Grant Richards'.

This was an interesting deviation from OUP's best-known imprints. As he later explained to Theodore Watts-Dunton, one of his authors, chief editors and preface writers:

> 'Oxford Printed at the University Press' is used chiefly for Bibles and Prayerbooks. 'Oxford at the Clarendon Press' for school books and educational works issued by order of the Delegates of the Press in the interests of learning (this form of imprint has sometimes been objected to unreasonably, as repellent to readers who are seeking amusement rather than instruction) and the imprint which we have now adopted for the World's Classics is used in many of our more popular books and is generally accepted as a pledge for the accuracy of the text.[34]

The distinctions made here are curious, and point to the extreme care that publishers gave to the ways in which their productions appealed. Here Frowde is anxious to appeal simultaneously to the potential purchaser's two main desires: for enjoyment, and for the distinction conferred by the recognition of authentic scholarship. Frowde's name was obviously thought to combine these needs in a way that the names 'Oxford' and 'Clarendon' by themselves could not. Throughout the period his name appears on OUP's list announcements in the trade papers, where Cambridge merely uses the name of its University Press.

---

[32] Letter No. 239 to Charles Cannan, 11 November 1904. Letterbooks of Henry Frowde, OUP Archives.

[33] Letter No. 52 to Mr Moring, 22 August 1905. Letterbooks of Henry Frowde, OUP Archives.

[34] Letter No. 288 to Theodore Watts-Dunton, 12 January 1906. Letterbooks of Henry Frowde, OUP Archives.

What OUP seem to be trying to cultivate here is a relationship with the reading public which is friendly, paternal, and rather more personal in its associations than the hallowed institutionalism implied by some of its other imprints. This was part of a larger trend in the popularising of 'great literature' that saw magazines like *The Reader* running competitions in which entrants had to identify quotations from a cheap classic – proof if nothing else is of the extraordinary sameness of many of these series' constituents.[35] But it was also part of a calculated move on OUP's part to appeal to a wider market, to be invited into homes which might feel the names OUP or Clarendon were not suitable for them, or more schoolroom than self-help, or too scholarly to be interesting. By the turn of the century the names and meanings of these imprints were sufficiently part of common knowledge for Gissing to have put them to his customary use in *Our Friend the Charlatan* (1901). In this novel the modern young reformer May Tomalin is trying to impress her wealthy old Aunt with her philanthropy and her education, jointly designed to disguise her own lowliness. "'I take a great interest in the condition of the poor"', May tells her Aunt, Lady Ogram:

> 'Really!' exclaimed Lady Ogram. 'What do you do?'
> 'We have a little society for extending civilization among the ignorant and the neglected. Just now we are trying to teach them how to make use of the free library, to direct their choice of books ... I know a family, shockingly poor, living, four of them, in two rooms, – who have promised me to give an hour every Sunday to "Piers the Plowman"; I have made them a present of the little Clarendon Press edition, which has excellent notes. Presently I shall set them a little examination paper, very simple, of course.'[36]

Gissing's point (inevitably) is to expose May's lower-middle-class vulgarity through the absurdity of her expectation that the lower classes could ever appreciate so lofty a gift. To give them Anglo-Saxon poetry at all is to cast pearls before swine. To give them a Clarendon Press edition is to add diamonds to the mix. Frowde was so keen to make the series a success for OUP under his name – and so convinced, perhaps, that his name was a crucial element in that success – that he took the trouble to write to the editor of the *Western Mail* to correct an error in their announcement of the series: 'I should like to point out that it is I who purchased the series, and that there is no such institution as the Oxford and Cambridge University Press'.[37] Apparently the collaborative enterprise of the 1881 Revised Version was a thing of the past. And the strategy worked. So successful was the association of Frowde's name with good, cheap, durable books that in 1925 Aldous Huxley 'credited him with the invention of India paper, which made it possible to get "a million words of reading matter into a

<hr>

[35]   *The Periodical*, December 1907, p. 199.
[36]   George Gissing, *Our Friend the Charlatan* (London, 1901), p. 154.
[37]   Letter No. 433 to the Editor of the *Western Mail*, 8 November 1905. Letterbooks of Henry Frowde, OUP Archives.

rucksack and hardly feel the difference"'.[38] True or not, the series was an unqualified success; by 1907 almost two million copies had been sold.[39]

What OUP were determined to offer, it seems, was a series that combined education with respectability, the wide horizons of world literature with the conservatism of the English middle-class family. Frowde's name, like Smith's at the bookstall or Humphrey Milford's on OUP Prayer books, inscribed the dangerous new public spaces of the modern world with the familiar and fatherly. Scholarship was a stated aim from the first: Frowde asserted in many letters that 'I only propose to add novels of the first rank',[40] that 'I should like to lift some of the new volumes a little above the bare reprint style', that 'new vigour will be infused into the series', and that 'important additions are to be made'.[41] And some of these claims, at least, were true. Figures 3.2 and 3.3 demonstrate the development of the series in its early days under Richards. Figure 3.2 shows how, building on the balanced mix of his initial list of 25, Richards adds a further 14 volumes during 1903, including novels by Eliot, Hawthorne and Dickens, poetry by Burns and Longfellow, essays by Emerson, Hume, Peacock and Buckle, and classic works by Pope, Gibbon, Dryden and Machiavelli. In 1905, the first year of Frowde's control of the series, we see Richards's last additions in the shape of novels by Theodore Watts-Dunton (a best seller and one of the series' few living authors), Charlotte Bronte, George Eliot and George Borrow, poems by Browning, and a long list of more serious works such as further volumes of Gibbon, Buckle and Chaucer, and works by Adam Smith, Carlyle, Thomas à Kempis, Tolstoy, Montaigne and Peacock. Thus far the mixture is fairly typical of the constituents of most classics series.

By 1907, Frowde had increased the list from 66 to 135 volumes (counting two-volume entries as one). The breakdown of subjects is as follows: biography – eight; drama – five (counting Shakespeare as one); essays, letters and speeches – 22; fiction – 38; history – six; poetry – 23; philosophy and political science – eight; science – two; translations – 14; travel – two; and miscellaneous – seven.[42] The series announcements in the trades around this period demonstrate Frowde's commitment to widening the pool in order to create, as his publicity put it 'the cheapest and the most charming series of classics in existence'.[43] The announcement for 1906 includes Sheridan's Plays; George Eliot's *Silas Marner*, 'The Lifted Veil' and 'Brother Jacob'; Burke's Works; Defoe's *Captain Singleton*; Dr Johnson's Lives of the Poets; Matthew Arnold's Poems; Mrs Gaskell's *Mary Barton* and *Ruth*; Holmes's *Professor at the Breakfast Table*; Scott's Lives of the Novelists; Holmes's *Poet at the Breakfast Table*; Motley's

---

[38]   Sutcliffe, *OUP*, p.188.
[39]   *The Periodical*, Vol. 39, May 1907, p. 124.
[40]   Letter No. 180 to George Meredith, 15 December 1905. Letterbooks of Henry Frowde, OUP Archives.
[41]   Letter No 197 to Watts-Dunton, 16 December 1905. Letterbooks of Henry Frowde, OUP Archives.
[42]   *The Periodical*, Vol. 39, May 1907, pp. 124–5.
[43]   *Bookman*, Vol. 30, April 1906, p. v.

THE

LIFE AND OPINIONS

OF

TRISTRAM SHANDY

GENTLEMAN

BY

LAURENCE STERNE

LONDON

GRANT RICHARDS
48 LEICESTER SQUARE
1903

Figure 3.2 Frontispiece and title page from *The Life and Opinions of Tristram Shandy, Gentleman* (The World's Classics No. 40) by Sterne, Laurence edited by Richards, Grant (1903). By permission of Oxford University Press and the John Spiers Collection of Victorian and Edwardian Fiction

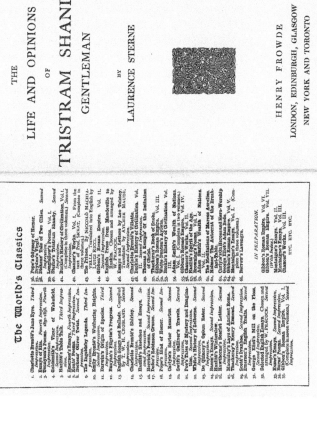

Figure 3.3 Frontispiece and title page from *The Life and Opinions of Tristram Shandy, Gentleman* (World's Classics No. 40) by Sterne, Laurence edited by Frowde, Henry (1905). By permission of Oxford University Press and the John Spiers Collection of Victorian and Edwardian Fiction

Rise of the Dutch Republic; Essays and Sketches by Leigh Hunt; Seven Plays by
Sophocles and Seven Plays by Aeschylus.[44] This policy of widening the reach of the
cheap reprints and reproducing the books in well-bound, pocket-sized versions was
immediately successful, and, of course, spawned imitators. In 1906 the *Publishers'
Circular* carried an advert for Routledge's New Universal Library, whose volumes
were sized at $6^1/_8 \times 3^3/_4$ inches, 'the size of THE WORLD'S CLASSICS, which
has proved so attractive to the public all over the world'.[45] Before 1914 Frowde had
widened the pool even further, including still less obvious (and now largely forgotten)
'classic' titles such as Douglas Jerrold's *Mrs Candle's Curtain Lectures*, Richard
Cobbold's *Margaret Catchpole* and Jane Porter's *The Scottish Chiefs.*[46]

The winning formula of a wider range of titles presented with more scholarly
authority than anyone else's was not Frowde's only concern. He assured correspondents
that 'as in any other series printed at OUP writers can rely on the accuracy of the
text – which differentiates the World's Classics from other cheap reissues'.[47] But
he also ensured that the series remained within acceptable (and conservative) limits
by keeping a firm hand on the editorial reins. His main concern was, in fact, less
to populate the series with masterpieces than to make certain of three rather more
prosaic details. These considerations somewhat complicate the familiar notions that
a 'great' or 'classic' book is one that has stood the test of time, and that its sudden
cheapness enabled the newly-literate working classes to break out of the yoke of
ignorance once and for all.

A primary consideration for Frowde – as for most classics publishers – was that
the chosen books were out of copyright or, if not, that they were cheap. As he told
several correspondents who suggested books for inclusion in the series, the profit
margin was very small and a great number of copies had to be sold in order for a
particular book to be successful. An author or copyright holder could expect to receive
only a halfpenny royalty on all sold at 1s or 1s 6d; 1d on all sold at 2s or 2s 6d; or a
royalty of £20 for each 10,000 sold of the whole impression.[48] This meant that for
Frowde's purposes a non-copyright work provided the best return, particularly if
he could publish it before anyone else did. So keen a copyright-watcher was he, in
fact, that in 1904 he wrote to his solicitor Rivington to enquire whether the current
42-year copyright period covered printing as well as publication, and whether he
might have a selection of Browning's poems (published in 1864) ready for sale the
minute the copyright expired. The reply informed him that he might have the poems
set up in type, but not printed before the copyright ran out at midnight on 20 August

---

[44]   *Bookman*, Vol. 31, October 1906, p. 51.
[45]   *Publishers' Circular*, 7 January 1905, p. 3.
[46]   Sutcliffe, p. 142.
[47]   Letter No 197 to Watts-Dunton, 16 December 1905. Letterbooks of Henry Frowde, OUP
       Archives.
[48]   Letter No. 178 to Watts-Dunton, 14 December 1905. Letterbooks of Henry Frowde, OUP
       Archives.

1906.[49] He also kept his eyes open for new possibilities that might have been missed by his opponents (particularly his main rival, J.M. Dent, whose Everyman series was – not coincidentally – started the same year that Frowde took over the World's Classics). Writing his thanks to copyright holder Dr Furnivall for permission to publish Ronald Gower's life of *Joan of Arc* in the World's Classics, for example, he indicates just how obscure such a book had become; even the legal copyright holder didn't seem able to provide him with a copy. 'I am searching for a copy among the second-hand bookstalls', Frowde writes, 'and as soon as I can procure one I will let you know whether, in my opinion, it is suitable for the series'.[50]

Just as important, the works had to be of the right length to enable a standardised form that looked good on the shelf and on thinner paper fitted into a pocket. Frowde sometimes included a personal but critically sidelined favorite of one of his superiors or colleagues as a favor. But in October 1905 he wrote to Milford rejecting his suggestion that the World's Classics should produce an edition of Greek plays on the grounds that: 'all the books in the World's Classics are uniform as to size of type and quality of paper and I desire to keep them so. They ought to contain from 300 to 500 pages per volume. The type which you are proposing to use for Churton Collins's single plays would not do for the World's Classics'.[51] It was not, in fact, strictly true that 'all' the World's Classics were uniform as to size. Some occupied two volumes, and some, particularly those essential classic staples inherited from Grant Richards, such as Macaulay's *Lays of Ancient Rome*, were far shorter. The *Lays* is a mere 113 pages in total.[52] But once Frowde took over, uniformity and appropriateness became more important issues. Sutcliffe suggests in his history of OUP that the additions of certain books to the World's Classics 'could scarcely be accounted for without a knowledge of Charles Cannan's private reading habits or Milford's taste for adventure stories',[53] but in fact most of those suggestions appeared in the Boys' Classics and Parson's Handbook series also purchased from Richards rather than in the World's Classics, and were there somewhat less out of place. Frowde generally had an unerring sense of which books were suitable for his vision of a classics series.

Finally, the books had to be inoffensive to the lower- and middle-class family reader. The World's Classics walked a curiously fine line between the edifying and scholarly and the generally acceptable, Frowde declining to reprint certain books in this series (Fielding was conspicuously absent in these early years, for example, though as we

49 Letters No. 493 to Mr Rivington, 10 March 1905 and No. 8, acknowledging Rivington's response, 14 March 1905. Letterbooks of Henry Frowde, OUP Archives.
50 Letter No. 388 to Dr Furnivall, 1 May 1907. Letterbooks of Henry Frowde, OUP Archives.
51 Letter No. 383 to Mr Milford, 27 October 1905. Letterbooks of Henry Frowde, OUP Archives.
52 I am indebted to Professor John Spiers for pointing this out, and for loaning me the *Lays* from among his extensive collection of Victorian and Edwardian fiction.
53 Sutcliffe, *OUP*, p. 142.

have seen he was very present in other cheap series). This is similar to the line taken by W.H. Smith's in withholding books such as Moore's *Esther Waters* from their stalls only for the sake of consistency with their library, a tactic which revealed not only that their stalls policy contained something of a muck-and-brass element compared with their circulating library, but that the ban carried an implicit class prejudice. If a book was unsuitable for the working- or middle-class family (due to its core constituency of women and children), it was, like OUP's books, nonetheless available to the scholar – male or female – who had sufficient education, standing, funds and knowledge.

More importantly, though, the World's Classics did not just refuse to reprint certain books; they also expurgated some that they had chosen to include. In some ways this is a rather surprising editorial policy which seems to sit somewhat uncomfortably with OUP's public persona. Altick notes that several cheap series capitalised on a famous author's name by including what were, in effect, merely 'haphazard selections' of a masterpiece[54] similar to the Reader's Digest Condensed Classics popularised later in the century, but this was not Frowde's policy; he was an agent for a learned Press, and as he explained to Watts-Dunton on 12 January 1906, he felt he had a certain duty to the text: 'I am endeavouring to discover the texts which were followed by Mr Grant Richards and am having the volumes very carefully read. We are finding many misprints and are having them corrected … in all future ones we propose to follow the most reliable texts, and they will be set up with our usual care at Oxford University Press, this will be conspicuously announced upon them'.[55] But in reality the laudable pursuit of scholarship was not quite so straightforward: as Sutcliffe notes, 'well into the twentieth century a double standard prevailed. Expensive complete texts could be made available for the elite, for "ripe scholars": for the masses expurgated editions would be required reading for many years to come'.[56]

Few records of specific editorial meetings survive in the Press's archive – if indeed they were ever kept – but the letter books and author files provide a clue as to how the expurgation policy may have operated. One new edition which gave Frowde problems was a collection of '24 Tales of Tolstoy', translated by Aylmer Maude. Following Maude's visit to his offices on 27 October 1905, Frowde agreed to print the tales but stipulated that he would be reading the copy with extreme care and that he intended to retain all expurgation rights. A note in the Tolstoy file made that same day reads: 'Copy received for 16. We have examined part of it, and we should have to omit from our book such passages as that marked on page 13. Such an omission would not affect the story in the least'.[57] No page 13 – and indeed, no manuscript – now exists, but it is possible to surmise from information which does survive exactly what Frowde was inclined to object to. In that same file is a typewritten list of the 24 tales,

---

54 Altick, p. 309.
55 Letter No. 288 to Watts Dunton, 12 January 1906. Letterbooks of Henry Frowde, OUP Archives.
56 Sutcliffe, *OUP*, p. 143.
57 Report on '24 Tales by Tolstoy', 27 October 1905, Ref: 010095/1364, OUP Archives.

apparently furnished by Maude, four of which ('The Bear Hunt', 'Three Old Men' [sic], 'Françoise' and 'The Surat Coffee-House') have been marked with blue crosses. Apparently having had his fears confirmed, Frowde wrote to Maude reiterating the terms of their agreement: 'If I desire to omit any passages such as that I showed you this morning I am at liberty to do so'.[58] Maude replied by return: 'I ... agree (rather reluctantly) to leave you with the ultimate decision about any passage that you feel must be omitted from my translations. But I must stipulate that no omission shall be made without my being informed thereof; and I would strongly urge upon you the undesirability of lightly tampering with such harmless, if slightly coarse, expressions as the great Russian writer characteristically puts into the mouths of some of his characters. It would sometimes be better to omit a story than to mutilate it'.[59] Frowde, however, evidently had no compunctions about mutilating the Great Russian writer, or anyone else, if it suited his purposes to do so. 'Coarse' expressions had to go. And he didn't mind omitting an entire tale which the acknowledged world expert on Tolstoy felt was of crucial importance to the collection. 'I want to know whether you will include the story 'Françoise', which I enclose herewith', Maude wrote to him on 16 November 1905. 'It was selected by Tolstoy because of its strongly moral tendency, and was modified by him to strengthen the impression it is calculated to produce on normal minds. The story deals, however, with matters more or less tabooed in English literature, and will probably be considered immoral by people who remain untouched by the author's feeling, and are capable only of judging a book by the class of subjects it treats of. Personally, I should include the story, both for the sake of completeness, and because it is one not included in any English edition of Tolstoy's works. In fact, I feel it would be mutilating the volume to leave it out'.[60]

Frowde remained unaffected by the expert's opinion. In the end he accepted only 23 of the tales, writing to Maude that 'the tale "Francoise" [sic], the copy for which I now return had better be omitted from our book, and I should be glad if you could find some other to take its place; if not we must have 23 only. To include it would mean a very much reduced sale for the book, nor should we be promoting the study of Tolstoy's works as we desire to do'.[61] For Frowde, the overriding principle was that 'classics' had to be wholesome as much as instructional. Any reader who thought their shilling was furnishing them with the best and most complete texts that world literature could impart was sorely mistaken.

There is evidence in this archive that the World's Classics was not alone in offering such watered-down fare. John Aubrey's *Brief Lives of the Poets*, edited by Andrew Clark, was considered inappropriate for the World's Classics as late as 1931,[62] and

58 Letter from Frowde to Aylmer Maude, 28 October 1905. Ref: as above.
59 Letter from Maude to Frowde, 28 October 1905. Ref: as above.
60 Letter from Maude to Frowde, 16 November 1905. Ref: as above.
61 Quoted in Sutcliffe, *OUP*, p. 144.
62 Letter from Humphrey Milford to G.F. Cumberlage, 16 December 1931. Ref: L.B.1219, OUP archives.

the Clarendon Press edition was heavily expurgated. This had irritated one Mr
P.W.F. Lodge so much that he felt obliged to write Milford in 1915: 'I am returning
the copy of Aubrey's *Lives* kindly sent on approval. I regret to find it much too
incomplete to be of use. Continually the footnotes repeat "four lines of the text are
here suppressed"; "six lines of the text are here suppressed"; "eight lines…etc.", e.g.
p. 185 Vol. II. So, that one would be working in the dark using it'.[63] This criticism
apparently had little effect. Scholars were still writing to the Press as late as the
1940s to complain that the new two-guinea edition of the *Lives* 'cannot be relied on
except for suggestive dots!'[64] It should be remembered here that Clarendon Press
editions, like the World's Classics, were aimed at schools and the self-educated, and
that the protection of these 'innocent' readers was very much a nineteenth century
trope. 'I think that it is rather scandalous in 1942', the Oxford scholar continued,
'to reprint a text at 2 guineas (a price to frighten off schoolboys and schoolgirls and
even smutalogues!) with arbitrary deletions and no note on the title page to warn
the serious and adult purchaser that his morals are being taken care of by careful
emasculation, willy-nilly'.[65]

The assumption of a class of reader with superior knowledge (the Oxford
scholar's 'serious adult' male with what Maude called a 'normal mind') who knew
the difference between art and immorality is crucial, for it is manifestly not the reader
for whom publishers produced their hundreds of thousands of 'classics'. Instead,
publishers tended by the end of the century to assume a patriarchal, teacherly role,
a role which embraced the critic, the scholar, the editor, sometimes the novelist, but
excluded absolutely the Board School reader bent on a course of self-help. For this
reader, the 'careful emasculation' of literature was a necessary procedure performed
behind closed doors.

'The Husks of Books': Cheap Classics and Cultural Distinction

Bourdieu has produced a useful model for describing the effects of a sudden increase
in the number of possessors of a class-distinctive asset such as literary knowledge. In
his model, this diminishing of the 'rarity and distinctive value' of the asset results in
a 'threatening [of] the distinction of the older possessors'. This threat causes a 'deep
ambivalence' about 'everything concerned with the democratisation of culture' and
prompts the development of a 'dual discourse on the relations between the institutions
of cultural diffusion and the public'.[66] Ambivalence and its resulting dual discourse
are in evidence not only in the division between those novelists and critics who (like

---

63   Letter from P.W.F. Lodge to Humphrey Milford, 15 November 1915. Ref: as above.
64   Letter from Exeter College, Oxford to Kenneth Sisam, 16 June 1942. Ref: as above.
65   Letter from Exeter College, Oxford to Kenneth Sisam, 16 June 1942. OUP archives.
66   Bourdieu, *Distinction*, p. 229.

Edward G. Salmon),[67] thought the provision of cheap classics a good thing and those (like Gissing) who abhorred the very idea, but also in the manner in which the praise was offered. The Secretary to the Chairman of the London School Board accepted his presentation copy of Routledge's World Library's *Aesop* with thanks, saying 'In bringing good, wholesome literature within reach of the poor it will supply a long-felt need'. Another of the dignitaries who received a copy responded loftily: 'in view of the rapid increase of education I cannot doubt that they will be appreciated by the class for whom they are intended'.[68] Here there is a combination of philanthropy and patronage, in both cases serving to distance the speakers from the classic-buyer. As Bourdieu suggests, 'All critics declare not only their judgement of the work but also their claim to the right to think about and judge it. In short, they take part in a struggle for the monopoly of legitimate discourse about the work of art and consequently in the production of value of the work of art'.[69]

In England at the close of the nineteenth century, there is clearly a 'dual discourse' occasioned by the democratisation of culture and the rise of mass production. It means that the legitimate culture designated 'classic literature' becomes accessible to the lower classes only when it has been permitted, authenticated and ultimately cheapened by the upper strata, whether these are the aristocrats and officials who endorse the books or the professionals and intellectuals who edit and publish them. In the literary field as a whole, the struggle between these older possessors of cultural distinction and the new players is won by a shift in the stakes; by, in effect, de-emphasising the literary work *as literature* so that its aesthetics, its publisher, its price and its textual verity become active as currency. Edwin Clayhanger's recognition of the social significance of his neighbour's calf-bound editions which prompts him to buy some of his own signals his desire to progress from son of a printer to budding architect, to move from the artisan into the professional class. Machine-tooled prize-books are suddenly shown up as inferior; Edwin has become in this moment in his own eyes one who knows and sees in a way that his father, though financially successful, will never know or see. Once enlightened, 'it was astounding to Edwin how blind he had been to the romance of existence in the Five Towns' (p. 161).

In fact Bennett was filled with ambivalence about the aspirant middle classes. He defended them all his life and regularly and proudly noted his rising income in his journal. But in his articles he frequently displays a sense of discomfort and even contempt about their tastes and activities which is lent humour but not quite robbed of

---

67   In 'What the Working Classes Read', *Nineteenth Century*, Vol. 20, July 1886, p. 116, Salmon writes: 'It is a matter for regret that, with the many means of disseminating among them [i.e. the working classes] the masterpieces of the English language, more energy is not exerted in bringing home to them the inherent attractions of Shakespeare, Scott, Marryat, Dickens, Lytton, Eliot'.

68   Recommendations inside front cover of Routledge's World Library edition of *Aesop's Fables* (London, 1886)

69   Bourdieu, *The Field of Cultural Production*, pp. 35–6.

its sting by his open acknowledgement that he is one of their number. In an article in the *New Age* in 1908 he explored the question of the readership for his own books:

> When my morbid curiosity is upon me, I stroll into Mudie's or the Times Book Club, or I hover round Smith's bookstall at Charing Cross.
>
> The crowd at these places is the prosperous crowd, the crowd which grumbles at income-tax and pays it ... I see at the counter people on whose foreheads it is written that they know themselves to be the salt of the earth. Their assured, curt voices, their proud carriage, their clothes, the similarity of their manner, all show that they belong to a caste and that the caste has been successful in the struggle for life. It is called the middle class, but it ought to be called the upper class for nearly everything is below it ... When they have nothing to do, they say, in effect, 'Let's go out and spend something.' And they go out. They spend their lives in spending. They deliberately gaze into shop windows in order to discover an outlet for their money. You can catch them at it any day.[70]

The reduction of middle-class life to simple currency implied by the repetition of the word 'spend' highlights Bennett's anxiety about its wasted potential. Time and money become interchangeable. Having been 'successful in the struggle for life' the middle classes then exchange that life for commodities, as though life itself can only be realised through its power to purchase. But Bennett also recognises the middle class's drive to improve as well as to prove itself through spending on the acquisition of 'culture', and on that point he is equally damning:

> Do you know anybody who really buys new books? Have you ever heard tell of such a being? Of course, there are Franklinish and self-improving young men (and conceivably women) who buy cheap editions of works which the world will not willingly let die: the Temple Classics, Everyman's Library, the World's Classics, the Universal Library. Such volumes are to be found in many refined and strenuous homes, oftener unopened than opened – but still there! But does this estimable practice aid the living author to send his children to school in decent clothes?[71]

For Bennett, the drive to purchase 'culture' is not only marked by an unpatriotic Americanness, it is also a transparent and pointless practice. 'Estimable' and 'refined' are both rendered ironic here by the word 'strenuous', a recognition that the bourgeois (like Gissing's Nancy Lord trying to impress her suitor in the library) simply tries too hard. But Bennett also devalues the 'classics' themselves: for him a work which has endured has done so for purely commercial reasons. The classic-reader is a dupe and modern literature (not to mention the living writer) is the poorer for it. Nor, in Bennett's view, is there any advantage in the collection of 'classics'. They are 'oftener

---

[70]   Arnold Bennett, *Books and Persons: Being Comments on a Past Epoch 1908–1911* (London, 1917), pp. 88–90.

[71]   Bennett, *Books and Persons*, p. 33.

unopened than opened'. They unsex women (whom Bennett – typically – can only just conceive of as purchasers of self-help). And they can't, by their very nature, really 'help' at all. Edwin's promise to himself to embark on a strict course of study is consistently broken. He occasionally 'saw the material of happiness ahead, in the faithful execution of his resolves for self-perfecting' (p. 211), but more often than not 'his systems of reading never worked for more than a month at a time' (p. 144). Ambivalence lies at the heart of *Clayhanger*. For Bennett, the modern middle-class subject is constructed through contradiction. Edwin is 'happy in the stress of one immense and complex resolve' (p. 144), to improve himself, and to fail.

Even when the fictional lower-middle-class reader does stick to a plan and actually read the classics, his/her reading is devalued by those in the strata above who, like the Schlegel sisters, are liable to dismiss the 'strenuous' attempts of a Leonard Bast to relate to them. 'Should he and those like him be given free libraries?' Helen Schlegel tells her friends she was asked during a debate. Her answer is a resounding: 'No! He doesn't want more books to read, but to read books rightly' (p. 139). This manner of 'reading rightly' is never, of course, revealed, except that it is not 'reciting the names of books feverishly' (p. 146). To the Schlegels, Leonard Bast's 'brain is filled with the husks of books, culture' and it is 'horrible; we want him to wash out his brain and go to the real thing' (p. 150). But, like 'reading rightly', the 'real thing' remains a secret. And, not being in on it, readers like Bast will always fail.

The failure is built into the possibility, not just in the novels of Bennett, Gissing and Forster, but in the nature of the field which has produced the culture of self-help. The classics series is one of those phenomena which Bourdieu describes as 'entirely organised to give the impression of bringing legitimate culture within the reach of all, by combining two normally exclusive characteristics, immediate accessibility and the outward signs of cultural legitimacy'.[72] In this instance the tension between the 'two normally exclusive characteristics' is resolved by a renewed emphasis on 'outward signs' which paradoxically, like Leonard Bast's 'husks of books', will always be mere illusion. To those who 'know', the classic series is already stripped of any real cultural capital. It designates its possessor as 'strenuous', as Bourdieu's petite-bourgeois who, 'always liable to know too much or too little … is condemned endlessly to amass disparate, often devalued information which is to legitimate knowledge as his stamp collection is to an art collection, a miniature culture'.[73] The classics series outwardly disseminates legitimate culture by being finite, cheap and durable, possessing the pretence of aesthetics as well as a legitimised text. But it simultaneously devalues what it gives by those same processes. The much-valued Arnoldian aesthetic is mass-produced; mid-century hopes for enlightenment through learning and new technologies have spawned only beauty's poor, plain and far-too-numerous cousins. The book is part of a finite number which implies a limit to legitimate culture, something prosaic which, like the set of encyclopaedias which contain the world, can be bought and owned.

---

[72] Bourdieu, *Distinction*, p. 323.
[73] Bourdieu, *Distinction*, pp. 328–9.

However carefully authenticated as a text, it is liable to expurgation and moral and artistic narrowness. It is stamped with the words 'classic' and, in the case of my own example, 'Henry Frowde' and/or 'Oxford University Press', all of which mark it as authentic but also mark its purchaser as one who did not 'naturally' already 'know'.

In *Outline of a Theory of Practice* Bourdieu describes the mechanisms of objectification through which the cultural product might be legitimised – and the legitimisers lifted above the rising tide. Through a socially recognised standard of professional or academic qualifications, individuals are able to operate without the need for further legitimisation, the title or status or qualification alone being sufficient:

> Once this state of affairs is established, relations of power and domination no longer exist directly between individuals; they are set up in pure objectivity between institutions, i.e. between socially guaranteed qualifications and socially defined positions, and through them, between the social mechanisms which produce and guarantee both the social value of the qualifications and the positions and also the distribution of these social attributes, among biological individuals.[74]

The notion of a power relation which has become institutionalised, almost invisible, is crucial if a phenomenon such as the classics series is to succeed commercially without posing a threat to the dominance of its older cultural possessors. There are several mechanisms through which this is achieved in the case of my own example, though they are to a great extent also true of other publishers of classics series.

First, the association with Oxford University Press provides academic respectability and an assurance of the authenticity of the text, a fact which gives World's Classics an edge over most of its competitors who, as Feltes has noted, tend to be 'enterprising' publishers aspiring to a 'list' rather than the other way around. Second, as we have seen, the name of Henry Frowde furnishes the promise of friendly, paternal guidance through morality as well as accessibility, making the World's Classics books that can safely, as well as usefully, be brought into the home. Frowde even colour-coded his books (green for history, maroon for fiction, blue for essays and poetry) and endorsed the 'fiction is a lower class of literature' view by offering for sale at 1s 6d or 2s 6d boxed presentation volumes, bound in buckram, gilt-edged and with a silk marker, of any World's Classic *except* novels. Third, the adoption by OUP of the scholarly introduction written by a well-known and respected scholar, critic or writer promises a 'way in' to the text which will fill in the gaps in the self-taught reader's knowledge and also reward him or her by endorsing his/her choice. The more informative and scholarly the introduction and the more culturally legitimate the writer of it, the more rewarded and vindicated the reader feels. And, like the critic, the preface writer is legitimised through his or her own act of legitimisation.

---

[74]   Bourdieu, *Outline of a Theory of Practice*, pp. 187–8.

OUP by no means invented the introduction: these appear in many a classics series prior to 1905. Cassell's National Library, Routledge's World and Railway Libraries, Chandos Classics, the Minerva Library of Famous Books and the Temple Classics, to name but a few, predate the World's Classics and have an introduction or preface of some kind. These differ widely in length, form and content, and in some cases are merely prefatory notes with author dates. But by the time Frowde took over the World's Classics (which under Richards had contained at best only the author's dates), there was a strong move towards the famous or otherwise legitimate name introduction on the part of most classics publishers. The King's Classics series issued Eliot's *Silas Marner* in 1907 with an introduction by Richard Garnett, keeper of Printed Books at the British Museum. Cassell's well-known editor Henry Morley, Professor of English Language and Literature variously at King's, Queens and University Colleges, London, introduced its National Library.[75] Heinemann's Favourite Classics used Edmund Gosse on a number of occasions. Frowde was quick to adopt the practice – partly, no doubt, because his main rival was Dent's Everyman which, as we have seen in the example of its *Aesop's Fables*, featured thorough and scholarly introductions. He expended considerable energy in hunting down big names for his introductions, bagging (among others) G.K. Chesterton, Edmund Gosse, A.T. Quiller-Couch and Swinburne, and offering Lord Rosebury 25 guineas for the introduction to a work of his choice instead of the usual 10.[76] This was a considerable sum: even in the 1920s Virginia Woolf was only able to command 13 guineas.[77]

One of Frowde's favourite and most prolific early introduction writers, though, was Theodore Watts-Dunton, a writer and critic of some standing (though he was in his seventies by 1905 and his career was probably past its best).[78] He was one of the few living authors represented in the World's Classics; Grant Richards had chosen to include his 1898 bestseller *Aylwin* and – possibly as a means of keeping its author onside – Frowde kept the book. Watts-Dunton became a key player on the World's Classics editorial team, suggesting both books for the series and big names to introduce them. He had carved a name for himself in the 1870s and 1880s by vying with Hall Caine for the right to be considered D.G. Rossetti's closest confidante during the poet's final years, and to produce the definitive biography. His name appears frequently not only in Hall Caine's correspondence with Rossetti, but in the correspondence of numerous other players in the drama, and the tone of these letters gives an indication of the importance to an aspiring writer of the association with an established name.

---

[75] *Dictionary of National Biography*, Vol. XIII, pp. 975–6.

[76] Letter No. 185 to Mrs Drew, 31 October 1905. Letterbooks of Henry Frowde, OUP Archives.

[77] This was for an introduction to Sterne's *Sentimental Journey*. Subsequently Leonard Woolf refused all the Press's requests to reissue his wife's works in the World's Classics. Attempts were made – and refusals received – from the 1930s to at least the 1950s. Ref: World's Classics Suggestions File, OUP Archives.

[78] Sutcliffe, *OUP*, p. 143.

On 24 July 1882, Watts (he later, in a splendid piece of writerly self-mythologising, added the Dunton by deed poll) wrote to Rossetti's brother William that 'a lot of fellows will scribble about [Rossetti] and vulgarise his name'.[79] Another acquaintance of the famous family, William Bell Scott, wrote to a friend on 13 June:

> Watts was here yesterday after dinner in a state of simmer – I might say boiling over, about Sharp and Caine having prepared themselves as rival acrobats to write books about DGR! He says Gabriel on his death bed begged him to let no-one else write 'a Life' – to write it himself – if it was necessary. He had prevailed on Caine to be quiet, but suddenly the other hanger-on whom as Watts says 'I have brought a little into notice, and who was seeing me daily and hourly' has, without mentioning his intention, got Macmillan to commission him a book of 300 pages as the intimate friend of the deceased! and then Caine says, 'Well! if *he* does it I shall too!' ... Watts is cut out of the game and in despair. 'Rossetti has fallen among the Philistines' is his commentary, 'and I can't help him!'

The ferocity of the competition to achieve professional standing as a writer is palpable here, and it indicates how volatile the market for literature had become by the 1880s. It is also marked by the desire, expressed by Watts through the dubbing of his rivals as Philistines, to achieve this standing at the highest possible cultural level. Watts at least was somewhat successful: *Aylwin* was reviewed ecstatically by the *Bookman* in November 1898,[80] his doings (even his health) were commented on regularly in all the trade papers, and when he died on 6 June 1914, aged 81, the *Publishers' Circular* printed a respectful obituary.[81] There is none of the critical ambivalence associated with his name such as often appeared in connection with his younger and far more commercially successful rival Hall Caine. Watts managed to avoid the somewhat contradictory charges of Philistinism, immorality and pandering to a mass market which dogged Caine throughout his career. He hung onto his reputation as a distinguished scholar and critic, producing poetry and essays as well as novels and contributing to such upstanding journals as the *Athenaeum*. His association with the World's Classics was advantageous to Frowde and Watts himself made money out of it: Frowde paid ten guineas for an introduction (a far better remuneration than the £20 per 10,000 copies which he paid for *Aylwin*) and Watts wrote dozens of them. He was able to offer the added inducement of an acquaintance with the ageing Swinburne, to whom he introduced Frowde in January 1906. Frowde persuaded Swinburne to write a preface to the World's Classics Shakespeare series on the strength of this meeting.

---

79   All extracts from letters concerning Rossetti taken from William E. Fredeman, '"Fundamental Brainwork": the Correspondence Between Dante Gabriel Rossetti and Thomas Hall Caine', *Journal of the Australasian Universities of Language and Literature Association: A Journal of Literary Criticism, Philology and Linguistics*, Queensland, Australia, Vol. 52 (1979), pp. 211–12.

80   *Bookman*, November 1898, pp. 37–9.

81   *Publishers' Circular*, 7 November 1914, p. 465.

The scholarly introduction was, in fact, perceived by the editors of the classics series to be at least as valuable as the work itself, and in some cases more so. It legitimised the text in a degree directly proportionate to the social standing of its author (where a Gosse, a Watts or even a Swinburne was worth only 10 guineas per introduction, a Lord was worth 25). Just as important, it enabled an objectification of the cheap classic which served to separate the class for whom it was produced from the class which produced, encouraged and endorsed it. As Bourdieu has explained in his fullest delineation of his model of the cultural field, endorsements operate in two directions at once, legitimising not only the work, but also the legitimiser: 'A consecrated writer is the one who has the power to consecrate and to win assent when he or she consecrates an author or a work – with a preface, a favourable review, a prize, etc.'.[82]

The cheap classic series is a product of an explosion in the numbers of literate people with money to spend on books, of a new emphasis on the middle-class home as a display case and reading as a key to social advancement. From the point of view of the consumer, to buy a cheap classic series and display it in its own bookcase[83] was to announce that one knew enough to value 'culture' sufficiently to want to own and display it rather than borrow it from a Free Library. It showed an investment in self-help not only for oneself, but also for one's family. There were degrees of investment possible, from the Pocket Edition on Oxford India Paper to the $6^{1/8} \times 3^{3/4}$-inch version, ranging in price from 1s in cloth to 1s 6d in leather and available in boxes (bar novels, of course) for giving as gifts. The cheap classic declared its purchaser to be a person serious about 'literature'.

It was, however, incapable of elevating its purchaser to the level which self-help and the assimilation of legitimate culture were meant to facilitate, for it inevitably declared its purchaser to be serious above all about aspiration and display. To the consumer, the cheap classic might be a thing of beauty, an item of furniture which, aping the sober uniform rows of leather-bound gilded volumes in the library of the eighteenth-century gentleman, turned the middle-class parlour into a reading room in spirit if not in practice. But to the producer and the true intellectual it was a facsimile, designed to take in the 'strenuous' and culturally anxious class of reader created by the democratisation of literature and eternally separated from true knowledge, not by a lack of ability, but by a subtle shifting of the goalposts. Even pulled from a pocket on the bus or the train, it marked its reader as ostentatiously serious-minded. Bennett was not alone in his contempt for the cheap classic and what it represented. Henry Frowde himself, despite his commitment to the quality and breadth of the World's Classics, wrote privately to Charles Cannan, the Secretary to the Delegates:

---

[82] Bourdieu, *The Field of Cultural Production*, p. 42.
[83] Advertised by OUP alongside their list announcements for the series at prices ranging from 5s for oak to 33s 6d for mahogany.

> A set of the volumes of the World's Classics which are at present in print go to you to-night, and I am sending sets to two or three of the Delegates who have expressed an interest in the little books. I desire to send a set to each Delegate, but understand that some of them may be unwilling to give house room to cheap reprints of this character. I will therefore defer the dispatch of the remaining parcels till next Thursday in case you should have to send me the names of any who will not accept them.[84]

Frowde's tone here is almost one of embarrassment, the World's Classics dismissed as inferior 'characters', poor relations who might stamp the mighty scholars who made up the Board of Delegates (who presumably preferred expensive unexpurgated editions) with the taint of 'the abyss'. Morality, cheapness and abundance are here, among the elite, unmistakable markers of inferiority whatever the contents of the book.

Even the scholarly preface came under attack, despite being so lauded in advertisements and so crucial to the maintenance of the dual discourse which enabled financial gain to exist alongside cultural hegemony. At the very start of the period – in the same year, in fact, that the New Revised Version appeared – an anonymous contributor to the *Contemporary Review* issued a warning about the results of the spread of learning which is aimed directly at the cult of self-help. It prefigures both Bennett's dismay at the pervasive influence of the 'American' model of middle-classness (so often seen throughout the period as the epitome of all that was wrong with modernity) and Forster's 'right way of reading':

> There are not wanting signs in the air that, while the taste for literature of some sort is daily increasing, the taste for serious study of any kind is diminishing among the great mass of the English people. We seem to have caught the contagion of American rapid living and rapid reading, so that, if we go on devouring new books as omnivorously as we have lately been doing, a true student will soon be as rare as a dodo, and a true *litterateur* be as old-fashioned a spectacle as a true scholar is now. A very unmistakable indication of the state of matters is to be found in the super-abundance of cheap manuals, with boiled-down biography and ready-made criticism on such abstruse subjects as Byron's Poems, and easy, off-hand estimates of such obscure individuals as Hume and Gibbon, not to speak of Dr. Johnson and Oliver Goldsmith ... the public now seems too idle to read perfectly legible books for itself, and to form common-sense opinions concerning them, without the interposition of some *petit maitre* ... People read so much now and reflect so little.[85]

'Serious study', the 'true student', the 'true *litterateur*' and 'reflection' are all persistently invoked here as ideals, but nowhere explained. To the *Contemporary Review*'s largely middle-class audience there was no doubt a certain comfort in this. He or she is addressed as among the 'already knowing', as outside the mass of

---

84   Letter No. 87, to Charles Cannan, 29 November 1905. Letterbooks of Henry Frowde, OUP Archives.

85   'Some Recent Books', *Contemporary Review*, Vol. 39, February 1881, pp. 312–13.

'people' who, cramming themselves greedily with Byron, Hume, Gibbon, Johnson and Goldsmith (all, perhaps not coincidentally, constituents of the well-known Chandos Classics series at the time) form the subject of the article. But to the Board School-educated crammer, desperately trying to make up for centuries of lost time, this is an early indication that spend as s/he might on the best cheap editions of the 'classics' available, read as many as s/he could of those recommended by the highest authority possible, s/he will never – can never – be a 'true *litterateur*', for like the Saint of an earlier time, the 'real' reader is born and not self-made.

Chapter 4

'The Little Woman' and 'The Boomster': Marie Corelli, Hall Caine and the Literary Field of the 1890s

The Power to Consecrate: The Critic as Novelist

The 'true scholar/litterateur' does not just consume the highest-level cultural products. S/he also writes prefaces, helps to determine the selection and establishment of the canon and legitimises his or her own choices in articles which appear in the quality quarterly or monthly magazines such as *Athenaeum*, the *Fortnightly Review*, *Contemporary Review* and *Nineteenth Century*. And s/he is frequently also an author of fiction in his or her own right. Edmund Gosse, Theodore Watts-Dunton, Walter Besant, Arnold Bennett and many others were novelists as well as critics, journalists and/or preface writers, and their work appeared as serials in these periodicals alongside 'serious' criticism as well as in book form.

That this list of examples is all male is not accidental. Women novelists who wrote criticism were predictably rarer than their male counterparts, though there were notable exceptions including Constance Garnett, George Eliot and Mrs Humphry Ward, and it is difficult to be certain in some cases whether an author was male or female. Most critical articles were unsigned long after signature became common practice for other periodical entries such as fiction. As Laurel Brake has shown, the records of these periodicals indicate that anonymity had a number of benefits. Among them were 'log-rolling' or 'booming' (the inflation of the merits of a friend's work), the employment of women and newcomers and the production of a periodical with unity of tone, which the conflicting views of 'star-turns' might undermine.[1]

Nonetheless, signature was becoming increasingly acceptable in the 'quality' journals throughout the late Victorian period and the publication of a collected edition of a critic's articles served both to double profits for author and publisher and to ensure future markets for the author's 'quality' offerings. For these writers, clearly, carving a niche in the right kind of journals could enable a first novel to be taken far more seriously than that of an unknown newcomer, however talented. This too was a practice well recognised by publishers. As Brake further suggests: 'by attracting new

---

[1] Laurel Brake, *Print in Transition 1850–1910: Studies in Media and Book History* (Basingstoke, 2001), pp. 15–16.

and established authors to their highly paying and prestigious journals, the publishers aimed to secure authors for their firms' lists'.[2]

This was of obvious importance for the publisher. But it was of even greater importance for the author. One could not, of course, review one's own work, even anonymously, without serious consequences: self-publicity was a cardinal sin amongst the field's dominators and in so closed a shop it would have been difficult to hide. But a network of the right friends, a good literary pedigree and the right strategies for keeping out and distinguishing oneself from newcomers could help an author to occupy a position of dominance through the consecration implied by the term 'serious author' or 'artist'. This position, like all positions in a cultural field, is completely dependent upon the interactions of agents in the field as a whole. In this case, though, a large part of its power comes from disguising these relationships in favour of a belief in the autonomy of the artist, his or her 'purity' and difference from ordinary mortals and indifference to the market – a belief, even, that s/he is 'touched by God'. Clearly, though, the rarity of women's names amongst critical reviews etc. was a crucial factor in ensuring that this sub-field of cultural production was also male dominated. In the late nineteenth century, to be a 'pure', 'autonomous', 'touched-by-God' artist, one pretty much had to be male as well as educated, published in the right places and supported by the right people. The strategies adopted by male and female novelists with artistic ambitions were therefore, of necessity, very different.

In the previous chapters I suggested that a book's format, appearance, point of sale, availability and intended audience could play almost as great a part in determining its status in the field as what it contained. But however it is comprised, this status is not fixed but something dynamic and volatile and sometimes subject to extraordinary critical about-faces. This can be illustrated with a single well-known example. Zola's brand of realism, 'naturalism', was considered immoral and offensive in the 1880s, so much so that in 1888 it led to the banning of his works and the imprisonment of his English translator-publisher Henry Vizetelly after a hounding by the National Vigilance Association. Both Zola and Vizetelly were defended by certain writers – among them George Moore – who saw the expurgation or banning of his work as an outrage, a shackling of 'art' to the lumbering waggon of middle-class moral values. The debate struck a chord with many writers; as Keating notes, 'even the critics and novelists who did not particularly admire his work were still able to praise its iconoclastic, liberating effect'.[3] By the time Zola was exiled to England in 1898 in the midst of a romantic revival, however, he was already old hat.

Peter Keating suggests that Zola's final acceptance was due to the growing realisation that French naturalism was never going to infect England, but this is to down play somewhat the nuances of the changing terrain on which the debate continued. The strand of the relationship between art and the market which figured

---

2   Brake, p. 14.
3   Peter Keating, *The Haunted Study: A Social History of the English Novel 1875–1914* (London, 1989), pp. 250–51.

in the 1890s as an opposition between immorality/realism and decency/romance was usually couched in terms of the protection of the 'Young Person' – for which we may read women of all ages as well as children and adolescent girls. In the 1890s Thomas Hardy, Walter Besant and Eliza Lynn Linton, amongst others, entered into this debate in the *New Review* under the title 'Candour in Fiction'. Superficially, what was at stake here was the old issue of censorship affecting the progress of art. If the realism of a Hardy or a Zola led to the banning of his works in order to protect the 'Young Person', then only romantic revivalists or toned-down realism could find an audience and the general tendency was regressive. It was also, according to Linton, feminising, for a 'strong-headed and masculine nation [was] cherishing a feeble, futile, milk-and-water literature'.[4] But, as N.N. Feltes has suggested, underlying Hardy's solution to the problem – that new books should be cheap enough for fathers to buy them for the family rather than having to subscribe to a circulating library that might distribute books of which he disapproved – was a radical re-working of the whole publishing structure in favour of the controlled inclusion of women as both producers and consumers of 'quality' fiction. What the debate in fact represented was a crisis in novel production, becoming a question of 'what publishing practices best accommodate or contain realistic or romantic ideology ... what synthetic aesthetic ideology might best serve the commodity-text of the new patriarchal-capitalist mode of production'.[5]

Feltes's Marxist approach here privileges the publisher as an example of the machinations of capitalism, to the detriment, perhaps, of a more resistive model, though the imminent change in publishing structures was not a simple reflection of changing consumer tastes either. Consumer desires cannot be ruled out. As my first two chapters attempted to show, the consumer's needs and desires were extremely important to the producers and distributors of books in this period and also quite thoroughly accommodated (even if, as I showed in Chapter 3, that accommodation meant a simultaneous downgrading of the symbolic value of those acquisitions). But neither is this imminent change of crucial importance only to the consumer on whom I concentrated in those chapters, or to the publisher on whom both Feltes and Brake choose to concentrate and to whom I devoted my last chapter. Any change in a cultural field is, after all, a result of the struggles in which all its agents are perennially engaged, and this includes the 'apparent' producers – the authors – whom I have thus far largely ignored. In fact, the enormous shifts in production and distribution practices which I have outlined and which became particularly apparent in the 1890s had a profound effect on authors, for these shifts informed – and were informed by – not only how authors and their work were marketed, but also what they wrote. Implicit in Feltes's example of the 'Candour in Fiction' debate is the struggle for dominance in the field in

---

4   Eliza Lynn Linton, 'Candour in English Fiction', *New Review*, Vol. 2 (1890), p. 14.
5   N.N. Feltes, *Literary Capital and the Late Victorian Novel* (Madison, WN, 1993), p. 104.

which all cultural producers, including or perhaps especially authors, are perpetually engaged. It is, on one level, merely Hardy, Linton and Besant conducting a skirmish, not only on the battleground of literary form, but also on that of gender.

In these final chapters I will attempt to reconstruct some aspects of the struggles of some unexpectedly popular writers in a field of purists inclined to dismiss their work. Many of those purists have themselves at one time or another been written out of literary history in favour of a proto-modernist or modernist hagiology, and some have only recently been re-evaluated by critics (further proof of the field's eternal dynamism, and the slipperiness of generic definitions). But the relationships between literary 'artists' and the popular authors with whom they rubbed shoulders from 1880 to the First World War are important in any attempt to map out the ideological landscape from which modernism – by which I mean a new and purer purism, however we define it temporally or stylistically – emerged. Further, it is in the realm of the 'popular', particularly where these are publishing phenomena, that we find most clearly articulated those nuances of gender and class which tend to be obscured or simplified by what Bourdieu calls the 'charismatic ideology' which renders less visible the discourses around high art. As he explains:

> The 'charismatic' ideology which is the ultimate basis of belief in the value of a work of art and which is therefore the basis of functioning of the field of production and circulation of cultural commodities, is undoubtedly the main obstacle to a rigorous science of the production of the value of cultural goods. It is this ideology which directs attention to the apparent producer, the painter, writer or composer, in short, the 'author', suppressing the question of what authorizes the author, what creates the authority with which authors authorize.[6]

I ask a number of specific questions in these chapters in an attempt to find out 'what authorizes the author' and 'what creates the authority with which authors authorize'. What did it mean, for example, when a book was contentious enough to be banned by a public library or a bookstall and thought of as 'art' by its author, but also denigrated by the discerning critic due to its popularity, its marketing, or its author's gender (with all the slipperiness of definition which that term implies)? Can we find evidence in the texts themselves for the volatility of this position? How is it informed by the conditions of its production? What position did its author occupy – and *think* s/he occupied – with respect to literary form, gender, race, morality and class, and what can that tell us about the field at the time? Rather than think about the shifts in the romance/realism debate in terms of a 'synthetic aesthetic ideology' as Feltes does, I want to suggest that its attempted synthesis created only a new kind of antithesis. Since this is a characteristic strategy of the dominant cultural possessors when threatened by new assailants, this should not come as a surprise. But, properly unpacked, it should

---

6   Pierre Bourdieu, *The Field of Cultural Production: Essays on Art and Literature*, ed. Randal Johnson (Cambridge, 1995), p. 76.

tell us something about those elements of the relationship between art and the market that cannot be explained simply in terms of either aesthetics or economics.

Hall Caine and the 'Realist' Romance

There is a striking image near the end of Sir (Thomas Henry) Hall Caine's first moderately successful book, *Recollections of Dante Gabriel Rossetti* (1882). It is of the painter-poet's last moments attended by a small group consisting of his family and close friends. After several days of anxiety this group had begun to feel sanguine enough about their patient to leave his side, but after a shriek from the nurse, Caine writes: 'we hurried into Rossetti's room and found him in convulsions. Mr Watts raised him on one side, whilst I raised him on the other ... there were a few moments of suspense, and then we saw him die in our arms'.[7]

This image is important for a number of reasons. First, it is probably invented. Caine's most recent biographer Vivien Allen has checked the account against a number of others, including the diaries of Rossetti's brother William. The latter gives a somewhat different version which, while agreeing that Watts was there supporting Rossetti from the right, makes no mention of Caine cradling the dying man but notes merely that he was 'in and out' of the room.[8] Second, Caine's self-construction as one of Rossetti's most loyal and intimate friends was vital in enabling his entry into the literary field and he wasted no time in exploiting it. Third, the placing of himself on one side of Rossetti with the much-older Theodore Watts on the other, equal partners at the moment of loss, serves to equate him with the (then) well-respected poet/critic, marking out the position in the field that he desired to occupy.

As it was the *Recollections* which helped to establish him as a serious writer, Caine's pre-emptive self-image was not misplaced. His articles and reviews had appeared in various papers and journals (though not in the 'qualities') for several years spent as a jobbing journalist, most consistently for the *Liverpool Mercury*. But he had produced only one critical work in book form before the biography, *Sonnets of Three Centuries: An Anthology*, published in 1882 during Rossetti's last illness. It finally sold out its first print run of 1,000 copies after a kind review or two (notably one in the *Athenaeum* which could well have been written by Watts since he wrote for it regularly and often 'boomed' the work of his friends). But it was never reprinted. *Recollections* was the first biography of Rossetti, appearing in October 1882, a mere six months after the poet's death. It sold quite well, elicited some high-level praise (from Edmund Gosse for example) and was re-edited and reprinted in time for the centenary in 1928, almost at the end of Caine's life and long after he had become one of the best-known and highest-paid authors of his day.

---

7   Hall Caine, *Recollections of Dante Gabriel Rossetti* (London, 1882), p. 295.
8   Vivien Allen, *Hall Caine: Portrait of a Victorian Romancer* (Sheffield, 1997), p. 146.

There is something fitting about the bracketing of Caine's spectacular career with the two editions of the book that was of such importance to it. All concerned – including Caine – acknowledged that Rossetti had wanted Watts to write it, but this didn't stop Caine from striking while the iron was hot or Watts from prevaricating until 1895. There was – superficially at least – no apparent problem with this. But the careful respect that Watts and Caine extended to each other in print – and also, it should be noted, through a close friendship that lasted until Watts's death in 1914 – had a less respectful side which is of central importance to their professional positions. They almost fell out over Caine's *Life of Coleridge* in 1887 because Caine had ignored Watts's expertise on the neo-Romantics, dismissing him in print. Watts forgave him, but the episode is indicative of a sense of professional rivalry between the two men.[9] This rivalry was already keen at the time of the Rossetti biography. As I noted in the previous chapter, Watts wrote to William on 24 July 1882, three months after Rossetti's death, that 'a lot of fellows will scribble about [Rossetti] and vulgarize his name'. It will be remembered, too, that the letters of other friends of the family at the same period describe a Watts who was 'cut out of the game and in despair', in fact 'boiling over' at being pre-empted by Caine in the matter of the biography, and who complained that his revered friend had 'fallen among the Philistines and I can't help him'.[10] The attitude of these correspondents, including William, towards Rossetti's 'hangers-on' is clear: this is a game being played for the highest stakes – establishment in a dominant position in the literary field.

Other letters, this time between Caine and William Sharp, who had known Rossetti longer, confirm their positions as rivals in this game. As Fredeman describes it Caine had sent Sharp a 'bitter and piqued diatribe'[11] following the announcement of Sharp's own book on the poet and received an equally piqued one in reply, which categorically denied that Sharp was attempting a coup since he had assumed his book would come out a couple of months after Caine's and was of a different stamp altogether. 'Whatever I may be in a literary sense', Sharp wrote huffily, 'I hope at least I am a gentleman … I had come to like you, and to hope that our friendship would grow and fructify. But if you consider my conduct only in the light of what you designate as "journalistic sharp practice", there must be an end to our friendship'.[12] Further letters between the two Rossetti satellites testify to the fact that their friendship endured. But one of them, written by Sharp after Caine's book had come out, indicates that the rivalry remained: 'unlike yours, my book is on his work, not on the man and his opinions: and in such a case the public want "Rossetti", not Rossetti's opinion of "yours truly"'.[13]

---

[9]   Allen, p. 185.

[10]   William E. Fredeman, 'Fundamental Brainwork: the Correspondence Between Dante Gabriel Rossetti and Thomas Hall Caine', *Journal of the Australasian Universities Language and Literature Association*, Queensland, Australia, Vol. 52 (1979), p. 212.

[11]   Fredeman, p. 212.

[12]   Fredeman, p. 214.

[13]   Fredeman, p. 214.

This letter sets out an interesting opposition, indicating that there was an acknowledged divide in the 1880s between the gentleman critic who produced objective, disinterested works, and the self-aggrandising writer who used famous connections to boom his own work. This was not the last time Caine was to be scornfully relegated to the latter category. In spite of all he could do even his moderately successful critical writing could not save him from the charge of self-interest. Designated less than pure in Bourdieu's sense of the term in that it smacked of the market, obvious self-interest must of course always elbow its perpetrator into an inferior position in the literary field. This was precisely what Caine was trying to do to Sharp when he accused him of 'journalistic sharp practice'. What came to be called the New Journalism – pithy, succinct, market-driven, made for rapid reading and achieving its apotheosis in the traveller's newspaper – was already by this time coming to stand for all that was crass and tasteless about the rapidly expanding author's profession. Gissing was only the most famous of those who wrote disgustedly on this topic: while *New Grub Street*'s Jasper Milvain enduringly sums up the type he has antecedents and siblings in many places.

The Rossetti family's reaction to the biography is telling, for in this instance they were acting as the ultimate 'legitimisers' of Caine's book. Without their endorsement it would never have been written, and if they disapproved it would damage Caine's reputation amongst all the friends and contacts he had worked so hard to make. In the event, while William was pleased to discover that Caine had handled the biography with a certain amount of discretion, William's wife Lucy was furious over his treatment of the Madox Browns's son Oliver, her brother, and never completely forgave him. This volatile position, the difficulty not just of making but also of keeping influential friends, marks Caine's personal struggle between a desire for critical acceptance and an equal desire (or need, since he was supporting his entire family) for money. It was to dog him throughout his career and embroil him in debates that have crucial referents in contemporary gender and class ideologies.

Quite apart from its reception, the text of *Recollections* indicates the terms on which at least part of this debate was to be conducted. The book can therefore tell us a lot about Caine's position in the literary field both before and after his meteoric rise to bestsellerdom. While carefully respectful of Watts as the chosen biographer and most intimate friend, Caine declares from the outset that Watts's focus and interests are much wider than this and might mean (as in the event it so happened) that the 'official' biography would be years in the writing:

> though I know that whenever Mr. Watts sets pen to paper in pursuance of such purpose, and in fulfillment of such charge, he will afford us a recognisable portrait of the man, vivified by picturesque illustration, the like of which few other writers could compass, I also know from what Rossetti told me of his friend's immersion in all kinds and varieties of life, that years (perhaps many years) may elapse before such a biography is given to the world.[14]

---

[14] Hall Caine, *Recollections*, p. vii.

This undermining of Watts's fitness for the job as a result of his lack of due focus on its object is here presented as having come from Rossetti himself. Like the earlier parts of the preface in which Caine reports a conversation between the poet and himself concerning the value to the world of their own literary correspondence, this loaded apologia justifies Caine's biography with its inclusion of their letters. It does so in terms of a service to the world of art, something pure and disinterested that goes against Caine's own better judgement but comes in the form of an edict from the Great Man himself:

> From this moment I regarded the publication of his letters as in some sort of trust; and though I must have withheld them for some years if I had consulted my own wishes simply, I yielded to the necessity that they should be published at once, rather than run any risk of their not being published at all.[15]

This is an indication of Caine's acute sense of rivalry with the critic and poet who was already a well-respected writer in the *Athenaeum* (amongst other journals), a renowned literary scholar, and who was to become a far more serious novelist. An article about *Aylwin* having reached its twentieth edition in six years and thereby joined the ranks of 'art that endures' was written by Ernest Rhys (himself a well-known critic and preface-writer) in 1904. It declares that Watts first became known to the public with his criticism before Rossetti's death:

> The first acquaintance most of us made with the writings of Mr. Watts-Dunton – Theodore Watts as he was then – was in the famous 'Athenaeum' articles of about 1876 onwards ... we may trace the same rich and fertile stream of original criticism – creative criticism – in many of the prose writings which have since appeared over his own signature ... one might not accept their judgement, one might quarrel with the reviewer, but never on the ground of his being mechanical or irresponsible. Vivid and vital, and sure of himself, he breathed a larger air than that of the mere coteries; he spoke from the centre.[16]

Watts also, Rhys goes on, wrote 'that omniscient famous article', the entry on Poetry in the *Encyclopaedia Brittanica*.[17] Being known as a critic and reviewer was obviously extremely important to the way in which one's first novel was received. Watts's position gained him the legitimising power of the preface-writer for the World's Classics series, the friendship of Swinburne whom (being a tireless ageing-artist chaser) he also nursed to the end of his life, and a place for his own novel *Aylwin* on the World's Classics list. None of these accolades were to be Caine's. A self-starter and an inadequate player in the game, Caine could never resist parading his own merits however hard he tried.

---

15   Hall Caine, *Recollections*, p. vii.
16   Ernest Rhys, 'Aylwin', *Bookman*, Vol. 27, November 1904, pp. 67–8.
17   Rhys, p. 70.

The biography demonstrates exactly this propensity. It is filled with carefully selected passages from Rossetti's letters which praise Caine's own work and critical faculties while undermining those of Watts as well as those of other writer acquaintances including, in its original version, those of Oliver Madox Brown. This is what annoyed Lucy so much and she made him remove the offending passages. Several of the letters which Caine chose to include trumpet Rossetti's respect for Caine's opinion, which extended so far, apparently, that he included a short story which Caine had admired in the new (1881) edition of his poetry and changed an ambiguous line in the poem called 'The Portrait'. Several more letters indicate that Caine thought himself closer to the poet's true vision than Watts. While Rossetti agreed to leave 'Nuptial Sleep' and certain passages of 'Cloud Confines' out of the new edition because Watts said so and he considered 'Mr. Watts's opinion upon a matter of criticism ... to be almost final',[18] privately both Rossetti and Caine liked them. All the careful respect for Watts in these extracts cannot disguise Caine's self-image as the more intrinsically poetic of the two of them. Well might Sharp say the book was about 'yours truly'. This rivalry – publicly unacknowledged, at least on Watts's part – did not affect their friendship. But it did affect their respective positions in the field. Watts, the barrister-turned-poet, was respected and canonised as a serious writer all his life. Caine, the builder's assistant-turned-jobbing-journalist, was berated for his ambition and his popularity most of his.

Caine's instinct for turning his experiences into money without being able to hide the fact was finally to bring the consequences of such a strategy to the surface in the shape of his rejection by some of the field's key players. Rossetti's family never wrote or spoke to him again after the publication of *The Prodigal Son* (1904), which blatantly used the episode of Rossetti's burying of his compositions in his wife's grave and his subsequent exhumation of them for money. Intriguingly, though, Watts also used his experiences as Rossetti's friend – including the grave-robbing theme – in his only novel *Aylwin*, but for a number of important reasons he didn't suffer for it. It is worth examining Watts's novel since its fate was so very different from that of any of Caine's.

Aylwin is a romance set in Wales and the London of the Pre-Raphaelite Brotherhood. In its sensationalism (in the nineteenth-century sense of the term)[19] and its Gothic overtones it differs only in degree from the romances of either Caine (who already had eight successful novels under his belt by this time) or Corelli (who had more than a dozen, and whose position as Caine's greatest rival I will explore in a moment). Watts's hero, Henry Aylwin, is a child cripple who is cured by the miracles of modern science and reaches manhood strong, rational, and doubly manly due to the memory of his childhood: 'Those who say that physical infirmity does

---

18   Hall Caine, *Recollections*, p. 150.
19   In 1895, one critic described 'the very essence of sensationalism' as 'a succession of thrilling surprises conducted out of situations that are practically impossible'. Frederic Harrison, 'Charlotte Bronte's Place in Literature' (London, 1895), p. 17.

not feminize the character', Henry tells us, 'have not had my experience'.[20] Henry has gypsy blood, for which (in the 1890s at least) read a partial belief in and affinity with all things spiritual.[21] Henry himself fights the spiritualist urge after his cure by science, partly because his father is a spiritualist and it annoys his mother. D'Arcy (the novel's Rossetti) asks him: '"You do not believe in a supernatural world?" "My disbelief of it," I said, "is something more than an exercise of the reason. It is a passion, an angry passion"' (p. 223). But the book's project is to convince its hero (and reader) that rationalism alone is inadequate even in a modern world. Like Caine – and like Corelli – Watts super-imposes spiritualism onto the text of God's word in order to arrive at truth and a happy ending, either on earth or in heaven or both. Openness to new interpretations of God's Word which proves its applicability in a modern world, its possible co-existence with science, is crucial to all three writers and there is nothing in Watts's treatment of these themes which sets it apart.

His plot is relatively simple. Henry Aylwin is the second son of a wealthy landowner who has a secret belief in the supernatural due to the loss of his first much-loved Roman Catholic wife. Aylwin senior dies and is buried wearing a jewelled cross, 'The Moonlight Cross of the Gnostics' which was her most cherished possession. He protects this with a curse taken straight from the Bible (the 109th Psalm), which threatens destitution to the children of anyone who desecrates the tomb. Henry has been in love with Winnie, the heroine, since they were both children in Wales, though his mother disapproves on class grounds. Winnie's drunken father is killed by a landslide while stealing the Moonlight Cross and his corpse ends up at the bottom of the cliff, inviting one of Watts's flights of sensationalism:

> Bolt upright it stood, staring with horribly distorted features, as in terror, the crown of the head smashed by a fallen gravestone. Upon his breast glittered the rubies and diamonds and beryls of the cross, sparkling in the light of the moon, and seeming to be endowed with conscious life. (p. 96)

Both Henry and Winnie fall ill after this episode, Henry because he gets drenched in the sea trying to prevent Winnie from seeing her father's corpse, Winnie because she finds out about it anyway and goes mad. By the time he has recovered from his fever, she has disappeared. He spends the rest of the book wandering through Wales and London looking for her with the help of Sinfi Lovell, a Gypsy whose visions tell him he will marry Winnie in the end. He follows Winnie's trail from poverty as a witless match-seller in the hands of a well-meaning bawd to unconscious fame as the model of

---

20   Theodore Watts-Dunton, *Aylwin* (London, 1898), p. 26. All subsequent references are to this edition and will appear parenthetically in the text.

21   Watts, long fascinated by gypsies (as well as ageing writers with influence) had courted the friendship of the then-famous gypsy chronicler George Borrow and after his death had edited and written the preface to Borrow's works in a number of editions, including the World's Classics.

the Pre-Raphaelite painting fraternity, where she figures as a cross between Elizabeth Siddal and Ophelia. There he meets D'Arcy (Rossetti). Having found out that Winnie is apparently dead, Henry descends into melancholia. Returning to the book's favourite theme of death, graveyards and exhumation, he describes his state thus:

> Dead! Dead! rang through me like a funeral knell: all the superstructure of Hope's sophisms was shattered in a moment like a house of cards: my imagination flew away to all the London graveyards I had ever heard of; and there, in the part divided by the pauper line, my soul hovered over a grave newly made, and then dived down from coffin to coffin, one piled above another, till it reached Winifred, lying pressed down by the superincumbent mass; those eyes staring.
> Yes, that night I was mad! (p. 310).

Compare this Gothic outpouring of grief and remorse with Caine's description of his hero Oscar Stephensson's behavior in a similar situation. Caine's composer-hero, the prodigal son of the novel's title, has wronged his young wife Thora by falling in love with someone else (as Rossetti did) and driven her to her grave by neglect (as Rossetti did), though he has yet to bury the only copies of his compositions wrapped in her hair and then exhume them in order to make his name with them (as Rossetti did). That comes later. Here, overcome with remorse, he is lamenting beside the corpse and his madness of grief, like Henry's, is expressed in terms of a passionate desire not to be parted from her body.

> 'My sweet girl!' said Oscar, stretching both arms over the bed, 'forgive me for all my failures of duty. Oh, what I would give to forget them now, but I can't, I can't! You are gone, and I can never make amends'.
> Thinking to put an end to a scene which was touching everybody too deeply, the Governor signed to the man in the shirt-sleeves, but when the man stepped forward Oscar's grief broke out afresh, and in the vehemence of his sorrow his tongue lost all control of itself.
> 'Not yet!' he cried. 'O God! Thora! My wife! My sweet young wife! Let me look at her face again! How bright and happy it used to be, and now it is leaving me like this! Forgive me, my angel! Say you forgive me before you go! I cannot live without your forgiveness! I wronged you and sinned against you, but you were good and your childlike heart was from God!'
> The desolate cry rang through the room, and each of those who heard the revelation of the naked soul read it by the light of his own.[22]

Watts's description of the madness of grief is every bit as melodramatic as Caine's, and considerably more romantic. The differences in style between the two novels are important.

---

[22] Hall Caine, *The Prodigal Son* (London, 1904), p. 220. All subsequent references are to this edition and appear parenthetically in the text.

Peter Brooks has defined melodrama as a 'moral occult', an offshoot of the drive of romance which 'represents both the urge towards resacralization and the impossibility of conceiving sacrilization other than in personal terms'.[23] Both Caine's novel and Watts's can be described as a search for a moral occult, personalising the moral universe via their heroes' long journeys to enlightenment and moral truth through superstition. For Brooks also, the melodrama 'tends to diverge from the Gothic novel in its optimism, its claim that the moral imagination can open up the angelic spheres as well as the demonic depths and can allay the threat of moral chaos'.[24] Again, both novels enact precisely this optimism. Oscar is redeemed at the end of *The Prodigal Son* through his renunciation of sin, his anonymous financial reparations to his brother, mother and daughter, and his final realisation that forgiveness will come, if only in heaven. His journey proves the existence of God in a universe devoted to selfishness. Henry is redeemed at the end of *Aylwin* by the angelic self-sacrifice of Sinfi, which reunites him with Winnie. He gets to prove his manhood through suffering, have his rationalism thoroughly shaken up and mingled with a healthy dose of quasi-religious superstition, and then he gets the girl.

Aylwin, it has to be said, is closer to the Gothic in every respect, deviating from its nightmare prescription only in the manner indicated by Brooks and in every way more excessive than *The Prodigal Son*. As N.N. Feltes has pointed out, Caine's style of romance is tempered by realism, and this was recognised in the reviews: the *Westminster Review* hailed his arrival on the scene in 1887 in exactly these terms: 'Mr Caine's romance is the romance of reality. He has recognised that fiction is the essence of fact, that the improbable is the reflex of the probable. He combines moral sanity with imaginative fervour, truth of emotion with strength of passion; and thus succeeds in that combination of the familiar with the unfamiliar, that blending of the commonplace with the unusual which must ever remain the essence of the highest romantic achievement'.[25] For this critic, Caine is purifying realism: 'He is not afraid to handle "delicate" matters of life and action, and to speak plain English in relation thereto; yet his books have the effect of a moral tonic – no line of them unfit for the purest eye, no sentiment that would not grace the most fleckless manhood. Zola himself never wrote a more truly realistic work than "A Son of Hagar"; only, the realism of "Nana" is to the realism of "Hagar" as the realism of a pig-stye to that of a mountain dell'.[26] He is, as Feltes suggests, championing the 'softer feminine virtues in a world of patriarchal anger and brutality'.[27] But it is important to note that he is also seen as championing the harder virtues of masculinity in a world of popular feminine slush: 'Both his published fictions', the *Westminster Review* asserts, 'afford evidence of a

---

23   Peter Brooks, *The Melodramatic Imagination: Balzac, Henry James, Melodrama and the Mode of Excess* (1976; London, 1995), p. 16.
24   Brooks, p. 20.
25   'A New Novelist', *Westminster Review*, Vol. 128, October 1887, p. 843.
26   'A New Novelist', pp. 842–3.
27   Feltes, p. 118.

pronounced individuality of genius which is calculated to count as a potent factor in the prevailing romantic movement'.[28]

A number of recent critics have figured the period's literary field in terms of an opposition between realism/art/masculinity and romance/the market/femininity. Rachel Bowlby, for example, finds evidence in Dreiser's work 'that what modern realist art can offer is a specifically masculine form of artistic preference which avoids the weakness of feminine sentimentality'.[29] Feltes sees Caine's arrival on the scene and propulsion to bestsellerdom at the hands of the new entrepreneurial publisher William Heinemann as an example of canny capitalism working around this opposition. For him, many of Caine's 'elements of textual ideology enact that overlapping of "realism" and "romance" in the popular ideology of the early nineties, gratifying as well the economic purposes and artistic pretensions of a popular, entrepreneurial publisher in the emerging literary mode of production'.[30]

Feltes' reading of the realism-romance resolution as a market-driven compromise is probably accurate as far as it goes. But as I will demonstrate, Caine's injection of realism into romance could not save him from charges of Philistinism ('economic purposes') or turn his own or his publisher's 'artistic pretensions' into genuine capital in the symbolic marketplace. Nor, for that matter, did the publication of Watts's best-selling melodramatic romance get him accused of 'femininity' or hurt his position in the literary field. The 'solution' did not actually result in a happy homogenising of the market for books. In fact, the notion of a binary opposition, while useful, is somewhat complicated by the story of Watts's 'success' and its juxtaposition with Caine's 'failure' in the market for symbolic goods. It indicates that any analysis that focuses on the text – or even the publishing industry in relation to the text – in these binary terms is liable to miss something crucial. In order to arrive at even the beginnings of an understanding of the ways in which gender, class and the ideology of reading interacted it is necessary to consider the text in the context, not only of its production and its reception, but also of their impact on its author's relation to the literary field as a whole.

Bourdieu does not adequately explore the relationship between gender and class, or consider the respective values and impact of gendered artistic productions. But he does at least provide us with frameworks in which we can begin to trace these relationships for ourselves. As Toril Moi has pointed out, Bourdieu's gender model might not be perfect (and indeed, it frequently repeats arguments which feminists have known for decades) but it does enable us to 'reconceptualize gender as a social category in a way which undercuts the traditional essentialist/non-essentialist divide'.[31] The

---

28 'A New Novelist', p. 842.
29 Rachel Bowlby, *Just Looking: Consumer Culture in Dreiser, Gissing and Zola* (London, 1985), p. 123.
30 Feltes, p. 118.
31 Toril Moi, 'Appropriating Bourdieu: Feminist Theory and Pierre Bourdieu's Sociology of Culture', *What is a Woman and Other Essays* (Oxford, 1990), p. 267.

consideration of gender as social category is extremely useful as a way of thinking through its place in a given field. In a patriarchal society such as England in the nineteenth and early twentieth centuries, contrary to what Peter McDonald implies in his male-centred narrative, it is a crucial part of what creates symbolic capital. Bourdieu suggests in *Masculine Domination* that 'dualisms, deeply rooted in things (structures) and in bodies, do not spring from a simple effect of verbal naming and cannot be abolished by an act of performative magic, since the genders, far from being simple "roles" that can be played at will ... are inscribed in bodies and in a universe from which they derive their strength'.[32] This suggests, significantly, that the mere act of 'reclaiming' realism or romance for masculinity, as some critics have claimed, is insufficient and ultimately futile in terms of patriarchal cultural capital; the nature of the literary field in the 1880s and 1890s means that feminisation is attached to the realm of the popular, the 'chatty' and lowbrow and socially fluid, rather than to the legitimised, serious products of artistic endeavour. 'Naming', an act of 'performative magic', is unable to change this fundamental rule – though shades of meaning and capital might adhere to its different stages.

With his 'pronounced' and 'potent' romances, Caine is apparently attempting a compromise between the polar opposites realism/art/masculinity and romance/the market/femininity and he has, for the *Westminster Review* critic at least, succeeded admirably, having 'indubitably proved that it is possible to be artistic without being immoral, and to paint the heart's emotions without wallowing in the heart's riot'.[33] On one level this is merely a new phase in the debate about realism versus respectability that had figured so largely in the arguments over novels throughout the latter half of the century. Then the question had perennially been: how can women and children be protected from inappropriate reading without damaging the progress of art? And the answer had perennially been censorship, both of the content of books and of the means of their distribution. As Chapter 1 demonstrated, the male-dominated literary canon – 'Fiction as Art' – emerged in part as an antidote to and compromise with the public's voracious appetite for novels that were suspected of having a feminising and therefore morally ambiguous effect. Feltes suggests, along similar lines, that the 'Candour in Fiction' debate of the 1890s must be seen as evidence of the emergence of publishing as a 'patriarchal/capitalist' mode of production in that, 'trivialized as "the Young Person", women are inconceivable as serious producers of novels. This structures publishing as protective and paternal'.[34]

It is undoubtedly true that not only was the canon male-dominated, generally including only George Eliot and Jane Austen, but that publishers' lists gave far greater precedence to male authors of serious new literature. In advertising its list of over 200 star contributors to the *Nineteenth Century* as an inducement to subscribe, for example (a list which included, incidentally, Edmund Gosse, Theodore Watts and Sir

---

[32] Pierre Bourdieu, *Masculine Domination* (Cambridge, 2001), p. 103.
[33] 'A New Novelist', p. 843.
[34] Feltes, p. 109.

James Lubbock, but not Hall Caine), the publisher Kegan, Paul, Trench, Trubner and Co. included only fourteen women, and of these seven were titled, that is, justified as contributors by virtue of their class.[35] The problem with Feltes's model, though, is that it over-simplifies the nuances of gender and class in the relations between art and the market. While it is true that by the 1890s both the public's demand for novels and the outcry over 'candour' had begun to be answered by the reconfiguration of the structure of the industry (including its distributors like Smith's) as paternal and protective, there still remained a vestige of concern over the 'feminising effects' of novels – and particularly popular novels – even when these were written and published by men. This was true to such an extent that, the *Westminster Review*'s critic notwithstanding, in 1898 (the year *Aylwin* came out), Joseph Conrad was writing disgustedly to a friend that:

> Hall Caine is a kind of male Marie Corelli. He is the great master of the art of self-advertising. He is always being interviewed by reporters and is simply mad with vanity. He is a megalomaniac, who thinks himself the greatest man of the century, quite a prodigy. He maintains that the lower part of his face is like Shakespeare and the upper like Jesus Christ. (This gives you an idea about the man) ... One should say that he certainly made more than 60 thousand rubles on this book. His publisher is my publisher too – and I know it from this source. For the American edition he got almost another 60,000 rubles.[36]

Conrad's charges are revealing. Caine is financially successful, vain, a self-publicist who blasphemes against both Jesus the Son of God and Shakespeare the god of Art, and it is insulting (because humiliating, given his earnings) to have to rub shoulders with him in the same publishing house. All these things serve to 'feminise' Caine, reducing him to a 'kind of male Marie Corelli'.

Conrad, of course, was persistently bitter about his own inability to make money, despite the critical acclaim being accorded to his work. But his private attacks on Caine, his own personal *bête noir*, are indicative of a wider perception of self-construction, popularity, financial success and 'booming' as somehow 'feminine' qualities which have very little to do with the contents of a book. Even if it can only be articulated privately, the linking of popularity and Philistinism with femininity is a pervasive trope. In the same letter Conrad dismisses Grant Allen's controversial success *The Woman Who Did* as belonging to the Caine and Corelli school, read only by 'Philistines', and – intriguingly – mentions *Aylwin* as a 'curiosity success', a result of friendships with celebrities and the fact that Watts has 'crammed them all into his book'.[37] For Conrad, Watts is no richer in cultural capital than Caine. But the way in which Watts

---

[35] *Macmillan's Magazine*, April 1890, pp. 12–13. Reprinted in Brake, p. 17.
[36] Joseph Conrad, Letter to Aniela Zagorska, Christmas 1898, in *The Collected Letters of Joseph Conrad, II, 1898–1902*, ed. Frederick R. Karl (Cambridge, 1986), pp. 137–8.
[37] Conrad, Letter to Aniela Zagorska, p. 138.

played the game meant that by 1904 when *The Prodigal Son* was published, becoming an instant bestseller and ruining forever Caine's relationship with the Rossettis and a number of their influential friends, Watts's novel was being canonised as a World's Classic by Grant Richards.

The differences in the handling of the portraits of Rossetti in the two novels are even more crucial than their differences of style if we are to understand the rules of the game at that period. Where Caine simply lifts the dramatic events of the burial and exhumation from Rossetti's life and transposes them onto Oscar Stephensson, Watts relies upon the reader's *a priori* knowledge of these events to clarify the mystery with which he surrounds his Rossetti character D'Arcy. Without this *a priori* knowledge the plot certainly still makes sufficient sense. The reader can simply put the following exchange (which is never explained) down to D'Arcy's tragic past which, due to his characterisation as a man of a private nature, we do not need to have spelled out for us. But *with* this knowledge, the following takes on a whole new set of meanings.

It occurs during our hero's second meeting with D'Arcy, when he accompanies the famous painter to Jamrach's menagerie to look at wild animals to add to his backyard collection (a passion borrowed straight from Rossetti's life). Jamrach shows them (as a rather convenient sideline) some precious jewellery, and one of the crucifixes resembles the Moonlight Cross. Henry pulls out the real version and, on seeing and somewhat mysteriously recognising it, D'Arcy seems awe-struck: "'Put it away, put it away! The thing seems to be alive!'" (p. 222). The only way the reader can understand this response is through the conversation that happens on the next page, after Henry has explained his connection with the cross and asked what D'Arcy would do in his situation:

> He looked at me and said, 'As it is evident that we are going to be intimate friends, I may as well confess to you at once that I am a mystic'.
> 'When did you become so?'
> 'When? Ask any man who has passionately loved a woman and lost her; ask him at what moment mysticism was forced upon him – at what moment he felt that he must either accept a spiritualistic theory of the universe or go mad; ask him this, and he will tell you that it was at that moment when he first looked upon her as she lay dead, with Corruption's foul fingers waiting to soil and stain. What are you going to do with the cross?'
> 'Lock it up as safely as I can'. I said, 'what else is there to do with it?'
> He looked into my face and said, 'You are a rationalist'.
> 'I am'.
> 'You do not believe in a supernatural world?'
> 'My disbelief of it', I said, 'is something more than an exercise of the reason. It is a passion, an angry passion. But what should you do with the cross if you were in my place?'
> 'Put it back in the tomb'.
> I had great difficulty in suppressing my ridicule, but I merely said, 'That would be, as I have told you, to insure its being stolen again'.
> 'There is the promise to the dead man or woman on whose breast it lay'.

'This I intend to keep in the spirit like a reasonable man – not in the letter like –'
'Promises to the dead must be kept to the letter, or no peace can come to the bereaved heart. You are talking to a man who knows!' (pp. 223–4)

This is all that is said on the subject of D'Arcy's past or his 'promise'. For the uninitiated, D'Arcy is simply a spiritualist who has an interest in its icons, including famous mystical jewels. But for the knowing, D'Arcy/Rossetti has recognised the Cross as representative of broken promises to the dead.

The Rossetti story was fairly common knowledge by this time, though Caine at least glossed over it in his biography.[38] The important thing is the use to which the story is put. In *Aylwin*, D'Arcy goes on to be the means of re-uniting Henry and Winnie. First he rescues her from her trance-like existence in a London hovel by convincing everyone she is dead. Then he whisks her away to paint her in his country studio. Then, after realising she is Henry's long lost love, he employs a magnetism specialist to transfer her mad fits to Sinfi the Gypsy (with Sinfi's consent), thereby restoring her memory – and her 'life'. Watts merely hints at Rossetti's dark past (the 'one who knows' remark is never explained) and even redeems it. He has Rossetti's fictional counterpart not only persuade someone to honour a promise to the dead by replacing something stolen from a coffin (Henry replaces the cross in his father's grave at D'Arcy's urging, thus *reversing* the real story), but he actually *raises* the 'dead', restoring Winnie the Lizzie Siddal character to consciousness and her astonished faithful lover. On one level this is a rewriting of the Rossetti story, a restitution of the Artist's tarnished reputation via the spiritual medium of the romance. Caine, by contrast, lifts the facts as he knows them, transposes them onto Oscar the prodigal and then, after subjecting him to a lifetime of repentance as a lonely and melancholy figure for whom fame is but a poor reward, has his wife forgive him from beyond the grave before God kills him off. If the 'game' here were biographical honesty, Caine would have won hands down.

But the 'game' is far subtler than that. The *Recollections* and *The Prodigal Son* demonstrate that Watts, unlike Caine, understood that it is fine – even necessary – to use one's famous connections. But in order to maintain a dominant position as an artist it is not enough merely to disavow selfish motives. One must present one's homage to and use of them in a form that flatters without ever looking like toadying. It must appear as a true and faithful likeness (and therefore valuable to the world) yet keep real truth in the family by speaking a language which is comprehensible only to the initiated. The value to the world of this portrait must always therefore be

---

[38] Certainly by 1904 when *The Prodigal Son* was published the *Bookman*'s reviewer assumed a general familiarity with the story, summing up the hero's situation thus: 'when the disaster befell he had, like Rossetti, buried his compositions and his ambition (he is a musical composer) in the grave of his wife as the expression of his remorse and then he had allowed them to be exhumed at the call of vanity and love of the other woman'. J.E. Hodder Williams, *Bookman*, Vol. 27, November 1904, p. 74.

secretly and silently limited: once again we have a situation that excludes anyone who is not already 'one who knows'. As one reviewer of *Aylwin* put it: 'It will be read with delight by multitudes who may scarcely reflect at all on its deeper meaning'.[39] At the risk of pushing the metaphor too hard, in the above example Caine exhumes Rossetti's scandalous money motive while Watts ensures that it stays firmly buried. Using the latter strategy serves not only to protect one's important friends, but also to consecrate oneself as an 'artist'.

This is, of course, only one of the many strategies which Watts and men like him adopted, consciously or not, in their successful bids to gain and hold onto their cultural dominance. Watts, a barrister by profession who was thereby provided with the right class background, if not the right cultural goods to make it as a *litterateur*, pursued famous men so that he could write articles about them and use their endorsements of his work, elbowing his way to prominence as a critic, poet and preface-writer. This meant that his 'curiosity' success *Aylwin* was reviewed in the right places (*The Times*, *Athenaeum*, *Literature* and *Literary World*, among others) and noticed by the right people. Consequently it was liked and admired by Grant Richards sufficiently for him to elevate it to the level of a 'classic' in his new series. Once OUP took over and Frowde found Watts useful as an advisor, preface-writer and friend to the stars, there was no reason to drop the novel and its status as 'classic' was assured for a few more years. But the possibility was created by Watts himself. Silently, subtly, he edged his way to the top and took his 'rightful' place over the popular writers who, like Caine, could only envy from across the art/market divide. As Bourdieu explains, within 'charismatic ideology' and its structures of belief, 'excellence … consists in being what one is with reserve and understatement, urbanely hinting at the immensity of one's means by the economy of one's means, refusing the assertive, attention-seeking strategies which expose the pretensions of the young pretenders'.[40]

The Reviewing of Gender

Since we are beginning, perhaps, to point towards a problematising of that oft-quoted divide between realism/masculinity/art and romance/femininity/the market, the politics of the period's dominant literary forms are worth considering here. As we have seen, Peter Brooks sees Romanticism (and particularly its revival in the late nineteenth century) as:

> a reaction to desacralization [which] both reasserted the need for some version of the Sacred and offered further proof of the irremediable loss of the Sacred in its traditional,

---

[39]   Review of *Aylwin*, *Daily Chronicle*, no date. Reproduced at end of text of fifteenth edition, 1899.
[40]   Bourdieu, *The Field*, p. 83.

categorical, unifying form. Mythmaking could now only be individual, personal; and the promulgation of ethical imperatives had to depend on an individual act of self-understanding that would then – by an imaginative or even terroristic leap – be offered as the foundation for a general ethics.[41]

Both Watts's novel and Caine's enact this leap via the lonely heroes of their *bildungsroman*. Despite Caine's injection of realism into the romance, noticed and much praised by the critics at the time, he is clearly still predominantly a writer of the classical romance.

For Brooks, further, melodrama is Romanticism's near-cousin. It is opposed to 'naturalistic realism' and it is 'radically democratic' in that it strives to 'make its representations clear to everyone' This is a property that, of course, makes it a prime force in the market and a prime target for attack by the aesthetic purists. It is a victory over repression of all kinds, using its expressive language to articulate what cannot normally be expressed.[42] The Romance in this model, then, is democratic and self-contradictory, 'female', perhaps, because it is both conventional *and* dangerous, on the one hand reliant upon prescription and on the other defiantly speaking the unspeakable. It is both culturally repressed and inherently, generically crying aloud its liberation from repression.

Rita Felski takes issue with Brooks's claim for the melodrama as a victory over repression, however. 'The refusal of realism', she suggests, 'can just as easily be allied to conservative ideological agendas and the inscription of normative ideals of femininity; within the domain of the sentimental and the melodramatic ... the transgressive may not be completely removed from the banal'.[43] Felski's reading sounds close to one late nineteenth-century understanding of realism and romance as binary opposites, the one apparently too inclined to reveal sordid truths to the 'Young Person', the other too inclined to be silly and over-emotional. Brooks's, perhaps, represents a different but equally common contemporary reading of the opposition as one between pre-destination and democracy, with all the inflections of gender and class which those terms invoke and all the contentions which the invocation of those issues invariably raises.

What Felski's critique of Brooks points to without really resolving, though, is a problem shared by many other critics who claim either transgressive or conservative tendencies for a set of formally linked cultural products based on textual evidence alone. Watts's 'classic' novel, for example, is certainly on a textual level a melodramatic 'refusal of realism' which inscribes conservative ideals of femininity – the objectified, swooning virgin Winnie victorious in love over the kindly, racially-Othered Gypsy whore Sinfi, whose hyper-feminine qualities of raw nature, instinct and a nurturing selflessness make possible the lovers' spiritual union. It is also, though, on the same

---

[41] Brooks, p. 15.
[42] Brooks, p. 42.
[43] Rita Felski, *The Gender of Modernity* (Cambridge, MA, 1995), p. 126.

level a victory over normative ideals of *masculinity* in that its melodrama allows, encourages, and even insists upon its hero's 'feminine' qualities of superstition, tears and a selfless, spiritual love. On this level Watts's novel is no different than Caine's, which also demands that its hero suffers, cries, loses the love of parents and child in order to learn what they mean, and finds out the value of spiritual over sexual love. But the text alone – whether we categorise it as 'realism' or 'romance', and even if we accept that such generic definitions are themselves radically unstable – cannot tell us what a book 'meant'. Only *Aylwin* and *The Prodigal Son*'s positions in the literary field can explain the 'classic' status of one and the 'bestseller' status of the other when both reached the top of the bestseller lists and went through dozens of editions.[44]

It is not, then, the intrinsic value as romance or realism, feminine or masculine of Watts-Dunton's novels (or Caine's, or Corelli's) which we need to investigate, but the ways in which this value was constructed within a particular belief system. Conrad's construction of Caine as a 'male Marie Corelli' provides a vital clue here. I have suggested that on an ideological level it was sales figures, blatant self-advertisement and financial success which 'feminised' popular literature in the 1880s and 1890s, rather than the formal properties of either realism or romance. But what did that mean for a popular female writer like Marie Corelli? Given that she was obviously more liable to be dismissed by the 'litterateur', what strategies were open to her in making her assault on the dominant positions? Peter D. McDonald has demonstrated through his intricate analysis of Conan Doyle that, despite anything he could do, his reputation as a popular author was determined by his position in 'the sharply polarized literary field of the 1890s',[45] and that the field categorised all its authors in this manner. What is lacking in McDonald's account, however, is even a tacit acknowledgement that gender might have a crucial effect on a popular author's position, complicating – and polarising – it still further.

Caine courted – and wrote about – famous connections, allied himself with a dynamic new publisher in William Heinemann, and politicised himself to the extent that his views and his polemical writings on anti-semitism – particularly *The White Prophet* (1909) – alienated him from a number of influential friends and previously

---

[44]   Another useful recent account is Nicholas Daly's. His reading of the 'romances' of Haggard, Stevenson and Stoker sees them as an attempt to 're-masculinise' the popular romance, reclaiming it as a male form after the mold of Walter Scott. According to Daly: 'The romance ... could at once purify British fiction of foreign contaminants and re-masculinize it'. But, as he goes on to point out without commenting on the significance of the fact, though '*King Solomon's Mines* and *She* have not been out of print since ... it is only comparatively recently that they have come in for academic attention, and the consecration implied by a World's Classic reprint' (Daly, *Modernism, Romance and the fin-de-siecle: Popular Fiction and British Culture 1880–1914* (Cambridge, 1999), pp. 19; 151) The long-delayed consecration is of some importance, however.

[45]   Peter D. McDonald, *British Literary Culture and Publishing Practice 1880–1914* (Cambridge, 1997), p. 171.

devoted fans. He is absolutely a man of his age; his Christian Socialism motivated a high Victorian sense of duty towards society's victims, particularly women and the casualties of Empire. He used his popularity to cement his position as a public man and do some genuine good. *The White Prophet* drew attention to iniquities in the British system of rule in Egypt and advocated the uniting of the world's religions, and while it made him plenty of enemies it also drew the admiration of many who recognised its worth. He eloquently defended the book before the Jewish Literary Society at the invitation of Baron L. Benas, and Heinemann published this defense in pamphlet form. He took a similar approach to the 'Woman Question', advocating reform of the marriage laws in several novels and popular plays and causing a sensation with *The Woman Thou Gavest Me* (1913). Although only available on request at Mudie's and Smith's and banned altogether in several public libraries, the novel 'was re-printed five times before the end of 1913, when nearly half a million copies had been sold'.[46] This in spite of the fans who said they'd never read his books again after being outraged by *The White Prophet*. Popularity – when one was a man – was not apparently damaged by contentious politics, and it enabled many vexed issues to be kept before the public. This works both ways, too. While Caine probably did some good, the controversy that he continually aroused also served quite usefully to keep his name before the public in the latter half of his career. Further, it was as a man that his greatest honour was to be bestowed: he was knighted in 1917 as much for his services to the war effort as for his services to literature.[47]

For Corelli, few if any of these options were available. Like Caine, she arrived on the scene in need of money in order to support her family. Caine's dual roles as a journalist and builder's apprentice supported his parents, siblings and a girl called Mary who at fourteen became the mother of his first child. Corelli's attempts at a musical and then a literary career supported a father (Charles Mackay, whose literary reputation was declining fast), a half brother (Eric, whom she tried hard to establish as a poet but from whom she received only mockery and ceaseless demands for money), and a companion, Bertha Vyver. In dire financial straits (which she afterwards denied), as a late-Victorian single woman she could hardly do what Caine and Watts did and move into the house of a dying, reclusive and scandalous poet without raising the wrong eyebrows and being forever subordinated to his literary reputation. The structure of society – and the literary field – in the 1880s meant far fewer options for an ambitious single woman writer, especially if she was the illegitimate daughter of a minor poet and his housekeeper. Like Caine, she understood that self-construction was not only possible but also necessary in a world of profound social and artistic change. Unlike Caine, she had severely limited means for affecting this strategy.

Unable to get her critical essays published, she turned to novels and began as she meant to go on, creating an image of herself as a talented, aristocratic young girl-genius in need of male patronage. When she submitted her first novel *Lifted Up*

---

46   Allen, p. 351.
47   Allen, p. 367.

to George Bentley in 1886 she was 31 years old but told him she was 17. The book appalled Bentley's readers (one of whom, significantly, was Hall Caine) but aroused Bentley's curiosity sufficiently for him to take a chance on it under the revised title *A Romance of Two Worlds*. The title change was prophetic. Under Corelli the romance was partially reclaimed from re-masculinisers like Haggard, Caine and Stevenson. It was re-instated in a powerful position which, while firmly entrenching the old, established 'feminine' aspects of the popular romance with all the complex web of dangers about unleashed sexual and social forces which 'femininity' was thought to imply, managed to appeal also to Tennyson, Gladstone and the Prince of Wales and to be paraphrased in pulpits across the country. Corelli's brand of romance straddled the divisions of class and gender, aroused both religious fervor and moral outrage, and was as vigorously defended by its author for its artistic merits as attacked by critics for its mass appeal. It was a romance, not just of two worlds, but of several.

Nicola Diane Thompson has argued that the way in which a work is reviewed in the Victorian period is crucial to an understanding of its 'value'. She does not call this process part of a cultural 'field' in Bourdieu's terms, but her analysis works with precisely this kind of interactive model, placing reviewing as part of a set of interlocking practices:

> The review, as a genre, has to place the literary work in a certain framework in order to come to terms with it: it has to label, name, and put the work in context before it can proceed to analyze and evaluate it. One of the ways in which this naming takes place is through definition of the 'type' of work it is; another way is through comparison or juxtaposition of the reviewed work with other works.[48]

Thompson also suggests, like many other recent critics, that 'masculinity was identified with high culture (and male readers), rather than with popular culture (and female readers)', and that 'the term "masculine" was short-hand for a thumbs-up sign of approval'.[49] She provides several examples of the way this works. The most notable of these is her analysis of the reviews of Charles Reade's novels which, it was assumed, were read largely by men. Her account is invaluable, though due to its rooting in the middle of the century it is unable to account for the way in which reviews of later male- and female-authored popular novels were also gendered, in spite of the gender make-up of their readerships. This was a new development, congruent with the rise of a mass reading public, and it is crucial.

Caine's early reviews were filled with 'male' imagery and iconography which tended to emphasise power and potency, forcefulness, endurance and scale of vision: 'it is impossible to deny originality and rude power to this saga', said *The Times* of *The Bondman* in 1890, 'impossible not to admire its forceful directness and the colossal

---

[48]   Nicola Diane Thompson, *Reviewing Sex: Gender and the Reception of the Victorian Novel* (London, 1996), p. 10.
[49]   Thompson, p. 20.

grandeur of its leading characters'. Gladstone wrote that it was 'a work of which I recognise the freshness, vigour and sustained interest, no less than its integrity of aim'.[50] As we have seen, *The Westminster Review* claimed a new, clean masculinity for Caine's realist romances:

> He combines moral sanity with imaginative fervour, truth of emotion with strength of passion; and thus succeeds in that combination of the commonplace with the unusual which must ever remain the essence of the highest romantic achievement. This power of transmuting the ordinary into the marvellous by means of an imaginative manipulation which, though daring and vivid, yet keeps itself within the bounds of the truly artistic, is the main factor of differentiation between the novel and the romance.[51]

There is a curious (though common) ambiguity here about what – exactly – constitutes the 'bounds of the truly artistic'. For this reviewer it is a compromise between the 'ordinary' and the 'marvellous', though s/he doesn't say how much of either makes for a 'novel' or a 'romance'. S/he does say, however, that 'what readers want in a novel, and indeed what the conditions of true novelistic art demand, is narrative, not dissertation'. For this critic, George Eliot (by this time long established as an honorary member of the canon) was 'dull' precisely because 'she explained and dilated upon' the actions of her characters rather than allowing 'action, incident, emotion' to speak for themselves. Here George Eliot clearly represents both a too-masculine use of reason and a too-feminine avoidance of action which serves to undermine her position as a canonised novelist; she would, the critic asserts, have done better to have written 'one novel and half a dozen volumes of essays'.[52] By contrast, the reviewer goes on, Haggard has rejected the realism that is one of 'only two provinces … open to the incursions of the novelist' in favour of 'supernaturalism'. But this too is inadequate, for it crosses the line of believability beyond which 'our sympathies refuse to go without at least a strong feeling of artistic violation'. Haggard is, at best, merely a 'pregnant sign of reaction' against realism.[53]

What sets Caine apart, apparently, is the fact that he is 'essentially a man of letters'. The reviewer claims 'high powers of critical exposition' for him, naming the critical books he wrote before he published his first novel, including *Recollections*. Here we have a novelist who (unlike Eliot) knows how to keep essays apart from fiction, and (unlike Haggard) fiction within the bounds of the possible. In Thompson's terms he is 'masculinised' by the labelling, naming and contextualisation which, forming the framework of the review, compare him favourably to both a woman novelist (Eliot) and a more 'feminine' (because less realistic) male novelist (Haggard) and claim for him the ultimate potency – criticism.

---

[50]   John St John, *William Heinemann: A Century of Publishing* (London, 1990), p. 3.
[51]   'A New Novelist', p. 843.
[52]   'A New Novelist', p. 841.
[53]   'A New Novelist', p. 841.

Despite the similarities, this is a somewhat changed terrain from that of the 1850s and 1860s when Charles Reade was being reviewed and also compared to Eliot. An appreciation of Reade's works by Ouida in 1882 declares: 'the novels of this virile and vigorous master have been amongst the few English novels in which I have ever found delight ... There is an heroic grandeur in his treatment of these themes, and one feels that he ought to have been a great and adventurous soldier or singer of war'.[54] Two years later, after Reade's death, another review claims that while Eliot is far superior in certain aspects, particularly her 'refined and thoughtful' characterisations, she lacks the 'general animation' of Reade: 'the superiority of the male novelist is so obvious and so enormous that any comparison between the full robust proportions of his breathing figures and the stiff thin outlines of George Eliot's phantasmal puppets would be unfair if it were not unavoidable'. The reviewer then goes on to praise the 'variety of life, the vigour of action, the straightforward and easy mastery' in Reade's novels, and even compares him to Shakespeare.[55] This is a criticism of Eliot which is repeated in the review of Caine's work quoted above; Eliot's dullness, introspection and lack of action work in both cases to the male novelist's advantage by figuring his *work* as male compared to hers.

Despite being marketed as a 'sensation novelist' at railway bookstalls Reade was considered in his day to be as important a novelist as Dickens, Thackeray or Fielding, and if the early reviews of Caine's work are any indication he was being prepared for a similar place. The invocation of his critical writing and the representation of him as a young man of letters positions him with Watts, whose *Aylwin* was reviewed in precisely these terms by F.H. Groome in the *Bookman* in 1898:

> It seems but the other day I was lamenting in The Bookman that Mr Watts-Dunton – he then was Mr. Watts – was ... a literary celebrity who had produced not one single book. Since then we have had his grand 'Jubilee Greeting at Spithead' and his exquisite 'Coming of Love' [both books of poems], and now this novel; surely the Essays will follow, and the Life of Rossetti, and who knows what else besides? ... Novelty and truth are 'Aylwin's' chief characteristics, a rare combination nowadays ... If it could have been published anonymously or pseudonymously, and with a different title, it would, I feel sure, have been hailed by our leading critics as the first-fruits of the genius of some new 'marvellous boy', this although every page bears marks of the ripest maturity ... 'Aylwin' is a passionate love-story, with a mystical idée mère ... the plot may sound sensational, melodramatic, but that is where the master's art comes in; this eerie phantasmagoria reads just like sober fact, like what might, like what must indeed have been ... It is not everyone can write like that.[56]

---

54   Ouida, 'Charles Reade', *Gentleman's Magazine*, Vol. 253, July–December 1882, pp. 494–7.
55   A.C. Swinburne, 'Charles Reade', *Nineteenth Century*, Vol. 16, October 1884, pp. 550–67.
56   F.H. Groome, 'Aylwin', *Bookman*, Vol. 25, November 1898, pp. 37–9.

Here once again we have a history of critical writing leading to expectations of a novel and a melodrama made 'masterful' by realism. In this case also, we have a novel's 'art' authenticated by association: the review is accompanied by Rossetti's drawing of the author. It is significant too that, for this reviewer, the novel is saved from classification as the first fruits of a boy-genius precisely by its author's literary reputation. To be 'masterful' as a novelist is evidently a quality not intrinsic to the novel itself, but dependent on one's prior status, even if (or especially if) this is as a critic and not a novelist.

Caine had worked hard to achieve this kind of reputation for himself, and if it was flawed in its infancy it was at least salvageable, if not to Conrad. It also had an interesting pay-off in terms of his parallel career as a dramatist: it was as a young critic that he was first invited to attend Henry Irving's backstage parties in the Beefsteak room, and Irving's admiration for Caine's work somewhat complicates his position in the literary field, as I will shortly demonstrate. But as a novelist his burgeoning reputation was short-lived. Three years after he released his first novel, Caine left the well-established firm of Chatto and Windus and cast in his lot with the dynamic young publisher William Heinemann. With Heinemann he was to make publishing history when their third joint production *The Manxman* (1894) carried an announcement to the effect that it would appear only in single-volume format and not in the customary first-edition of three, thus completely bypassing the circulating libraries and going direct to the purchasing public.

Caine moved to Heinemann for the simple reason that he offered more money than Chatto. But the more aggressive advertising campaign and the change in first-issue format which the move occasioned signalled Caine's final departure from 'the world of letters' in favour of the world of booming, big sales and 'railway type' books, convenient to carry, cheap to buy, easy to read and, within a very few years, drawing the charge of indecency which to its author was a sign of 'art' and to its critics a sign of smutty popularity. No sign here of the consecration conferred on Reade even as he sold hugely at bookstalls. By the 1890s selling hugely to a mass public was a problem. Not for nothing had *Punch* dubbed Caine's third novel (*The Deemster*, 1887) 'The Boomster' and by the 1890s begun to apply the moniker to the author himself. Caine was known as one of Heinemann's most difficult and demanding authors as well as their most successful. As John St John notes in his history of the firm, 'he played a very active part in promoting his own books, sending the office a stream of letters in tiny crabbed handwriting, insisting on more advertising and advising on circularization and other methods of publicity'.[57]

By the early 1890s the reviews in certain quarters had begun to reflect this change in status, finding his self-publicity more irritating than his books were interesting, and this was a problem which he began to share with Corelli. She – famously – was so incensed by the scathing reviews of her first novels that she trained her Yorkshire terrier to tear them up and thereafter refused to allow her publisher to send out review

57   St John, p. 29.

copies at all. Some periodicals, like the *Bookman* and *Publishers' Circular*, seldom review her novels after this, and where reviews do appear in other publications they are likely to have been written by the author herself. But the tone of those that are written by genuine reviewers tend to indicate an indulgent, patronising mockery which smacks of an adverse gendering of her work as 'female' in conception, design and execution as well as form, even compared to later reviews of Caine's.

One of her severest detractors was Edmund Yates. He had founded *The World*, been an editor of *Temple Bar* and contributed to *All the Year Round* and the *Observer*. His comments on finally meeting – and liking – Corelli reveal the deeply prejudiced view he had formed of her writing, and point to the complexity of the issues involved in the 'gendering' of criticism. 'You are not in the least like what I fancied you might be. You don't look a bit literary – how is that? You've taken us all in! We expected a massive, strong-minded female, with her hair divided flat on each side, and a cameo in the middle of her forehead'.[58] The curious thing about this comment is its combination of flattery and scathing dismissal; Marie's books had persuaded him she was 'literary' and, as a literary woman, 'unfeminine'. Her public persona charmed him; evidently relieved to find a diminutive, vivacious woman rather than an Amazon he ceased to review her badly. To be a womanly woman writer was evidently less abhorrent than to be a serious 'literary' masculinised woman writer. Corelli well knew this and had her few publicity photographs retouched to make her look girlish, pretty and fragile, even when she was stout, stern and middle-aged.

She did not, however, pull her punches in her writing. The public persona was retouched so that the private/public might get through unmarked, and her combination of melodramatic romance and moralising polemic meant that, though Yates was off her back, the scathing attacks on her work continued in other quarters. For these critics she was again *too* feminine: the *Publishers' Circular* laughed at her polemic *Free Opinions Freely Expressed On Certain Phases of Modern Social Life and Conduct* (1905), declaring that while she probably had real grievances they could not be taken seriously. For their reviewer she makes 'naughty little insinuations' like a schoolgirl, and the book's sole merit lies in the fact that 'it is impossible to deny that a good deal of amusement is to be got out of these '"Free Opinions"'.[59] W.T. Stead, who was later to review *Temporal Power* (1902) and helped to get Corelli dropped from the King's tea-party list by suggesting that its characters were meant to represent Edward VII, Queen Alexandra and Chamberlain, started as he meant to go on with a review of *The Sorrows of Satan* (1895) which pegged her as a complaining shrew:

> A considerable section of the book is one long lampoon, spiteful and exaggerated, out of all semblance of truth, upon certain logrollers, publishers and critics against whom

---

58   Teresa Ransom, *The Mysterious Miss Marie Corelli: Queen of Victorian Bestsellers* (Stroud, 1999), p. 75.

59   'Review of Free Opinions Freely Expressed on Certain Phases of Modern Social Life and Conduct', *Publishers' Circular*, Vol. 82, 3 June 1905, pp. 621–2.

she has a grudge; but so great are the sorrows of Marie Corelli over her critics that she will probably not believe me when I say that one of the sorrows of her readers is that she should suffer so much and conceal it so little.[60]

The *Bookman* reviewed *God's Good Man: A Simple Love Story* (1904), seeing in it insufficient realism and putting it down as a melodramatic rant. While the reviewer says s/he agrees with 'Miss Corelli's denunciations of motor-cars, the "smart set", Bridge on Sunday, Englishwomen who smoke, absentee landlords, atheistic clergymen, and the murder of dogs by furious drivers on the high roads', s/he adds with an avuncular chuckle: 'I am a little more doubtful whether an American Duchess or two might not be tolerated under strict conditions'. Here the figure of a stereotypically fussy, conservative, dog-loving, matronly homebody is invoked with indulgent mockery. The reviewer goes on to point out several flaws in the book's form and composition, and concludes: 'some natural art, sweeping off the board these ready-made phrases, and toning down colour, would have been desirable … But the crowd that have sorrowed with Satan or glorified Barabbas and the religion of electricity worship unmistakable dyes. What do they care for creating Nature?'[61] The charges against Corelli here seem to be that she is both too conservative and too colourful, too religious and not religious enough, too outspoken and too commonplace, and above all that she is too popular. The review of *Aylwin*, which claimed for it an enduring place in literature and, therefore, consecration as 'Art' because it had gone through 20 editions in six years, was evidently placing a ceiling on the 'test of endurance'. Any more years or editions than that and a book became, apparently, merely 'popular' instead. Corelli and Caine both regularly went into a twentieth edition, and both remained in print with all their novels throughout their lives, though neither, as we know, has yet become a World's Classic and *Aylwin* has died with the rest.

My point here is that the terms on which a novel was reviewed in this period were not fixed, nor even reducible to a variety of subjective opinions, but shared a set of tropes which, chameleon-like in their ability to change their meaning according to their surroundings, not only militated against the woman writer but used its gendered terminology to militate also against the *popular* writer. 'It is better than Marie Corelli', Bennett said of Caine's *The Christian* in 1897, 'though not much better; it belongs to the same crowd as *The Sorrows of Satan*'.[62] And again, with characteristic wit: 'If Joseph Conrad is one Pole, Marie Corelli is surely the other'.[63] As with Conrad himself, here Corelli forms the function of yardstick, her name standing in for a type, interchangeable with a book's title. To be popular was bad enough. To be both

---

[60]   W.T. Stead, 'The Book of the Month: *The Sorrows of Satan* and of Marie Corelli', *Review of Reviews*, 12 October 1895, p. 453

[61]   'Review of *God's Good Man: A Simple Love Story*', *Bookman*, Vol. 27, October 1904, pp. 26–7.

[62]   Feltes, p. 128.

[63]   Bennett, *Books and Persons*, p. 32.

female and popular was, it seems, beyond the pale. But to be either was to be part of a shifting set of definitions of gender and class that had no fixed referent in science, in religion, or in art. As McDonald suggests, ' avant-garde and "popular" culture are reciprocally defined in and through ongoing cultural contest'.[64] The stakes shift constantly, endlessly. What McDonald neglects to explore, however, is the central role played by gender in that contest. 'Avant-garde' and 'popular' are by no means the only oppositions in the field in this period.

Marie Corelli and the Romance of Emancipation

Corelli and Caine adopted crucially different strategies to defend their economically successful positions and simultaneously try to improve their symbolic ones while claiming the artist's right of free speech. Caine, an active member of the Society of Authors, was from the first involved in the anti-censorship debates. Like Corelli, he was himself banned from both Mudie's and Smith's and from several public libraries, and like Corelli he believed the censorship issue to be detrimental to artists. Also like Corelli, he figured himself as among their number, and curiously enough several purists agreed.

Caine's early introduction to Henry Irving encouraged an interest in drama, and he wrote and produced many interpretations of his novels for the stage and, later, the screen. While his greatest successes were with melodramas in Drury Lane, which were as popular as his novels and as often critically panned, in 1887 he was commissioned to write a play by Irving himself – then, as now, considered one of the finest 'classical' directors of his day and renowned for his innovative aesthetic lighting. The play was banned by the Lord Chamberlain in the end due to its potentially inflammatory political content, and never staged, but the great actor/manager's interest in Caine's work has to be seen as complicating somewhat the position 'popular author' which he is often assumed to occupy. In addition, his novel *The Manxman* later attracted the fledgling director Alfred Hitchcock, who found in it sufficient material for a thoughtful and memorable early silent film. Hitchcock, like Irving, cannot easily be dismissed as an admirer. Caine's melding of realism and romance, his penchant for dramatic and sometimes contentious situations revolving around the contemporary politics of religion, race and gender, meant that he frequently hovered around the boundary between the 'artist' with something to say and the 'hack' with something to sell.

Caine, no stranger to censorship, seemed to remain unaffected by it. As we have seen, the biggest furore faced by him was over *The Woman Thou Gavest Me* (1913), his polemic on the 'Woman Question'. In it he felt free to express his – fairly liberal – opinions on divorce laws and the public treatment of illegitimacy, and its banning had no adverse affect on its sales. Corelli, on the other hand, expressed herself equally freely on the 'Woman Question', but as a woman writer she had to protect herself

---

[64]   McDonald, p. 173.

from the kinds of accusations which Yates had admitted to making. And she also, in the face of widespread denouncement of suffragettes and 'New Woman' novelists, had less political freedom in the public sphere. To be thought of as 'masculine' was in this case, in this climate, to lose the power to convince her readers that she spoke as a woman.

In order to avoid this she seized the moral high ground, denouncing suffragettes, bicycles, low-cut gowns and women smokers but championing changes in the law which put women in charge of their own careers, bodies, money and children. If this seems like a poor trade (and I'm not convinced that it does) she made up for it in her books. Her heroines may be winsome and conventionally beautiful but they are also powerful and fully sexualised, able to be simultaneously virtuous, passionately in love and able to consummate their passion with metaphor. Again, we might say that this is a poor substitute for the real thing. But, as Richard L. Kowalczyk points out, heterosexual union is the driving force behind Corelli's narratives, even if it is figured in a spiritual form: 'To use Corelli's imagery, the power of God is a masculine agency, ever active and yet incomplete. Mankind, the 'female' element in creation, can potentially develop an infinite number of psychic and spiritual identities and so may be considered an essence, either complementary or essential, to God's eternal nature … Most importantly, this relationship between God and man is never more clearly possible than in dream-like reverie or highly emotional states. Art is a culture's way of producing this intense state of feeling'.[65] For Corelli, the romance is the perfect literary form precisely because it provides the right atmosphere for this spiritual union; if the Bible is the spiritual sex manual, then Art is the wine and chocolates.

What we need to add to Kowalczyk's reading of Corelli's customary narrative engine, though, is an exploration of what it means for male and female characters to be figured in this 'feminised' spiritual role, and where that leaves merely mortal sexuality. If what got Caine banned from libraries in 1913 was his description of a woman seducing a lover who was trying to respect her married state, a model of transgressive femininity, what got Corelli banned in 1886 was her description in *Vendetta* of a man taking revenge for his wife's murder of him, a model of transgression by both sexes. Corelli persistently figures both men and women as equally capable of wrong, and equally capable of 'right', spiritual sex. In her representations of merely mortal sexuality, too, Corelli is equally liberal in permitting 'right' experiences to both men and women, and this is where she differs from Caine and where, perhaps, her version of the romance is more closely aligned to Brooks's model of a victory over repression. Here, in her 1902 novel *Temporal Power*, the famous socialist revolutionary Pasquin Leroy with whom the brave heroine Lotys is in love has just revealed himself to be the King. Lotys saves him from being murdered by their angry fellow rebels and as they say goodbye and return to the fight their relationship achieves its first consummation:

---

65   Richard L. Kowalczyk, 'In Vanished Summertime: Marie Corelli and Popular Culture', *Journal of Popular Culture*, Vol. 7 (1974), p. 856.

a flash of eyes in the darkness, and [she] heard her name breathed softly:
'Lotys!'
She grew dizzy and uncertain of her footing; she could not answer. Suddenly a strong arm caught her – she was drawn into a close, fierce, jealous clasp; warm lips caressed her hair, her brow, her eyes; and a voice whispered in her ear:
'You love me, Lotys! You love me! Hush – do not deny it – you cannot deny it! – You know it, as I know it! – you have told me you love me! You love me, my Love! You love me!'
Another moment – and the King passed quietly out of the door with a bland 'Goodnight' to Sholto, and joining his two companions, raised his hat to Lotys with a courteous salutation,
'Good-night, Madame!'
She stood in the doorway, shuddering violently from head to foot – watching his tall figure disappear in the shadows of the street. Then stretching out her hands blindly, she gave a faint cry, and murmuring something inarticulate to the alarmed Sholto, fell senseless at his feet'.[66]

Small wonder that, after a 'climax' like this, *both* protagonists and not just the King 'passed quietly out'. This hyper-indulgence in the minutiae of courtship in lieu of full sexual consummation is, as Brooks suggests, a common melodramatic device. But the important thing here is not that 'repressed' sexual desire is being given free rein (and that is important enough), but that in Corelli's books it can do so without impropriety. Lotys and the King (who is married) remain 'pure', their passion channeled into the marriage of socialism with the monarchy which replaces the soulless – and for Corelli sinful – marriage of a King with the icy Princess who is his earthly bride. For Corelli, 'true', earthly heterosexual love is a fully sanctioned enactment of the divine mating of Man and God. She was an enthusiastic and even sycophantic monarchist and her fiction, like much romance, was usually set amongst the elite of some distant land, but she also believed that the marriage of type-to-type merely in order to protect some human notion of class purity was a sin. In this sense her romances are truly democratic, and they enable women as well as men to participate fully in an idealised, but also fully sexualised world.

For Caine, by contrast, the same victory over repression is *always* a transgression, something which, while it may be the result of legal or social iniquities which force women into insupportable roles and situations, will *always* end up – and ought to end up – being punished by the narrative. Caine's favourite theme is two men in love with the same woman. She promises herself to one of them and then ends up having to break her vow because she loves the other one more. And invariably her sexualised object-choice is the wrong man, and it leads to suffering for all of them and usually death for at least one. Women are bones of contention characterised by poor judgement, possessing little agency but the choice of man on which to bestow their affections,

---

[66] Marie Corelli, *Temporal Power: A Study in Supremacy* (London, 1902), p. 494. All subsequent references are to this edition and appear parenthetically in the text.

and dependent always on the hero's powers of stoical self-command to extricate them from their predicaments. Caine's heroes are men precisely because they love weak, ultra-feminine women; the narrative journey is almost always a journey to spiritual enlightenment through the self-sacrifice which women demand. And sex is for bad women; good ones are sweet and childlike even after their marriages.

In *The Bondman* (1890) the idealised woman is Greeba, persistently figured as a child. After her decision to marry Red Jason because her true love Michael Sunlocks has deserted her, she appears with her 'womanly pride' apparently in full flood, but it is still linked exclusively to male protection; for her, the only choice is marriage to one of the men: 'Then her hope broke down. Sunlocks had forgotten her; perhaps he cared for her no longer; it might even be that he loved some one else. And so with the fall of her hope her womanly pride arose, and she asked herself very haughtily, but with tears in her big dark eyes, what it mattered to her after all. Only she was very lonely, and so weary and heartsick, and with no-one to look to for the cheer of life'.[67]

The Prodigal Son takes a further step in the direction of a revisioning of gender in a modern world; as well as two men in love with one woman, we have civilisation as degeneracy (represented by 'fast' society women and gambling) and – crucially – art as sex. Oscar the prodigal has been neglecting his sweet young Icelandic wife Thora, whom he stole from his brother Magnus. Thora realises even before their marriage that Oscar is no longer in love with her but with her sister Helga, who arrives from London in the latest fashions. Thora tries to compete by dressing fashionably in a dress ordered specially from London. But when she appears before her fiancé and her sister in it their reactions serve to cement Caine's view of the equation of 'society women' with degeneracy, and primitive cultures (usually Icelandic or Manx) with an ideal, classless, childlike femininity:

> Helga began to laugh, first in a smothered titter, but finally in an outright roar, whereupon Oscar, who had struggled not to smile, caught the contagion and joined her.
>
> Thora's pitiful face fell, and she said, with a crack in her voice –
>
> 'But what are you laughing at, Oscar?'
>
> 'My dear, dear child!' said Oscar; and Helga, who was still laughing, said –
>
> 'A little milliner! It makes her look like a little milliner!'
>
> 'No, no, not that', said Oscar. 'But it's not Thora. Thora is a sweet, simple Iceland maiden whose charm is her simplicity, whereas this –'
>
> 'I see', said Thora, and with her heart in her mouth she turned to go. (p. 95)

In this book Oscar is a weak man, Helga a predatory woman. His journey is about learning to reject sex in favour of love not, as in Corelli's fiction, about their melding in art and spirituality. In the following scene Oscar is neglecting his new career as a politician and instead giving free rein to his latent musical talent with Helga. This is the book's infidelity scene; as soon as Helga suggests he writes an opera 'a continual

---

[67]   Hall Caine, *The Bondman* (London, 1890), p. 158. All subsequent references are to this edition and appear parenthetically in the text.

fever burned in Oscar's blood' until it is done, and then they sit down at the organ in the cathedral to play it together:

> In this atmosphere of art and religion Oscar sat down at the organ, with Helga by his side, to try his anthem for the first time. The organ throbbed under his fingers, the empty cathedral shook like a sea cave under the boom of his waves of sound, and when he came to the end of his first reading he was quivering with excitement and Helga was in a fever … They played the piece again and again, and at every fresh playing their excitement increased until it reached the point of hysteria, and their voices in that silent place became as shrill as the wind on the mountain-top. At last they tried the words, and then their emotion knew no limit.
>
> The organ trembled and throbbed again, and then on the top of all other sounds came the sound of Helga's voice, like a human cry above the thundering waves of nature, sometimes weeping, sometimes raging, sometimes crouching, sometimes springing out of the surge, and finally sinking down to the soft whisper of 'Let there be peace' … In the intoxication of that moment, Oscar's hand swung down and took Helga's hand and held it, and their fingers trembled together and they seemed to hear the beating of each other's heart. They looked at each other, and his eyes were bloodshot and hers were wet. (pp. 87–8)

It is striking that this guilty desire takes place in an atmosphere of 'art and religion'. Oscar is here figured as Byronic, the romantic artist-as-hero who chooses individualism over social order, Nature over God, Art over Duty. And Caine punishes him royally for it. On this level, it is not just Rossetti's story that Oscar enacts, but the story of all Romantic artists who exhume desire for money, in this case Oscar's musical compositions figured as desire and exhumed at Helga's urging. For Caine, 'art' must be 'pure', free of the desire for earthly fame and fortune, and that makes Romanticism, the cult of the individual and the publicisation of his innermost self, an inferior form. It is precisely this refusal of the effects of the 'popular romance' which his novels frequently enact in their use of a form of realism, and which his early critics picked up on. Though in terms of his position in the field it is precisely his expression of the opposite opinion in print – alongside his enormous popularity – which ensures his inferiority as a player. Entering the 'Candour in Fiction' debate in 1890 with an article in the *Contemporary Review*, Caine nailed his colours to the mast. 'I grieve to see that a writer of pure and noble instincts, Thomas Hardy, in his recent protest against the painful narrowness of English fiction, has been betrayed into prescribing a remedy for the evil that is a thousand times worse than the disease', he wrote. 'Though there may be many Madame Bovarys in the world, the Madame Bovarys are not the women whom right-minded people want to know more about … Passion … not fact, lies at the root of the novelist's art'.[68] Unlike Watts, he failed to understand that discretion is the better part of validation.

---

[68]   Hall Caine, 'The New Watchwords of Fiction', *Contemporary Review*, Vol. 57 (April 1890), pp. 480–82.

For Corelli, however, both as critic *and* as novelist, the 'feminisation' potential of the romance was a positive thing, enabling a new kind of freedom for her female protagonists, and she unambiguously eschewed the kind of realism which dealt only with the surface of the known world. Her novels free her heroines, enabling them to travel to other realms as well as other countries. These heroines are consistently in charge when all hell breaks loose and often, at the end, defiantly independent, able to choose their own destiny in spite of gender or class. Asked by the now-revealed King of *Temporal Power* to be his mistress, told she is now 'the ruling power of the country' because he will do her bidding, Lotys asks him to remember his wife and sons, and refuses (p. 530). This is no conventional model of female purity, however, despite its conventional 'good' female refusal of sex. It is here – through the medium of the romance – transformed into political purity because the players in the drama are world leaders grappling with global as well as personal issues. The common contemporary gendered chain of responsibility which goes from female purity to the family and thence to the nation is here enacted, made manifest, but with one crucial omission. Here the chain of responsibility is simply between a woman and her own judgement of her role as a citizen. There is no family, no husband, and thus unmediated, it gives her real power. Corelli, a single, self-made woman, consistently insists that women are capable not just of making decisions on their own, but of playing an equal role in the affairs of the world.

When women do exist in partnership with men, they are frequently figured as tragically unable to conduct their own affairs, with far-reaching consequences. In *The Mighty Atom* (1896) the child hero, Lionel Valliscourt, is made ill and finally killed by his father's insistence on a strict secular upbringing which consists of endless lectures in science and rationalism, an embargo on tears, fresh air and the company of other children, and no time to play. Lionel's mother disapproves of this regime, but is consistently over-ruled by her husband, who thinks her proclivity for singing, laughter, faith and affection ill bred. Finally, unable to stand this punishing treatment of herself and her son any longer and convinced by the years with her husband to abandon her faith, she runs away with another man, leaving Lionel to his father. But the book does not punish her for this betrayal as it might. She is represented as weak and a little foolish, but the real villain of the piece, it is made clear, is Valliscourt. Lionel's mother is presented as doubly wronged, forced into a cruel and desperate act by a man, and by a system which does not permit her control of her own affairs. Her farewell letter to Valliscourt has the ring of truth, and is written with a considerable amount of empathy: 'I leave you without shame, and without remorse. While I was faithful to you, you made my life a misery … You have killed every womanly sentiment in me, – you have even separated me from my child. You have robbed me of God, of hope, of every sense of duty'.[69]

To Corelli the romance form itself was already politicised, and this made it 'Art': it will be remembered that when she was banned from Ealing Free Library in 1899 she

---

[69]   Marie Corelli, *The Mighty Atom* (London, 1896), p. 244.

wrote indignantly to the Library Association, allying herself with literary 'Great Men' such as Shakespeare, Sterne, Swift, Shelley and Byron. She also gave an important lecture on the subject of form to the Edinburgh Philosophical Society in 1901, in which she declared that:

> No king, no statesman – can do for a country what its romanticists and poets can – for the sovereignty of the truly inspired and imaginative soul is supreme, and as far above the conquests of Alexander. And when the last touch of idealistic fancy and poetic sentiment has been crushed out of us, and only the dry husks of realism are left to feed swine withal, then may we look for the end of everything that is worth cherishing and fighting for in our much boasted civilization.[70]

For Corelli, clearly, the romance is truly the only democratic art form; realism consistently fails to produce new fruit. Allying herself with wronged artists, Corelli sought to separate the public who enjoyed her books from the prudes who banned them. She used the endorsements of the Queen, the Prince of Wales, Gladstone and Tennyson as legitimisers, insisting that their requests for her books be announced in the leading papers. But she excused this self-publicity by insinuating that these exalted personages are of one mind with the 'public' who, she claimed, are 'in the main healthy-minded and honest' and with whom she 'by happy chance' had come straight into 'close and sympathetic union'[71] without the intervention of critics or friends on the Press. She also consistently heaped scorn on critics who could be bought. Compared with Caine's reliance on influential friends, Corelli is largely right to insist that she did it alone, and she later remembered the scathing rejection of her first book by him with justifiable bitterness and no small amount of retaliatory sarcasm:

> His strictures on my work were peculiarly bitter, though, strange to relate, he afterwards forgot the nature of his own report. For, on being introduced to me at a ball given by Miss Eastlake, when my name was made and my success assured, he blandly remarked before a select circle of interested auditors that he 'had had the pleasure of recommending my first book to Mr Bentley!' Comment on this were needless and unkind: he tells stories so admirably that I readily excuse him for his 'slip of memory', and accept the whole incident as a delightful example of his inventive faculty.[72]

Caine, for his part, doesn't mention her at all, but his own entry in this same volume is telling. Whereas it was as an autonomous but defenseless woman that Corelli sought to rescue herself from charges of 'booming' that would reduce her to the merely 'popular', it was as a journalist free to explore the seedier side of life that

---

[70] Marie Corelli, 'The Vanishing Gift', in *Free Opinions Freely Expressed On Certain Phases of Modern Social Life and Conduct* (London, 1905), p. 287.

[71] 'A Romance of Two Worlds by Marie Corelli', *My First Book*, ed. Jermone K. Jerome (London , 1894), pp. 215, 219:

[72] Corelli, *My First Book*, p. 207.

Caine sought to rescue his reputation from the 'feminising' effects of popularity and the form of the romance. He talks at length about his struggle to be recognised as a critic, taking his work from publisher to publisher, and advises the young hopeful to 'keep a good heart, even if you have to knock in vain at many doors, and kick about the backstairs of the house of letters. There is room enough inside'. He admits that writing novels has been simultaneously fulfilling and 'hard work', and he disavows pecuniary rewards. 'If it has been hard work it has also been a constant source of inspiration and I would not change it for all the glory and more than all the emoluments of the best-paid and the most illustrious profession in the world'.[73] In disavowing the Romantic notion of the divine inspiration of the artist he attempts to disavow also the feminine notion of romance as a genre and the artist as a passive vessel. And in playing down his earthly rewards (he became both wealthy and illustrious) he seeks to disavow any interest in his own popularity. Given the self-help nature of the book in which this entry appears, it is obviously a case of Caine performing 'higher-than-thou' in the literary field for the newest batch of uninitiated potential recruits. Once again he demonstrates that he knew the rules of the game, but not how to work them to his advantage.

By contrast, Corelli's entry denies not only influential friends but also hard work and monetary needs – a similar strategy to Caine's, but crucially and subtly different. It seems designed, in fact, as an answer to Caine's, successfully defeating his attempt to disavow the romantic notion of the artist by pointing out that starving in a garret is an equally romantic notion:

> It is an unromantic thing for an author to have had no vicissitudes. One cannot expect to be considered interesting, unless one has come up to London with the proverbial solitary 'shilling', and gone about hungry and footsore, begging from one hard-hearted publisher's house to another with one's perpetually rejected manuscript under one's arm … Now, I am obliged to confess that I have done none of these things, which, to quote the Prayer-book, I ought to have done. I have had no difficulty in making my career or winning my public. And I attribute my good fortune to the simple fact that I have always tried to write straight from my own heart to the hearts of others, regardless of opinions and indifferent to results. My object in writing has never been, and never will be, to concoct a mere story which shall bring me in a certain amount of cash or notoriety, but solely because I wish to say something which, be it ill or well said, is the candid and independent expression of a thought which I will have uttered at all risks … I had no particular need of money, and certainly no hankering after fame [with A Romance of Two Worlds] my notion was to offer it to Arrowsmith as a shilling railway volume, under the title 'Lifted Up'. But in the interim, as a kind of test of its merit or de-merit, I sent the manuscript to Mr George Bentley, head of the long-established and famous publishing firm.[74]

---

[73] 'The Shadow of a Crime by Hall Caine', in *My First Book*, p. 74.
[74] Corelli, in *My First Book*, pp. 206–7.

Here, Corelli's self-construction is of Bourdieu's 'pure' artist discovered by a lone discerning critic (and it should be noted that she both proclaims her own modesty and naivety and inflates Bentley's status in the literary field by positioning them in relation to the shilling railway novel, that benchmark by which all other books can be measured). Her story, however, is pure fabrication. She wanted both money and fame, she spent several years trying unsuccessfully to publish her articles and poetry, and she moved from Bentley to Methuen in 1893 because she was dissatisfied with Bentley's handling of her international editions, believing (correctly) that he was not taking full advantage of their financial possibilities.[75]

The game here between these two close rivals was for the right to proclaim 'pure' artistry, something that comes in Corelli's case straight from the heart, and in Caine's from the school of hard knocks. Caine built on his story in his autobiography of 1908, declaring once again that it was the masculine world of journalism that prepared him for novel writing. It was as an architect's apprentice and journalist for the *Builder* that he first came to London, and he declares that 'journalism, to be the best school for the novelist, must be the journalism of the police-court, the divorce-court, the hospital, and the jail, where human nature is real and stark, if vulgar and low – not the journalism of "society", where humanity is trying its poor best to wear a mask'.[76] This attempt to claim a masculine, professionalised realism was unsuccessful. By this time (1908), Caine's wealth, popularity and self-publicity had him pigeon-holed in the imagination of most reviewers. His autobiography was greeted in the *Bookman* by an article which had been prompted by his claims that he was brave to go on half salary of £100 p.a. from his job at the Liverpool Mercury in order to give himself more time to write novels. Better authors than Caine, the *Bookman* said, had had to abandon fiction because 'the novels didn't catch the public fancy ... knowing these things, and how more likely it was that a rude awakening must await the literary beginner who accepted Mr. Hall Caine's experiences as typical of the hard struggle that lay ahead of him, we put the question to a number of successful and popular novelists'. So they did, and all the responses that came in comment disparagingly that if their authors had only had £100 p.a. when they started, they would have thought themselves lucky.[77]

The gendered self-construction of these two romance novelists as a means of protecting themselves from complete dismissal as merely popular has a vital role to play in the way in which their successors – including writers who have been central to our critical thinking about modernism – approached fiction as a way of constructing and investigating identity. Rebecca West's comment on Corelli that 'she had a mind like any milliner's apprentice but she was something much more than a milliner's apprentice'[78] points to the integral class dimension of such a gendering. Corelli's

75   Ransom, *The Mysterious Miss Marie Corelli*, pp. 73–4.
76   Hall Caine, *My Story* (London, 1908), pp. 260–61.
77   'Early Struggles of Popular Novelists', *Bookman*, Vol. 35, January 1909, pp. 181–2.
78   Quoted in Eileen Bigland, *Marie Corelli: the Woman and the Legend* (London, 1953), p. 39.

novels were figured as lower class and female, not because they were written for a lower-class female audience, but because they were calculated to reach a much wider market, 'from the Doctor of Divinity ... to the tripper whose annual literary pleasure is Marie Corelli's latest book read on Margate Sands'.[79] Like Socialism or democracy or desire itself, Corelli was dangerous precisely because she reached so many, breaking down barriers, encouraging mass pleasure. For a reader, a Corelli novel was always going to inhabit that grey area which made reading her either an act of reverse snobbery or defiance or a guilty pleasure for anyone who was not a Royal, a Prime Minister or a Poet Laureate. Being 'banned unless asked for' did not put her on a par with the 'pure' artist for all her protestations: it merely drew attention to her qualities of seduction. And that meant a different brand of the popular feminine was necessary, one that either knew its place, or fought to be free of both place and popularity.

The binary opposition between popular/female/romance and art/male/realism is rendered radically unstable by the struggles of these two writers in a field in which they saw themselves as competing on equal terms with the 'pure' artist. Caine might be 'feminised' by his popularity, his self-imaging and his bracketing with Corelli. But she, paradoxically, was not a more 'feminine' woman because she wrote popular fiction. While being a literary woman unsexed her in Yates' critical imagination, her shift from a 'masculine' literary woman to a 'feminine' popular one after he met her is undercut by his subsequent nickname for her as 'dear little chap'. W.T. Stead called her a 'little woman' rather than a 'great one' because she couldn't keep her opinions out of her books; here the spoiling of 'art' is the despoiling of femininity: '"The Sorrows of Satan and Marie Corelli" is a great book by a little woman. "Little woman", that is the right phrase, and it is a thousand pities we should have the littleness of the woman thrust in every chapter before the attention of the reader, who, but for this, might have mistaken her for a woman to the height of whose genius very few of her sex could attain'.[80]

Corelli's defensive moralist stance is an integral part of her own construction of her femininity; like Caine, she believed that she was re-interpreting God's word through the form of the novel for a modern, increasingly secular audience which nonetheless had pure and healthy instincts. Unlike Caine, she believed there was a transfigured role for women to play in this new interpretation. The differences in the ways in which she and Caine were reviewed, their insistent differences in the form of their romances with the gendered reflections on morality, race, art and the market which their respective forms embodied, and the different strategies which they each adopted as players in the literary field, paved the way – and in fact demanded – new definitions of these positions by the writers who followed them.

---

[79]   Review of *Free Opinions Freely Expressed*, *Bookman*, Vol. 28, June 1905, p. 104.
[80]   W.T. Stead, 'The Book of the Month: "The Sorrows of Satan – and of Marie Corelli"', *Review of Reviews*, Vol. 12, October 1895, p. 453.

Chapter 5

'Mr Bennett and Mrs Barclay': The Literary Field before the First World War

Authorship and Art

In June 1911 the *Bookman*'s customary six-page opening feature was an exposition of the reputation of Dante Gabriel Rossetti contributed by Ford Madox Hueffer. The fact that Hueffer penned an article about Rossetti is neither surprising nor particularly significant since he was the nephew of William and Lucy Rossetti and the grandson of Ford Madox Brown and spent his early years surrounded by the Pre-Raphaelite Brotherhood (a habitus, we might suggest, tailor-made to produce a future purist). Nor should it surprise us to find, writing articles for a stolid belletristic journal, an author who had already made his name as editor of the *English Review* (which under his aegis published both Lawrence and Hardy as well as H.G. Wells), and was destined to become one of the earliest and most important contributors to the modernist movement. The close relationship that existed between the popular and the literary has been demonstrated many times. What is noteworthy, though, is the shift signalled by Hueffer's article in the perception of what comprises 'artistic reputation' itself. Hueffer agrees up to a point with the nineteenth-century view of Rossetti that he was, whatever else, the epitome of artistic excellence:

> In the popular estimation – in everybody's estimation – Rossetti was just a solar myth, a golden vision, a sort of Holy Grail that the young poets of the seventies pursued, but seldom saw. And I think this romantic vacuum was extraordinarily good for the seventies. It meant that they had the feeling – that everybody had the feeling – that somewhere in the world there was a glorious, a romantic figure, cloistered up and praying for the poetry, the romance, and the finer things of this world.[1]

The notion of a 'pure' artist existing in a 'romantic vacuum' and acting as the custodian of poetry, romance and the 'finer things' is a familiar one. It was this on which both Caine and Watts-Dunton had depended. But the truth, Hueffer goes on to explain now in 1911, was probably rather different. He agrees that there are two possible views of Rossetti, the common view through which 'for most of us he is the gentleman who dug his poems out of his wife's coffin',[2] and the critical view through whose purer gaze all that mattered was the work: 'none of the energetic gentlemen

---

[1] Ford Madox Hueffer, 'Dante Gabriel Rossetti', *Bookman*, Vol. 33, June 1911, p. 113.
[2] Hueffer, p. 119.

who boomed this poet-artist tried to do it by means of sarcophagic details. They did their work decently, talking only of the glorious sonority of the polysyllabic lines, of the romance, of the tenderness, of the splendour, of the morbidness, of the high moral purpose, of the mystic inner meaning'.[3] It is tempting to see these two viewpoints as being represented by Caine and Watts-Dunton, the one fatally interested in the grim details of Rossetti's life, the other just as studiously avoiding them. And here, perhaps, Hueffer clings to the old binary opposition between the common reader or popular author and the objective gentleman critic.

What has changed, though, now in the early twentieth century is the open acknowledgement that even 'pure' artists need – and get – the help of critics, and that this too is a form of booming: 'Rossetti's poems were boomed – just as my own works have been boomed, and just as the work of every writer of any position or merit must be boomed if he is to continue to live by his pen'.[4] No longer the easy separation between the 'artist' who writes for love and the greater good of art and the 'boomster' who does so for profit, what we are seeing here is an example of the increasing professionalisation of writing, an acceptance that financial rewards are a desirable and even necessary end of artistic endeavour. This professionalisation had been happening slowly throughout the 1880s and 1890s with the formation of the Society of Authors and changes in the laws governing intellectual property.[5] As Simon Eliot has suggested: 'the whole concept of the "man of letters", not as an inspired genius nor as a picturesque bohemian, but as a workaday professional, on a par in training, status and (with a bit of luck) income with a lawyer or a doctor, was the creation of this hopeful period'.[6] The change had come about relatively slowly and not without considerable opposition from the purists. But it was becoming more acceptable to expect suitable financial rewards for one's literary labours. Gissing's Grub Street was beginning to look outdated; by the death of Edward VII in May 1910 we see, if not exactly the end of the Victorian debate about art and the market, then at least the emergence of new forms of both.

Some of these forms were profoundly regressive, like the attempt of several authors in 1910, led by Edmund Gosse, to form a new body called the Academic Committee which, they claimed, would 'represent pure literature in the same way that the Royal Academy represents the Fine Arts, the Royal Society Science, and the British Academy learning'[7] but which refused to admit women. At a time of the rapid acceleration of militant female suffrage this seems like the last gasp of Victorian patriarchy and it

---

3   Hueffer, p. 114.

4   Hueffer, p. 113.

5   Peter Keating provides an extremely detailed chapter on this process in *The Haunted Study: A Social History of the Novel 1875–1914* (London, 1989), pp. 9–87.

6   Simon Eliot, 'Some Patterns and Trends in British Publishing 1800–1919', *Occasional Papers of the Bibliographical Society*, Vol. 8 (London, 1994) p. 14.

7   Samuel Hynes, *Edwardian Occasions: Essays on English Writing in the Early Twentieth Century* (London, 1972), pp. 194–5.

embroiled Gosse in fierce debates with Mrs Humphry Ward, Arnold Bennett and H.G. Wells, all of whom denounced its outmoded sexism, its stubborn adherence to an old model of 'real' literature as a masculine preserve. Gosse lost. But Victorian patriarchy was neither dead nor even close to being driven over the border. Some of the popular writing which women themselves produced in the 1910s was itself undergoing a kind of reactionary backlash.

Ann Ardis has suggested that 'early twentieth-century popular romance novelists were continuing the work of the *fin-de-siècle* New Woman writers – writing about sexuality, reworking the romance plot, and renegotiating women's access to the public sphere'. This was so, she suggests, because early twentieth-century women's suffrage campaigners had tended to banish female sexuality from their agendas in order 'to secure the respectability of "the cause"'.[8] Ardis is speaking largely of writers such as E.M. Hull (whose biggest success was *The Sheik*, 1919), but many of the pre-First World War popular romances, those by Elinor Glyn and Ethel M. Dell, for example, also revolved around sexuality. There was, however, a concurrent attraction by popular novelists and their readers in the pre-war period to a desexualised depiction of gender. This crucial aspect of the pre-war popular has often been overlooked. But it demonstrates the heterogeneity of popular representations of nationality and gender in this period, and this needs to be addressed more fully.

This 'purer' brand of the popular openly disavowed both the destabilising work of political emancipation performed by *fin-de-siècle* feminist narratives, and the spiritual liberation of the heroines of Corelli. Faced with what numerous critics have identified as some kind of crisis precipitated by the down turn of Britain's global and domestic economies and the apparent explosion of calls for equality by women, the Irish and the working classes,[9] as the first decade of the twentieth century drew to a close many of Britain's popular writers produced – and its readers overwhelmingly bought – books which recast Victorianism as a simpler age if not a golden one. The popular novel once more 'worlding' in the (often sexually) untamed spaces of Africa was one part of this backlash. John Buchan's *Prester John* (1910), with its central heroic white male pitched against a black villain and an overpowering feminised African landscape, looks back to Rider Haggard far more than it prefigures Richard Hannay. But a return to or stringent rewriting of Victorian moral codes was another. It will be remembered from Chapter One that it was in 1909 that the circulating libraries made a public announcement regarding their collective refusal to stock 'objectionable' books, and this must be seen as symptomatic of a highly anxious age. Moral purity

---

8   Ann Ardis, 'E.M. Hull, Mass Market Romance and the New Woman Novel in the Early Twentieth Century', *Women's Writing*, 3 (1996), p. 289.

9   Samuel Hynes, Thomas Harrison and Eric Hobsbawm are just three of the many historians who see the Edwardian period as 'sombre', characterised by 'a feeling of nostalgia for what has gone, and apprehension for what is to come'. Samuel Hynes, *The Edwardian Turn of Mind: The First World War and English Culture* (Princeton, New Jersey, 1969), p. 2.

crusades and organisations such as the National Council for Public Morals abounded, often (as ever) clustering around the period's art forms, both relatively old ones like fiction, and new ones like the cinema.

It would be simplistic to put this backlash down to the pressures of social and political upheaval alone. The hard facts of history are only part of what produces the literary work, its meanings and its cultural value. Here we might do well to heed Jonathan Rose's warning about the dangers of equating popular texts with majority attitudes and anxieties. Of course readers read other things alongside bestsellers – often conflicting things. They read classics, newspapers, magazines and non-fiction books. They got them from libraries and railway and second-hand bookstalls as well as bookshops. They went to the cinema and the music hall and/or the theatre and were bombarded with advertisements. Rose is right to insist on an awareness of the intertextual nature of existence. As I have tried to show throughout this book, readers had a wide choice of cultural material and almost as wide a choice of culturally loaded places from which to get it. But we must, I think, also be cautious about rejecting out of hand the possibility that some texts might speak to, for and about their own cultural moment, if only through fantasy, and that this might be a factor in their success.

Bourdieu provides us with a way of thinking through the relationship between history and literature that avoids both the sociological determinism rejected by Rose and the slightly risky brand of populism implied by his alternative. Bourdieu suggests that the text should not be seen as a product of a single teleology but situated as part of an intersection between the social and the cultural. For Bourdieu:

> To understand the practices of writers and artists, and not least their products, entails understanding that they are the result of the meeting of two histories: the history of the positions they occupy and the history of their dispositions. Although position helps to shape dispositions, the latter, in so far as they are the product of independent conditions, have an existence and efficacy of their own and can help to shape positions.[10]

This meeting of two histories includes the social and political conditions with which producers and consumers are surrounded in that those conditions contribute to a particular habitus. This has a direct bearing on both the kinds of books that a producer writes, and some of the ways in which a reader consumes them. Gissing's Nancy Lord serves as a useful model of the anxious, aspirant petit-bourgeois reader – appealing, perhaps, to real readers who shared Gissing's concerns about mass literacy.

But while it includes the social and political, this model of two histories prevents us from assuming too simple and direct a correlation between historical events and fictional ones, a dialectic that tends to obscure an important part of the cultural 'value' of the work and over-simplify its reception by readers. Without the history of 'dispositions' there could certainly have been no Nancy Lord who, as part of the

---

[10]   Bourdieu, *The Field of Cultural Production: Essays on Art and Literature*, ed. Randal Johnson (Cambridge, 1995), p. 61.

nineteenth century's new female middle classes, was literate, spared the need to work for a living, but socially anxious. But without the history of 'positions' in the cultural field she could never have been represented anxiously selecting Helmholtz over a popular novel in the library. In addition – and perhaps more importantly – alongside her own fictional fears Nancy displays the anxieties of one of the field's most anxious aspirant writers. Gissing's rejection of the popular, his horror at the instincts of the herd, articulates his fears over his own position in the field as much as anything else.

Positions and dispositions, then, when considered together, enable us to consider both literary form and literary reputation, and in turn – when placed within the sorts of social arenas which I explored in the first two chapters of this book – to draw some conclusions about symbolic meaning. It was the histories of both positions and dispositions with which I was concerned in the last chapter as I mapped out some of the forces at work in the literary field of the 1890s, and it is these two histories with which I will be concerned here. I want to explore how the dispositional influences at work on the positions 'popular male' and 'popular female author' as they existed by the end of the 1890s may have contributed to their altered symbolic value for the next generation of authors in the 1910s. I am seeking here, not to replace previous accounts of Edwardian middle-class fiction which concentrate on the concrete events of history, but to add to them an understanding of the place of this fiction in the literary field, which operates at least in part as a result of autonomous forces without direct reference to social history. In this way, I hope, we can find a more nuanced and less prejudiced relationship between popular and literary fiction that considers formal 'breaks with the past' (such as are often attributed to movements like modernism) the way they ought to be considered – not as unprecedented acts of genius, but as part of a much wider pattern governed by a range of forces within a field. As Bourdieu explains:

> Having established, in spite of the illusion of the constancy of the thing designated, which is encouraged by the constancy of the words artist, writer, bohemian, academy, etc., what each of the positions is at each moment, one still has to understand how those who occupy them have been formed and, more precisely, the shaping of the dispositions which help to lead them to these positions and to define their way of operating within them and staying within them.[11]

What Bourdieu does not reflect on in this early work is the different positions available to authors due to the effect on their *dispositions* of their gender. For example, in listing Mallarmé, Proust, Joyce and Woolf as prime examples of artists who have taken advantage of a 'historical heritage accumulated through collective labour against external constraints'[12] (who had, in other words, the requisite dispositions in terms of class, income and education to be able to emulate previous rebels in performing acts of artistic 'daring'), Bourdieu does not differentiate them. But far more than a

---

[11] Bourdieu, *The Field*, pp. 63–4.
[12] Ibid.

Proust, a Joyce or a Mallarmé, Woolf needed an independent income and a room of her own in order to safeguard her position in the field – and needed to write about those needs – precisely because both had always been more readily available to men than to women even of her own class. As Bourdieu later acknowledges in *Masculine Domination*, Woolf's gender contributed hugely to the kind of writer she became.[13] Polemical as well as experimental, essayist as well as novelist, she drew on both her dispositional possibilities and on the history of positions – the gendering of literary form – at least as far back as George Eliot. And it was against the authors of the 1900s and 1910s – both male and female – that she needed to define and maintain the position she claimed.

Ford Madox Hueffer's article on Rossetti signals one of the ways in which the position of 'writer' had come to operate by the first decade of the twentieth century. Professional, confident and openly earning a good living, the 'writer' had in many ways a more secure position now than ever before. But this position raises some questions. Where, in this new climate of commercialism, was 'art'? Even in Hueffer's pragmatic piece of journalism written for a middlebrow review that had never had a problem with the business end of books there is a touch of nostalgia for the good old days of the 1870s when 'everybody had the feeling that somewhere in the world there was a glorious, a romantic figure' – the artist. And in this climate of sexual frankness in both literary and popular writing, in a field which seemed to be attempting to close the symbolic if not qualitative gap between them, what was happening to the critical gendering of the popular woman author, and to the forms of novels themselves?

'Infuriating the Ungodly': The Popular Fiction of Florence Barclay

By the time Florence Barclay published her first novel *The Rosary* in 1909, Marie Corelli's heyday was practically over. As late as 1902 booksellers in 18 out of 23 areas surveyed nationwide confirmed *Temporal Power* as one of their biggest sellers.[14] In 1908 *Holy Orders* sold 112,450 copies and earned its author £7,505 10s.[15] But although her novels remained in print and continued to be circulated through second-hand bookstalls for some years to come, she wrote only three more major novels in her life, and of these only *The Life Everlasting* (1911) returns to the mystical themes of her earlier works. Devoting her time to articles and to fund-raising for Shakespeare's birthplace, where she lived, Corelli seems to have recognised that public tastes were

---

[13]   Pierre Bourdieu, *Masculine Domination* (Cambridge, 2001), pp. 69–78.

[14]   *Bookman*, Vol. 23, December 1902, p. 86. The demographics are interesting. *Temporal Power*, with its curious melding of socialism and the monarchy, is a top seller in East London, Manchester, Leeds, Croydon, Rugby, Ipswich, Stockport, Leamington, Wigan, Edinburgh, Aberdeen, Inverness and Dumfries. It doesn't rate as a seller at all in West London, Birmingham, Nottingham, Southampton, Torquay or Ventnor.

[15]   Teresa Ransom, *Marie Corelli: Queen of Victorian Bestsellers* (Stroud, 1999), p. 160.

changing and by 1911, as David Trotter notes, the literary agent J.B. Pinker privately felt that middle-class readers were getting 'beyond her'.[16]

On one level this is easily explained through social history. The anti-modern spiritualism and pseudo-scientific theology that she had perfected in the 1880s and 1890s seemed anachronistic in the age of the cinema and the motorcar. But on another level this rapid dating of her work must be placed within the shifting fields of the gendered literary forms around her. Corelli's heroines were rooted in a romantic revival that placed women at the centre of the global political stage. Their sexual energies were channeled, not always into motherhood, but into re-balancing the universe, or righting wrongs. In this respect Corelli wrote and rewrote herself. Hers was a single-woman-alone-but-for God philosophy, her novels the spaces in which she and her heroines could be both irreproachable as women and fully active as citizens. In that sense she is truly the contemporary of the suffragettes who '"banished the beast" of sexuality ... from their feminist agendas', as Ardis puts it.[17] Corelli affected to despise suffragettes, but she partly shared their mission.

Barclay is frequently described in contemporary journals as Corelli's natural successor. This is certainly true inasmuch as Barclay assumed Corelli's position in the field as the Queen of Bestsellers, and perhaps predictably they met and liked each other after the publication of *The Rosary* in 1909.[18] Predictably enough too, given their chronological closeness, they both made vast amounts of money out of romances which posited a firmly Christian view of the world. But their similarities are probably less important than their differences, which signal an important shift in the position 'popular female author'. While acknowledging the commonly accepted line of succession, Joseph MacAleer has situated Barclay as a bridging figure: 'Florence Barclay is an important case, an example of a popular author who bridged our two periods [that is, before and after the First World War], combining qualities of both ... she was in fact a much more transitional figure in popular fiction'[19]. This is so, he goes on to explain, because she first published before the war when the author still reigned supreme, but she was powered by an impressive publicity machine which heralded the dawn of the age of the publisher, the genre and the imprint. Mills and Boon commenced publishing in this period, albeit at first as a general publisher. Religious publishing survived only by diversifying into rigorously researched markets. But the idea of Barclay as either more transitional than other writers, or as Corelli's successor, is problematic for other equally important reasons.

The Rosary was something of a surprise hit. It was published – quite unusually for a first novel from an unknown author – simultaneously in Britain and America, for the simple reason that Barclay had sent the manuscript first to her sister in the United

---

16   David Trotter, *The English Novel in History 1895–1920* (London, 1993), p. 182.
17   Ardis, 'E.M. Hull', p. 289.
18   Ransome, p. 186.
19   Joseph MacAleer, *Popular Reading and Publishing in Britain 1914–1950* (Oxford, 1992), pp. 38–9.

States, and the sister sent it to Putnam and Sons of New York on Barclay's behalf. The plot is simple to the point of being facile. The Honourable Jane Champion is a 12-stone, plain, independently wealthy woman with an eccentric aunt, an admiring but married doctor friend, and a gift for gathering pretty young boys into her coterie. These bright young things spend their time in a halcyon pre-war round of parties, tennis and musical evenings while Jane amuses herself pairing them off and beating them all at golf. The hero, portrait artist Garth Dalmain (nicknamed 'Dal'), is one of the most beautiful and talented of her 'boys'. For Garth, love is a momentary obsession with a woman as object. The moment he has 'had' her (on canvas) his 'love' dies and he moves on. In one of many bantering conversations he tells Jane that he lives for beauty and could never marry anyone plain. Shortly thereafter he hears Jane sing for the first time – a soul-stirring rendition of 'The Rosary' – falls in love with her 'inner woman' and asks her to marry him. Noble Jane refuses after an honest hour spent alone in front of her mirror. Garth disappears, Jane tries to get over him by travelling the world, and while in Egypt she hears that he has been blinded in a shooting accident. Wanting to be with him but kept silent by her own pride and her respect for his, Jane secretly becomes his nurse under the name Rosemary, making herself so selflessly indispensable to him that the revelation of her real identity at the end performs the miracle of persuading him she has changed her mind through love, not pity. They get married, Garth turns from painting to music, and the latent mother in Jane is given free rein at last.

The book is described by Barclay's biographer (one of her daughters) as having received 'glowing reviews ... in every department of the Press'.[20] This is not, however, strictly true. *The Publishers' Circular* certainly thought it 'a charming novel', commenting that although 'the plot of this powerful and fascinating work is very slight ... of the heroine we can only say that for a plain woman we do not remember any heroine of fiction more attractive in a great many ways. Garth too is excellent and worthy the love of the Honourable Jane'.[21] But the *Bookman* reviewed the novel unenthusiastically, treating is as a light read of 'staccato emotion' and summarising the plot with wry tones: 'But alas! A woman's memory is sometimes a very, very long thing, and a heroine's ways are not to be set down and easily justifiable in cold print by a reviewer ... only when blindness has overtaken Garth can Mrs. Barclay bring herself to permit Jane to swallow the recollections of those cruel, cruel words and to take the cold plunge into the unplumbed depth of matrimony between the "woman" of thirty and the "boy" of twenty seven'.[22]

Hardly a glowing review. But although the book sold slowly at first, word of mouth worked its customary magic: by the end of its first year it had sold 150,000 copies and

---

[20] *The Life of Florence Barclay, by One of Her Daughters* (London and New York, 1921), p. 212. All subsequent references are to this edition and appear parenthetically in the text.

[21] *Publishers' Circular*, 25 December 1909, p. 916.

[22] *Bookman*, Vol. 37, February 1910, p. 239.

it went on selling well for almost a quarter of a century. Two editions a month were being printed at the height of its fame. 'The purple book was to be seen everywhere', Barclay's daughter gushes, 'in railway compartment, hotel lounge, and under the arms of busy people hurrying along the streets, while "F.B." was, as it were, the name of an old friend in thousands of English-speaking homes' (p. 213). It is necessary to view the author's enthusiasm with a certain amount of caution. The biography reads like the life of a saint, and in at least one of her pronouncements Barclay's daughter is inaccurate, as we have seen. Still, even in its hyperbole and allowing for the fact that this is the testimony of an obviously devoted daughter, the 'Life' provides some useful ways of thinking about Barclay's book. There is, for example, as I noted in my Introduction, a curious echo in the above quote of the words used to describe the 1881 publication of the revised New Testament. The new Bible, too, was seen 'in every omnibus, in every railway compartment, and even while walking along the public thoroughfare'.[23] In both cases the capacity to reach and unify a large, heterogeneous mass of readers in all the spaces of the modern world is presented as the greatest heights to which a text can aspire. If further proof were needed of the shift from organised religion to the spiritual in novels that occurred during this crucial period, then this is probably it.

But the comparison serves another purpose. In both cases the book in question is being hailed as a publishing phenomenon, but if in 1881 the New Revised Version had stirred up fears about the dangerous misinterpretation of God's word which mass literacy might enable, by 1909 *The Rosary* was being used as proof of the reverse. According to Barclay's daughter the audience for the novel was unified by its message of unquestioning faith: 'The busy men and women who form the majority of the reading public, and who read fiction by way of relaxation and enjoyment … ask merely to be pleased, rested, interested, amused, inspired to a more living faith in the beauty of human affection and the goodness of God. My mother was the friend of these ordinary readers – she was out to supply them with what they wanted' (pp. 241–2). Like Corelli, Barclay apparently believed in the herd's healthy instincts. Unlike Corelli, and as part of the early twentieth-century backlash against decadence, suffragism and the excesses of the *fin-de-siècle* and beyond, she believed that a rigid High Anglican framework was the best way of gratifying that need.

A glance at the popular novels round it helps us to understand why. *The Rosary* was preceded by the sexually risqué bestsellers of authors such as Robert Hichens (*The Garden of Allah*, 1904) and Elinor Glyn (*Three Weeks*, 1907), and followed by equally scandalous novels such as Ethel M. Dell's *The Way of an Eagle* (1912) and, most scandalous of all, E.M. Hull's *The Sheik* (1919), all of which engendered a barrage of criticism because they sold sexuality (even if they punished it in the end).[24] As David

---

23   Sutcliffe, p. 51.

24   It is worth noting that Caine's *The Prodigal Son* (1904) was, chronologically speaking, a product of this period, but properly belongs to the 1890s. It was only with *The Woman Thou Gavest Me* (1913) that he began to take real risks with infidelity narratives.

Trotter notes, now 'absolute sex sold more books than divinity, though few things could beat a skillful combination of the two'.[25] It is easy to see how a novel like *Three Weeks* could fall into the 'absolute sex' category, though it also, as Trotter further notes, turns sex into an 'absolute value' by presenting it as regenerative.[26] Paul Verdayne, the hero of *Three Weeks*, is 'just a splendid English young animal of the best class'.[27] He is meant to marry a pink-mouthed parson's daughter, Iabella Waring, who is 'quite six foot, and broad in proportion' (p. 10). She is also a product of the blurring between genders that was apparently a side effect of suffragism, modernity, the growth of the middle classes, and the spread of liberal education that encouraged women to behave like men. 'They were dressed almost alike, and at a little distance, but for the lady's scanty petticoat, it would have been difficult to distinguish her sex' (p. 10). Not his, oddly enough. In this novel English masculinity is latent and lazy rather than threatened, though there is a vague sense that women who dress like men and are beginning to look like them are stealing from the nation's fount of manhood, to its ultimate detriment.

Paul's rescue from mediocre marriage to androgyny comes in the shape of a trip to Lucerne during which he becomes obsessed by a Slavonic beauty. 'The Lady' irritates as well as obsesses him at first because she is so un-English. She has heavy waves of dark hair, sufficient to 'strangle' a man, quite unlike the blond fluffy locks he is used to. Her mouth is not 'large and pink and laughingly open like Isabella's, but straight and chiselled and red, red, red' (p. 17). The Lady, despite being a Queen (as we later discover) represents raw female sexuality. Her red lips are not painted but real. Her figure is 'so supple in its lines, it made him think of a snake' (p. 47). The Lady has phallic power; it is she who instigates their sexual relationship and she who ends it. Despite Glyn's self-defensive preface to the second edition (when the book was due to be released in the US) contending that the Lady is 'immensely cultivated, polished, blasée' (p. v), the primitive nature of her sexuality is summed up by the famous tigerskin rug seduction scene. As though to enhance the experience, Paul has already torn the silk lining from the rug, knowing that his Lady will prefer the feel of the raw skin. Indeed, as the euphemisms pour forth during this scene it's hard to know who, out of the Lady-Paul-tigerskin threesome, is making love to whom.

Three weeks later, though, Paul is banished, receiving only an annual letter from the Lady's old manservant to tell him first that she has borne him a son, and then that she has been murdered by her jealous husband. 'And so, as ever, the woman paid the price' (p. 302). Paul's son grows to rule in her stead and Paul is left manlier, more mature and more English than before. As Trotter suggests, he not only extends the Empire with his offspring, but he has also used its primitive energy to revitalise his English manhood.[28]

---

[25] Trotter, p. 182.
[26] Trotter, p. 182.
[27] Elinor Glyn, *Three Weeks*, 2nd edn (London, 1907), p. 13. All subsequent references are to this edition and appear parenthetically in the text.
[28] Trotter, p. 182.

Rejecting the sensuous worlds of novels like this, *The Rosary* returns the heroine to England, to the sound of well-bred banter over the clink of teacups. Nobody gets raped or kidnapped. Nobody is in danger of being murdered. Nobody seeks revenge on anybody else. But gone too are the opportunities for either the hero or the heroine to take part in political struggles, to commune with unfamiliar cultures of whatever realm, or to embody any sort of social crusade. Jane Champion is comfortably, completely, complacently English. *The Rosary* deals purely with heterosexual love under God's law, never stepping outside that prescription for happiness, or straying beyond the boundaries of its own neatly constructed sunshine-and-strawberries universe. While Jane does venture overseas on the advice of Dicky, her doctor friend, it is merely to climb pyramids and sit on verandas with other English people abroad, and when she returns home it is with a surge of patriotic delight that she sees English shores again:

> The white cliffs of Dover ... a strong white wall, emblem of the undeniable purity of England, the stainless honour and integrity of her throne, her church, her parliament, her courts of justice, and her dealings at home and abroad, whether with friend or foe. 'Strength and whiteness', thought Jane as she paced the steamer's deck.[29]

This smug English patriotism revolving around 'strength and whiteness' sums up the novel's hermetically sealed world. In the last years of the Empire under 'Edward the Peacemaker', Englishness in popular fiction frequently assumed this position, even as it posited a notion of national decay. Most often it is foreign encounters that regenerate: Paul Verdayne requires his Slavonic Lady to teach him how to be a red-blooded Englishman. Threats come more commonly from outside than from inside the country whose structural integrity was thought to be collapsing, thus displacing the anxiety: when licentious Boers threaten the heroine of Richard Dehan's 1910 bestseller *The Dop Doctor*, for example, she is saved by the alcoholic English doctor who has been abroad too long but is dried out and reAnglicised by her love just in time. Anarchists might ape Englishness but are never the real thing when placed beside genuine Englishness in novels such as Edgar Wallace's *The Four Just Men* (1905) and G.K. Chesterton's, *The Man Who Was Thursday* (1908), and the comparison serves, of course, to cement comfortable notions about identity.

On into the late teens and even after the war's exposure of the dangers of imperialism this trope continued. E.M. Hull's Sheik Ahmed Ben Hassan abducts tomboyish Englishwoman Diana Mayo, raping her 'into a recognition of the difference between men and women' as Trotter puts it.[30] Then, after Diana has fallen in love with him, he turns out to be an Englishman after all. Here we manage both unlicensed sadomasochistic sex with an exotic Other, and racial and moral purification through

---

[29] Florence Barclay, *The Rosary* (London and New York, 1909), p. 138. All subsequent references are to this edition and will appear parenthetically in the text.

[30] Trotter, p. 186.

love, a kind of redemption through social Darwinism. This might be a long step beyond Corelli. But it borrows from her manner of permitting adventures to heroines in the world's political arenas, if it leans more towards the woman-as-sexual-pawn than woman-as-active-citizen philosophy.

Barclay, in spite of her novel's obviously Edwardian racial and national assumptions (and now, significantly, eschewing the public spokesperson role assumed by late-Victorian authors such as Corelli and Caine), does something quite different, not only with Englishness, but also with gender. Jane and her Aunt the Duchess are drawn to college boys, amongst whom the Duchess becomes an honorary eccentric aunt and Jane appears as an honorary male. This is partly due to Jane's physique:

> She walked with the freedom of movement and swing of limb which indicate great strength and a body well under control. Her appearance was extraordinarily unlike that of all the pretty and graceful women grouped beneath the cedar tree. And yet it was in no sense masculine – or, to use a more appropriate word, mannish; for everything strong is masculine, but a woman who apes the appearance of strength which she does not possess, is mannish – rather was it so truly feminine that she could afford to adopt a severe simplicity of attire, which suited admirably the decided plainness of her features, and the almost massive proportions of her figure. (p. 17)

But it is also due to her golfing prowess: 'she drives like a rifle shot, and when she lofts, you'd think the ball was a swallow', Garth tells a friend admiringly (p. 11). And it owes a lot to her common sense. Garth calls her 'old chap' and expects her to take a 'sane and masculine view' of marriage (p. 37). When she is helped by the native bearer Schehati to climb the pyramids he calls her 'Nice gentleman-lady ... Real lady-gentleman' (p. 127). 'Had Jane overheard the remark it would not have offended her', the narrator tells us:

> for, though she held a masculine woman only one degree less in abhorrence than an effeminate man, she would have taken Schehati's compound noun as a tribute to the fact that she was well-groomed and independent, knowing her own mind, and, when she started out to go to a place, reaching it in the shortest possible time, without fidget, fuss, or flurry. These three feminine attributes were held in scorn by Jane, who knew herself to be so deeply womanly that she could afford in minor ways to be frankly unfeminine. (p. 130)

'Mannishness' and 'femininity' are apparently something of a problem, denoting superficiality, while 'masculinity' and 'womanliness' denote pure, admirable nature. Barclay posits a direct link between the Latinate male adjective and acceptable maleness, and the Anglo-Saxon female adjective and acceptable femaleness. There is an important class dimension to this linguistic pattern and it makes David Trotter's description of Jane as 'part Jane Eyre, part champion golfer'[31] somewhat misleading.

---

31   Trotter, p. 183.

Despite the obvious plot similarities – blind hero rescues fleeing orphan heroine from lifelong loneliness by appealing to her nurturing instincts – poor, plain Jane Eyre's position as dependent female relative is very different from rich, plain Jane Champion's independent, aristocratic social role. Sixty years of social change separate the two Janes. The 'champion golfer' idea is rather more important, however, and it provides a clue to the complexity of Jane Champion's social position in the 1900s.

Eric Hobsbawm has noted that the rise in women's sports after the 1870s – including the institution of the women's singles title at Wimbledon only six years after the men's – was of enormous importance:

> Though women's fashions did not dramatically express emancipation until after the First World War ... the escape of middle-class women from the twilit or lamp-lit cocoon of the bourgeois interior into the open air is significant, for it also implied, at least on certain occasions, escape from the movement inhibiting confinement of clothes and corsets ... sport ... made it possible for young men and women to meet as partners outside the confines of household and kinship.[32]

Jane's sensible attire and 'freedom of movement' are a direct result of this relaxation of the conventions governing the clothed female body, and her relations with men are equally free of traditional confines such as chaperonage, though they operate within other safety parameters. Hobsbawm also notes that until the 1890s golf had been an exclusively upper-class sport. Thereafter:

> Golf clubs were to play an important role in the (Anglo-Saxon) masculine world of middle-class professional men and businesswomen ... the social potential of this game, played on large, expensively constructed and maintained pieces of real estate by members of clubs designed to exclude socially and financially unacceptable outsiders, struck the new middle classes like a sudden revelation.[33]

Jane is a product, not just of her aristocratic heritage, but also of its appropriation by the middle classes. Her prowess at golf, like her build and attire, signal not just her freedom from Victorian stereotypes of femininity (though not from 'true' femininity – womanliness) but also her position as a confident handler of her own affairs. Socially, physically and emotionally she ranks not only with her friend Dicky the Doctor, but also with – or above – the boys whom she beats at golf. She is well able to participate – and succeed – in the middle-class masculine world of straight talking and keen competition.

Indeed, despite being independently wealthy she is also a professional of sorts: she was a trained nurse during the Boer War and is described as 'the real thing, mind you ... Miss Champion was in command there, and I can tell you she made them scoot.

---

[32] Eric Hobsbawm, *The Age of Empire: 1875–1914* (London, 1995), p. 205.
[33] Hobsbawm, pp. 182–3.

She did the work of ten, and expected others to do it too' (p. 222). She is capable of looking after herself as well as others, crucial talents in an age anxious about the very real decline in the number of domestic servants.[34] She is interested in politics (even though the novel does not permit her to participate), and she does not mind being alone. Though she is famous for reading on trains, it is because she desires to immerse herself in world affairs rather than because she requires either protection or escape: when traveling she reads the *Spectator*, not *Tit-Bits* or *Woman* or a popular novel, absorbing herself in things like 'the South African problem' (pp. 71–2). All this makes her a thoroughly modern woman, quite unlike Corelli's old-fashioned, anti-modern heroines, however much spiritual freedom they were allowed. It should be noted, too, that she owes a lot to the reworked depictions of femininity for which the New Woman novelists were famous, embracing their hard-won freedom from weakness, incompetence and restrictive clothing. But she is not uncomplicatedly modern, nor is Barclay free from the obsession with social degeneration which haunts the work of her fellow bestsellers. This is why her linguistic definition of the ideal man from the ideal woman is so important.

For Barclay, a middle or upper class man can clearly be artistic, sensitive, vain, Latinate, sartorially obsessed, and even childlike without being effeminate. '"Really, Dal"', Jane's Aunt the Duchess remarks to Dalmain, '"it is positively wicked for any man, off the stage, to look as picturesque as you do, in that pale violet shirt, and dark violet tie, and those white flannels. If I were your grandmother I should send you in to take them off. If you turn the heads of old dowagers such as I am, what chance have all these chickens?"' (p. 19). Jane is not oblivious to Garth's beauty either. But like her Aunt she admires it from the safety of her plainness and her maturity: 'As is often the case with plain people, great physical beauty appealed to her strongly … of the absolute perfection of his outward appearance, there was no question, and Jane looked at him now, much as his own mother might have looked, with honest admiration in her kind eyes' (p. 35). Just as clearly, for Barclay a middle- or upper-class woman can be strong, willful, plain, independent, sporty and – as in the above example – quite capable of objectifying male beauty and mixing freely with the opposite sex without being either 'mannish' or 'fast', though this only seems to be completely acceptable once she's over 30 (Jane's age).

Class and age, then, together serve to contain the slipperiness of gender and the dangers of desire in a post-Wilde, post-New Woman world. In this novel the strongest men are boy-children and the strongest women are masculinised mothers, and both are – ideally – firmly upper or middle class if not aristocratic. When Garth declares his love to Jane 'the mother in her awoke and realized how much of the maternal flows into the love of a true woman when she understands how largely the child-nature predominates in the man in love' (p. 106). This is complicated further by the description of a man in love as not just a child but also 'forceful, determined, ruling man – creation's king. The echo of the primeval forests. The roar of the lion is in them,

---

[34]   Hobsbawm, p. 180.

the fierceness of the tiger; the instinct of dominant possession' (p. 104). Here, despite its apparent role-reversal in the meeting of huge, strong, plain, sensible womanhood with slight, beautiful, creative, petulant masculinity, gender is something firm and innate and ordained by God. It cannot be unmade no matter how unstable its modern earthly referents might become. Love, as in Corelli's novels, apes the human's relation to God in that it recognises the need for a hierarchy in any pairing, whether spiritual or bodily. Being 'in love' makes God's pattern transparent, like magic ink in fire. The devout Englishwoman's job here is to recognise the gentle, caring but Anglo-Saxon and therefore pre-civilised quality of her own nature (which makes her subordinate) while simultaneously recognising the powerful, pure yet supremely civilised (that is, intellectual) qualities of the manhood which requires her guiding maternal hand. No surprises there. This is in many ways a nineteenth-century model of the biological determinism of gender which pretends to give women power by telling them how much their masters depend on them.

But there are crucial differences. If the romances of the 1880s and 1890s were driven by openness to new interpretations of God's word that prove its applicability in a modern world, *The Rosary* indicates that this is no longer necessary. Now we have a version of faith that has subsumed and naturalised new interpretations: 'The Rosary' is a modern song, and American to boot.[35] In the face of a flood of bestsellers about sex, Barclay renamed it 'love' and tamed it Corelli-style by marrying it to religious faith. In the face of the radical instability of that faith, as well as of gender and national identity, she embraced change by containing it within a fantasy of a stable, earthly, English upper middle class. Jane Champion is in many ways an answer and antidote to the rejected, mannish Isabelle Waring of *Three Weeks*. *The Rosary* is a call to plain, hefty parsons' daughters nationwide to hold up their heads again, and to emasculated Englishmen to look no further for a wife than the vicarage tea-party.

But it is insufficient simply to note Barclay's similarities to and differences from either Corelli or her own contemporaries. Remembering Bourdieu's insistence on the consideration of positions as well as dispositions, we need to examine *The Rosary's* success in terms of the subtle gendering of popularity and the not-so-subtle gendering of female-authored popularity within or against which it defined itself. In the previous chapter I suggested that the nineteenth-century classification of popular female-authored novels such as Corelli's as doubly feminised, and therefore both morally impure and unacceptable as real art, necessitated a new kind of female authorship. In order to rid themselves of their dismissal by critics (and by large numbers of conservative potential readers) who saw them as merely seductive, women writers must, I suggested, either demonstrate that they knew their place and were beyond

---

35 Written in 1898 by Ethelbert Nevin, the song is described as 'a highly successful adaptation of lush sentimentality to a religious mood', words which could just as easily apply to the novel. Sigmund Spaeth, *A History of Popular Music in America* (New York, 1948), p. 296.

reproach, or else (if they wanted to write serious novels) fight to be free of both place and popularity. In the first decades of the twentieth century this is exactly what began to happen. While Elinor Glyn, Ethel M. Dell and E.M. Hull went on writing books that, like Corelli's, got banned and condemned and therefore advertised by default, Florence Barclay wrote a book that knew its place and said so.

Barclay's 'feminine' popular novels purified the position 'popular woman writer' of its Corelli-like qualities of seduction (and any overly masculine tendency towards literariness) as much as they purified fictional English femininity of foreign contaminants. Barclay's own list of ideals and methods for novel-writing, reproduced not only in her daughter's biography but also in many interviews with the author herself, lay claim to exactly this object:

> Never to write a line which could introduce the taint of sin, or the shadow of shame, into any home. Never to draw a character which should tend to lower the ideals of those who, by means of my pen, make intimate acquaintance with a man or a woman of my own creating. There is enough sin in the world without an author's powers of imagination being used in order to add even fictitious sin to the amount. Too many bad, mean, morbid characters already alas! walk this earth. Why should writers add to their number and risk introducing them into beautiful homes where such people in actual life would never, for one moment, be tolerated? (p. 240)

Barclay here simultaneously sums up the longest-standing fears about mass literacy, and offers her work as its antidote. Her daughter, having repeated this claim, adds to it in a long validatory list. Barclay's work, she claims, purified the popular in all the dangerous modern spaces of its dissemination. As I demonstrated in Chapter 2, it apparently appealed to the businessman on a train and encouraged him to read – and take home – a better type of book instead of immersing himself in the 'history of some vile character and his viler doings as he travels up to business in the train' (pp. 243–4). But this was not all. Her books also, it seems, stopped the trashy fiction rot amongst public book borrowers as people 'read them to pieces in the libraries' (p. 218). They addressed urban alienation by making a reader forget 'the dull or sad world of his own life, the disappointing people of his acquaintance' (pp. 214–5). They saved honest booksellers from bankruptcy in the cruel contemporary world of rampant capitalism (p. 218). They unified society in their appeal 'to individuals of every type, from the royalty she revered to the working people she loved' (p. 219). They encouraged decadent Europeans to cultivate better instincts: '[The French translation of the novel] pleased my mother, for it showed that the French public does not necessarily want the kind of thing usually associated with the idea of a French novel' (p. 264). Her books even poured balm on the body and soul torn apart by modernity's most extreme expression, the First World War: 'How the wounded Tommies loved her books! One day she went into a hut at the Netley Red Cross Hospital, and she saw a man screened off because his wounds were so severe. He was reading *The Following of the Star*. [Barclay, 1915] She asked him gently if he liked it. "Yes", he said, "it makes me forget my pain"' (p. 219).

Barclay's daughter's posthumous biography is not only a result of filial devotion. It is also part of the well-oiled publicity machine that went into action once *The Rosary*'s winning combination of romance, religion and a stable England became a surprise hit. It is no accident that *The Life* was published by Putnams, Barclay's own publisher. Barclay became immersed in a round of tours of booksellers, book-signings, press interviews and trips to the US throughout which she peddled her vicar's wife (and daughter) philosophy. Photographs show either a solid Victorian matron covered from neck to toe in dark modest clothes and sitting upright in a chair reading fan mail or the Bible, or taming wild birds St Francis-style in her sunny vicarage garden.[36] The trades had realised by the time her second book came out that here was a winning formula and they had better be nice to it: the *Bookman* had completely reversed its opinion of her work by the time it reviewed *The Mistress of Shenstone* in 1911: 'From a quiet, rather conventional beginning, this story advances to an emotional, even thrilling succession of incidents … As the story nears its end things happen quickly, and the authoress rises to genuine strength and pathos'.[37]

All these publicity-driven claims signal one thing. Barclay was not, as her daughter spells out for us, interested in 'art'. She wrote for 'the people' not because, like Corelli, she thought them capable of recognising her as 'art' no matter how the critics howled, but because she was claiming for popularity a new kind of purity in the Bourdieuan sense, as well as claiming that her books purified popularity in the moral sense. This was a recent shift, the carving out of a markedly new position in the literary field. No longer did the art/market divide invented and institutionalised by the purists act in a unilateral manner to glorify literature and vilify bestsellers. Now apparently the herd were fighting back, claiming for themselves an exclusive kind of knowledge – the knowledge to demand, get and appreciate their own kind of literature, for their own kind of identity and world view. These people, Barclay's daughter claims, 'do not desire to have productions of literary "art" supplied to them, that their critical faculties may be exercised and their minds educated to a precise valuation of dramatic form, of powerful realism, high tragedy' (pp. 241–2). According to this justification her readers were of a new sort. They were those who had grown into their own literacy and were getting tired of being told how to use it. In this model the popular is the truest form of mass expression for it understands majority desires (contrary to what Jonathan Rose might prefer). In a neat reversal of values, it is the 'literary connoisseur' who is a poser, becoming a sham, a 'seeker after mere artistic effect' (pp. 241–2) which includes, of course, the depiction of sex.

While Barclay shares Corelli's belief in the sound instincts of the herd, then, she does not pretend to be an artist when she speaks for it. Hers is a tamer brand of creational femininity, a domesticated, devout and less ambitious brand that nurtures simpler tastes the way a mother nurtures her brood or a vicar his flock, presumably

---

[36] Such a photograph accompanied the review of *The Rosary* in the *Publishers' Circular*, 25 December 1909, p. 196, as well as littering the pages of the biography.
[37] *Bookman*, Vol. 39, February 1911, p. 250.

appeasing those consciences that were troubled by the exploits of more sexualised heroines. She balanced old-fashioned Englishness and a slightly updated version of femininity that managed to move with the times while somehow simultaneously seeming traditional. It was an inspired mixture that hit exactly the right tone. Barclay followed *The Rosary* with hit after hit, initially telling the stories of spin-off characters and then branching out fractionally to tell the equally tame, saccharine but unarguably page-turning stories of new Janes and Garths, equally English, equally middle class, the books all equally free of the taint of sex or any pretensions to be literary.

Unsurprisingly, in addition to her novels she also contributed seamlessly to the tide of nationalistic sentiment that enveloped the country during the first years of the First World War, lending her name to the war effort and writing stirring sentimental tracts such as *In Hoc Vince: The Story of a Red Cross Flag* (1915), in which a gallant officer stumbles upon a beleaguered flagless hospital surrounded by German troops who are firing on it, not knowing its function. The officer creates a flag out of old sheets and soldiers' blood and saves the day before being killed in action himself. Published (as usual) by Putnam's, the story (ostensibly a true one) was a commission, forming part of King Albert's Book which offered an outpouring of national sympathy and support to the King of the Belgians.[38]

Barclay's championing of the tastes of the popular audience was a relatively new move by an author in the field, calculated to establish a counter-current to the increasingly unstable poles of 'popularity' and 'literariness' which were being drawn uneasily together by their consensus over the treatment of sex. It placed her at the forefront of a strong current of popular expression which was hard to ignore, and which created a new and long-lasting critical backlash. When John Galsworthy told Q.D. Leavis that he admired Barclay as 'the Shakespeare of the Servants' Hall' he was not just acknowledging the servants' right to a literature of their own. That would have been bad enough. It was the fact that he permitted the popular some sort of qualitative value that prompted Leavis to remark that this was merely 'the fascinated envy of an ever-intellectual novelist for the lower organism that exudes vital energy as richly as a manure heap'.[39] She goes on to make an important comparison between Corelli, Barclay and Charlotte Bronte:

> Bad writing, false sentiment, sheer silliness, and a preposterous narrative are all carried along by the magnificent vitality of the author, as they are in *Jane Eyre*. Charlotte Bronte, one cannot but feel after comparing her early work with modern bestsellers, was only unlike them in being fortunate in her circumstances, which gave her a cultured background, and in the age in which she lived, which did not get between her and her spontaneities.[40]

---

38   Florence Barclay, *In Hoc Vince: The Story of a Red Cross Flag* (London, 1915).
39   Q.D. Leavis, *Fiction and the Reading Public* (1932; London, 1965), pp. 62–3.
40   Leavis, pp. 62–3.

Here the only difference between what we would now designate a 'classic' work and a long-forgotten bestseller is the disposition – the class background (informed by history) – of its author. For Leavis, ultimately, the work of authors such as Barclay is irritating simply because it is written for the lower classes. It clogs up half-educated minds with rubbish, giving the average reader no 'exhilarating shock' but merely 'the relief of meeting the expected'.[41] These books are a result of the dumbing down effects of mass literacy, and all that can be said for them is that they are clean rubbish: 'But the moral passion, though it may be a nuisance, is at least a respectable one', she concludes tiredly. 'At worst it could be accused of promoting the complacent virtue that infuriates the ungodly'.[42]

This, of course, was precisely Barclay's mission. Using the advantages of her dispositions as a mother and a wife (as well as a daughter) of the clergy, Barclay was instrumental in the forging of a new position in the field – the popular as harmless, clean escapism that doesn't pretend to be anything else. Other, more 'serious' authors around her naturally reflected this sea change.

'Like a Machine': Bennett and the Popular as Art

On one level Arnold Bennett must be thought of as arising out of the same historical moment as Caine and Corelli. He was 14 years Caine's junior but active as an editor, critic and journalist throughout the 1890s. His first novel *A Man From the North* was published in 1898, while Caine and Corelli were still at the height of their fame. *A Man From the North* is also tied formally to the work of Caine; as N.N. Feltes notes, it exhibits the same sort of compromise as Caine's first novel *A Son of Hagar*, published eleven years previously, in its 'commitment to both realism and romance'.[43] For Feltes, the novel 'at the very moment that it anticipates the modernist novel, is determined by the ideological struggles of the eighties and nineties [Bennett was] the bearer of historically determinate ideologies, like ... any writer'.[44]

Feltes's concern is to place writers like Bennett within a Marxist analysis of nineteenth-century publishing. But he hints above at the importance of Bennett as a transitional figure. This is certainly Woolf's summation of the contribution of authors such as Bennett to the history of the novel:

> I think that after the creative activity of the Victorian age it was quite necessary, not only for literature but for life, that someone should write the books that Mr Wells, Mr Bennett, and Mr Galsworthy have written. Yet what odd books they are! Sometimes

---

41 Leavis, p. 74.
42 Leavis, p. 66.
43 N.N. Feltes, *Literary Capital and the Late Victorian Novel* (Madison, WN, 1993), p. 134.
44 Feltes, p. 138.

> I wonder if we are right to call them books at all. For they leave one with so strange a feeling of incompleteness and dissatisfaction. In order to complete them it seems necessary to do something – to join a society or, more desperately, to write a cheque. That done, the restlessness is laid, the book is finished; it can be put back on the shelf and need never be read again.[45]

In some respects Woolf's opinion is understandable. As a writer deeply engaged with the political iniquities of the present, she did not want to have her conscience pricked by realistic details of bodily privation and social decay suffered back in the nineteenth century. For her, famously, 'on or about December 1910 human character' had 'changed'. 'All human relations have shifted', she wrote in 'Character in Fiction' in 1924, 'those between masters and servants, husbands and wives, parents and children. And when human relations change there is at the same time a change in religion, politics, conduct, literature'.[46] For Woolf, traditional nineteenth-century literary forms as espoused by Bennett, Galsworthy and Wells were inadequate to deal with this change. They were superficial, masculinist, outmoded. They objectified women and ignored the psychological and spiritual life. Like Forster's Schlegel sisters, for whom Leonard Bast was one who has 'failed to reach the life of the spirit', Woolf saw in these writers an infuriating obsession with the low, the material and bodily. 'If we tried to formulate our meaning in one word', she further explained in 'Modern Fiction', 'we should say that those three writers are materialists. It is because they are concerned not with the spirit but with the body that they have disappointed us, and left us with the feeling that the sooner English fiction turns its back on them, as politely as may be, and marches, if only into the desert, the better for its soul'.[47] The horrors of the First World War, a direct result of nineteenth-century thinking, had created an urgent need for a break with the destructive past.

But the reactionary side of early-twentieth-century literary purism – its politics, its tendency to abhor the tastes of a homogenous 'mass' actually comprised of the working- and lower-middle-classes, with all their diversity – also plays a part in the relationship between Bennett and Woolf, and it would be reductive to ignore this element. Bennett spoke to, for and about these very people. McDonald describes him as another 'provincial on the make', but admits that as a critic he 'spent much of his time giving practical advice to the Leonard Basts of Edwardian England', and that his novels were preoccupied 'with the disregarded, marginalized or despised, be they women, servants, provincials or suburbanites'.[48] Compare this to Woolf's preoccupations, with new representations of women, certainly, but only if these were the 'daughters of gentlemen', and her dismissal of Bennett takes on a new character,

---

45   Woolf, 'Character in Fiction' (1924), *The Essays of Virginia Woolf III: 1919–24*, ed. Andrew McNeillie (London, 1988), p. 427.
46   Woolf, 'Character in Fiction', pp. 421–2.
47   Woolf, 'Modern Fiction', p. 159.
48   McDonald, pp. 98–9.

one which engages overtly with the clash of authorial authority created by their very different dispositions. Even Woolf's comment about Bennett's novels making her want to do something desperate like 'write a cheque' is a wilful misreading of what Bennett himself described as his artistic mission in *The Author's Craft* (1914). There, he wrote that observation is 'a moral act' which stimulates charity. Not, though, 'the charity which signs cheques, but the more precious charity which puts itself to the trouble of understanding'.[49]

Woolf had a good reason for refusing to take part in any attempt to understand either her social inferiors, or her literary forebears. John Carey pulls no punches and calls this 'snobbery'.[50] I prefer to see it as the typical response of a newcomer in the field trying to establish her own position. Either way, the condemnation and the critical weight that it has carried ever since have tended to write out of literary history one of its most important figures. Bennett's literary practice certainly tends to look backwards rather than forwards. But most of his novels, and particularly the Clayhanger trilogy with which Woolf chose to take particular issue, demonstrate an acute interest in and awareness of the forces of history – at once productive and destructive – working on the present, and an active commitment to reflecting that fact in their narrative forms. Bennett's position in the field carries more importance than as a sort of disposable bridge across which 'Victorian creativity' and high modernism might meet to pass the literary baton, a view taken by both Feltes and by Woolf herself. All authors, as part of a shifting dynamic field, are transitional figures. What makes Bennett important is the strength and innovation of his own position-taking.

When Bennett's play *What the Public Wants* was published in book form in 1910 the *Bookman*'s reviewer greeted it as significant due to the seriousness of its subject matter:

> Yesterday the very superior critics settled it for us that the problem novel, the novel with a purpose, was necessarily inartistic; yet today those same critics are giving their highest praises to problem plays and plays with a purpose, and assuring us that the men who write them are the true artists among modern dramatists ... our own belief [is] that, other things being equal, the drama or the tale that teaches something and has a purpose behind it is superior to the book or the drama that does not and has not.[51]

The tired old war between 'realism' and 'romance' for the prize of serious artistry has not, by this account, changed much since the 1880s when Caine and Corelli were fighting to be recognised as artists. Here the claim is for Bennett's play to be thought of as artistic because it has a social conscience true to the spirit if not the letter of

---

[49] Arnold Bennett, *The Author's Craft* (London, 1914), pp. 17–18.
[50] John Carey, *The Intellectuals and the Masses: Pride and Prejudice among the Literary Intelligentsia, 1880–1939* (London and Boston, 1992), p. 178.
[51] A. St John Adcock, review of 'What the Public Wants', *Bookman*, Vol. 38, June 1910, p. 132.

realism. But in fact, as the Hueffer article in the *Bookman* indicates, the terrain was changing – and had already changed – quite dramatically. As early as 1901 Quiller-Couch was situating Bennett as an unusual figure, a writer who could both appeal to the masses and maintain his critical integrity: 'Mr. Bennett writes temperately. He has no mercy for the foolish belief (invented by certain popular novelists in self-defense) that the uneducated person for the moment known as The Man in the Street can teach the critic his business: but, though one of the artistic minority, he does not run about shouting Philistine'.[52] Bennett does not, according to Quiller-Couch, display the usual anxiety that attended the serious writer's position in the 1880s and 1890s. The 'certain popular novelists' mentioned here refers more specifically elsewhere in the review to Hall Caine, for whom the herd had instincts as healthy as – or healthier than – the critic. But it could equally include Marie Corelli, for whom also the public were 'healthy-minded and honest' enough to vouch for her artistry. Bennett apparently did not subscribe to the 'let the people decide' philosophy. But neither did he share the insecurity felt by a Watts-Dunton, in despair at his inability to save Rossetti from the Philistines. For Bennett, at the dawn of the twentieth century, the professional critic and writer had a secure, comfortable position that enabled him to judge and write for the 'knowledgeable' as well as for the 'masses', and to be equally happy doing either.

For Peter McDonald, it is precisely Bennett's adaptability which finally ensured his status as loser in the field. A competent serious novelist, he also wrote hugely successful fictional serials, and for McDonald we cannot separate these: it is only through reclaiming the serials which Bennett himself 'would happily have suppressed' that we are able, as historians and readers, to 'recover the dialectical energies of the major novels'.[53] In some ways this is true. Bennett had certainly adopted the chameleon-like qualities of the modern writer early on in his career, switching not only into and out of the voice of the public but also switching gender as the occasion demanded, and we cannot ignore this part of his professional life without misunderstanding his position in the literary field. Writing as 'Barbara' for *Woman*, for example, he reviewed Caine's *The Manxman* enthusiastically in 1894, admitting that 'I have been saying to myself that Mr. Hall Caine was an over-rated man', but that he thought *The Manxman* 'perfect'. Not, though, because he thought it art, but because he thought it perfectly suited to its audience. '*The Manxman*, for grandeur of perception, for breadth of treatment, for tear-compelling simple pathos, and for unforced humour of the true northern pawkiness, is unsurpassed in modern fiction'.[54] Without patronising his audience he manages to give his opinion that the book is 'perfect' for them. It has to be said that the selection of a female pseudonym signaled not only an increasing awareness of the power of women as consumers but also the common labeling of their needs as popular and herd-like rather than discerning. Still, whether under a male or female

---

[52]   Arthur Quiller-Couch, Review of Bennett's *Fame and Fiction*, *Bookman*, Vol. 21, October 1901, p. 22.
[53]   McDonald, p.117.
[54]   Arnold Bennett, writing as 'Barbara', 'Book Chat', *Woman*, 22 August 1894, p. 8.

pseudonym or writing as himself, Bennett successfully made the switch between the popular and the artistic with a notable (and, as it turned out, symbolically fatal) lack of self-consciousness.

He was not afraid to criticise the critics, seldom pandering to the educated consensus. Reviewing Wells's *Tono-Bungay* for the New Age in 1909, Bennett wrote of the book's art in terms of its ability to shock the complacent amongst the self-styled intelligentsia:

> I was ... in Frank Richardson's Bayswater. 'Wells?' exclaimed a smart, positive little woman – one of those creatures that have settled every question once and for all beyond re-opening, 'Wells? No! I draw the line at Wells. He stirs up the dregs. I don't mind the froth, but dregs I – will – not – have!' And silence reigned as we stared at the reputation of Wells lying dead on the carpet [On reading *Tono-Bungay*] I was filled with a holy joy because Wells had stirred up the dregs again, and more violently than ever. I rapturously reflected, 'How angry this will make them!'[55]

If Bennett here figures the smart knowledgeable set in gendered terms, using a common refrain to put down the speaker when he refers to her as a 'creature' and a 'little woman', he also figures it in class terms. Here, those who will be made angry by Wells are the smart Bayswater set who discuss literature, as well as the women who traditionally comprise its moral police. For Bennett 'the public' or 'the purists' were less of a problem than the educated middle classes who still felt that literature of whatever sort should be beholden to their own narrow sense of morality, while insisting on their right to judge it.

This was a position that infuriated Bennett throughout his career. While he too was one of the educated middle classes he consistently fought for artistic freedom. 'The backbone of the novel-reading public is excessively difficult to please', he wrote 'It quite honestly asks to be "taken out of itself", unaware that to be taken out of itself is the last thing it really desires. What it wants is to be confirmed in itself'.[56] This confirmation, though, Bennett was also quite capable of providing, not only in his popular journalism (such as his editorship of and reviews in *Woman* in the 1890s) but also in those of his novels written explicitly for that public such as *Grand Babylon Hotel* (1902) or *The Card* (1911). He was quite capable of mocking middle-class conservatism within popular novels themselves:

> Gladstone [who made Mrs Humphry Ward's reputation] had no sense of humour, at any rate when he ventured into literature. Nor has Mrs Humphry Ward. If she had she would not concoct those excruciating heroines of hers. She probably does not know that her heroines are capable of rousing temperaments such as my own to ecstasies of

---

55 Arnold Bennett, *Books and Persons: Being Comments on a Past Epoch 1908–1911* (London, 1917), p. 104.
56 Bennett, *Books and Persons*, p. 97.

> homicidal fury ... Oh, those men with strong chins and irreproachable wristbands! Oh, those cultured conversations! Oh, those pure English maids! That skittishness! That impulsiveness! That noxious winsomeness![57]

But he was also quite capable of defending popular novelists in print, even as he elsewhere maligned them. Corelli was a case in point. She may have been his yardstick for the lower end of the market, but he did at least understand that she served a purpose and should not be judged more harshly than other novelists of her type:

> I do not object to Mrs. Humphry Ward being reviewed with splendid prominence. I am quite willing to concede that a new book by her constitutes the matter of a piece of news, since it undoubtedly interests a large number of respectable and correct persons. A novel by Marie Corelli, however, constitutes the matter of a greater piece of news; yet I have seen no review of 'Holy Orders', even in a corner, of the *Guardian* ... If the answer be that Mrs. Humphry Ward's novels are better, as literature, than Miss Corelli's, I submit that the answer is insufficient, and lacking in Manchester sincerity.[58]

For Bennett, then, as for his contemporary Galsworthy when he replied to Q.D. Leavis, the popular was not 'art' but it did have its place. Bennett had a tolerance for differences in taste; his intolerance was reserved for those who either claimed artistic merit for the merely crowd pleasing or tried to shackle art to their own narrow worldview.

Bennett's struggle for the high positions of either 'pure' critic or 'pure' artist was therefore somewhat more complicated than the struggles of his forebears in the 1880s. He leaned heavily on the position as it had been defined in that period. His criticism, like Watts-Dunton's, appeared in the 'qualities', and he wrote extensively on such subjects as 'Literary Taste and How to Form it' (1911), an assumption of critical authority that seems to have worked. Rose's recent research has unearthed evidence of at least one working-class autodidact who built up a library almost exclusively by following Bennett's advice.[59] He was also instrumental in introducing the works of Chekhov and Dostoevsky to a general audience. But Bennett's journalism and his popular writing meant that he occupied a very different position from the kind of 'pure' gaze represented by Watts-Dunton who was introducing the cheap, male-dominated classics series in this same period. Unlike Watts-Dunton, Bennett wrote for money and said so.

For many this was not a problem. Not everyone thought of Bennett as a kind of Jasper Milvain figure, a vulgar, self-made man with a yacht and a mistress who, as Feltes puts it, had 'studied every detail of salesmanship'.[60] In the first decade of the

---

[57]   Bennett, *Books and Persons*, pp. 51–2.

[58]   Bennett, *Books and Persons*, p. 49.

[59]   Jonathan Rose, *The Intellectual Life of the British Working Classes* (New Haven and London, 2001), p. 191.

[60]   Feltes, p. 131.

twentieth century he was described with respect by many reviewers who saw him as the consummate professional author: 'There are men who must write in their own way and cannot make any sacrifice to popular taste if they are to retain their consciences', wrote F.G. Bettany in a 1911 appreciation of the author:

> There are others who adopt the course of providing the public with 'what the public wants', only to discover eventually that their capacity for achieving any nobler aim has somehow disappeared. There lies the danger of being too indulgent to the moods of 'the great beast'; doing the second best may impair the faculty for doing the best – the material may react on the artist. Mr. Bennett in his time has written plenty of 'popular' fiction, but he could always switch off his muse, at will, to the service of serious art … How has he contrived to keep the two sides of his fiction so long in tandem? Partly, I conceive, through his exceptional will power. The most methodic of writers, he has trained himself, when at his desk, to act like a machine.[61]

This image has real resonance when we remember how negatively machine-imagery was used a mere half-century previously. Now, it seems 'to act like a machine' is not to disseminate indiscriminately but to *control* the insidious psychological effects of popular literature. Professionalisation had arrived. Bennett himself cemented the image of a peaceful co-existence between modernity, literature and the masses in his 1908 series 'The Human Machine', written for *T.P.'s Weekly*, in which he doled out advice to the clerking classes.

Even in his appreciation Bettany does not encourage the reader to imagine that everything Bennett wrote was art. Some of it was merely 'journalistic … It is good journalism, of course, for Mr. Bennett is never less than thorough in anything he attacks, but it may be left out of account in any consideration of him as a serious artist. His claim to be in the front rank of our younger novelists depends on a relatively small group of books'.[62] But the *Bookman* was as happy to review his popular works such as *Grand Babylon Hotel* (1902) as it was to review the handful of more serious works such as *Clayhanger* (1910), and it did so in a manner that indicates a complete understanding of their differences in style and the different audiences for which they were intended. The former, for example, is described as 'a lively, rattling story … uncommonly readable throughout'[63] and the latter as 'an excellent and enduring work of fiction'.[64]

Bennett was not, of course, unusual in the breadth of his professional experience in this period. Wells and Galsworthy, like many other authors, were critics of some sort as well as novelists and/or dramatists. But despite Woolf's bracketing together of the names Wells, Galsworthy and Bennett under the term 'Edwardians' in 'Character in

---

[61] F.G. Bettany, 'Arnold Bennett: An Appreciation', *Bookman*, Vol. 39, March 1911, pp. 265–6.
[62] Bettany, p. 265.
[63] *Bookman*, Vol. 21, February 1902, p. 176.
[64] *Bookman*, Vol. 39, October 1910, p. 46.

Fiction' (1924), neither of the first two had quite the same prominence in the market as Bennett – or rather, they had prominence of a different type. The Oxford-educated Galsworthy, for example, Leavis's 'ever intellectual novelist', had always tended to be thought of in these terms rather than as a journalist or critic – his plays and novels had real impact on social reform, and in 1932 he received the Nobel Prize for literature. Wells was closer to Bennett in background and literary range, but he had a far more anxious relationship with the market. For example, he vehemently denied using agents, whom Bennett openly endorsed as necessary for the professional author. Wells even took out an advert in the *Author* that ran for a full year, from June 1913 to June 1914. This advert declared that: 'Mr. H.G. Wells does not employ an agent for his General Literary Business. Agents to whom he has entrusted specific transactions will be able to produce his authorisation. He will be obliged if Publishers and Editors will communicate directly with him in any doubtful case'. But, as Matthew Skelton has shown, Wells used as many as five agents during this period of his career, sometimes several at a time, apparently recognising that his work fell into several different categories as he attempted to move from sci-fi romances towards more experimental serious fiction, and that he needed expert help in placing it.[65] Convinced that he was writing new forms of fiction, he nonetheless gained a reputation for demanding high advances and energetic advertising for the work. Indeed, Skelton argues convincingly that Wells finally placed *Tono-Bungay*, one of his more experimental and controversial pieces, with Hueffer's *English Review* (in a year in which the journal also published Hardy, James, Lewis and Lawrence) not because he particularly shared its ethos with regard to the new and artistic, but because he – and his agent – had been unable to place it with a higher-paying publisher.[66]

The public disavowal of the privately vigorous pursuit of money had been a common strategy for assaulting the field's top positions for some years, as I demonstrated in the last chapter. Like Bennett, Wells was as much a part of the ideology of the 1890s as Caine and Corelli. An important distinction separates the two authors, however. Unlike Wells, Bennett did not apologise for or attempt to hide his profit-driven activities. He took as active a part in the debates about censorship as any of his contemporaries, but he was also convinced of the need for the full professionalisation of authorship, and that meant a dropping of the pretense about the purity and autonomy of 'art'.

Bennett's serious fiction occupies a unique and valuable position in the field as a result. However, despite McDonald's persuasive insistence that the serials symbolically informed the serious novels in that Bennett's championing of the professional author undermined his position as a literary novelist, his understanding of the field indicates that he deliberately set out to differentiate the two areas of his work, not only through

---

[65]   Matthew Skelton, 'Re-presenting H.G. Wells: The Literary Agency of London and Tono-Bungay', unpublished paper, SHARP conference, London, 10 July 2002. The quotation from Wells' advert above comes from this paper.

[66]   Skelton, 'Re-presenting H.G. Wells'.

his choice of subject matter and publisher (as exhaustively analysed by McDonald) but also through his choice of literary form. Bennett's attraction to 'realism' must be placed in the context of its position as a serious, 'masculine' art form in relation to the seductive or sanitised 'femininity' of the popular with which he was by this time extremely familiar, not only through his popular fiction, but also through his journalism and his editorship of *Woman*. He was, after all, one of the few critics who recognised that Post-Impressionism heralded a new age not just in art, but also in literature, and that realism was set to become outmoded.[67] Yet he did not abandon it entirely (although, as I will show, he innovatively modified many of its elements). His main concern during the first decades of the twentieth century was, in fact, not to be in the vanguard of literary revolution, but to be taken seriously as a novelist on terms which the literary field as it then existed would immediately recognise.

McDonald does go some way towards exploring this relationship. '[Bennett's] novels were not simply a social critique directed at purist intellectuals', he quite rightly argues, 'they were a literary challenge to the canonical English authors and, as importantly, to the popular serialists and their readers'. This, he goes on to suggest, 'is where the value of Bennett's own serials lies', in that they show us what the 'well-informed writer understood to be the preferences of the syndicates, newspapers and magazines; and, by extension, of what the editors perceived to be the tastes of the new mass readership'.[68] This is certainly valuable. But, fascinating as McDonald's analysis of Bennett's serials is, it does not actually help us in understanding the symbolic position occupied by the 'serious' novels, which in themselves provide us with a rich vein of material if we are interested in the roots of feminist modernism. It should be remembered that it was the form of his serious novels, not his serials, with which Woolf chose to take issue. If we are to approach an understanding of why and how that particular purist challenge worked, we need to accept that there was a crucial symbolic difference between these two major forms of Bennett's writing, and that it works at the dispositional levels of gender and class as well as the positional level of compromised artistic purity.

Bennett's literary project – the use of elements of realism to explore a despised class and to create a new kind of hero and heroine out of ordinary people – is visible in his earliest serious novels, though here the realism is of a purer and more recognisably nineteenth century form in that it comments upon, but does not attempt to analyse, its characters' social conditions. In these novels Bennett's interest is in the material effects of change, and the contrarily stultifying effects of social habit. In *A Man from the North* the hero, Richard Larch, is forced to settle for suburban mediocrity, conscious of dissatisfaction and disillusionment, but unable to break out of his sphere. In *The Old Wives' Tale*, Constance and Sophia Baines feel that their sphere is the centre of the whole world, and while Sophia escapes from the Five Towns to Paris, she is drawn inexorably back, and all her adventures come to in the end is the realisation that her former lover, Gerald Scales, 'had once been young, and that he had grown

---

67 Carey, p. 157.
68 McDonald, p. 107.

old, and was now dead'.[69] Bennett's mission here is to map time's changes through the generations, to indicate that time is the only enemy, the only victor, and the only certainty. One of the most important things he took from Naturalism was a conviction that every individual is worthy of notice, if only as a biological curiosity, and in these novels he indicates where the heart of his writing lies. Characters such as Samuel Povey demonstrate 'to the observant, the vein of greatness which runs through every soul without exception' (p. 215). But he is also under no illusions about literature's (and realism's) limitations: for him the most acute of observers can never penetrate the surface: 'No-one but Constance could realize all that Constance had been through, and all that her life had been to her' (p. 517).

In his next literary project, however, Bennett did something new. 'With "Clayhanger" Mr. Bennett takes a decided step forward', Lewis Melville wrote in 1910. 'It is far more ambitious than any novel he has published; and with it he carries on the tradition of the novelists who had the grand manner'. Melville likens Bennett not only to Trollope and Mrs Oliphant but also to Thackeray, a comparison that serves to raise the novel from the ranks of the mid-century bestsellers and place it amongst the classics. He also differentiates the novel from popular fiction in terms of its purpose:

> It is as if Mr. Bennett, like a certain other author, has determined to write a novel without a hero; only he has put in the hero's place a young man singularly unheroic and has made his study of this commonplace person so enthralling that probably the great British public will let him pass for a hero, which is as well, for while the public knows what it wants, it does not know what is good for it.[70]

The positing of *Clayhanger*'s social realism as a kind of intellectual tonic serves to separate it decisively from the popular crowd-pleaser. Other reviewers, while less enamoured of *Clayhanger*'s style, also wrote of it as a serious work. William Morton Payne in the Chicago *Dial* thought the novel's 700 pages were 'touched with such genius that we find them interesting against our will'.[71] The *Atlantic Monthly* stated: 'you have no sense of reading a book, only a half-painful, half-pleasant feeling of sharing human experience, difficult in a thousand homely ways'.[72] The British reviews were more mixed. The *Times Literary Supplement* felt that the novel's events were 'trivial' but acknowledged that they were capable of inducing a 'hypnotic trance' in the reader,[73] while the *Star* claimed that 'there are few novels that take you so

---

[69]   Arnold Bennet, *The Old Wives' Tale* (London, 1944), p. 485. All subsequent references are to this edition and appear parenthetically in the text.

[70]   Lewis Melville, review of *Clayhanger*, *Bookman*, Vol. 39, October 1910, p. 45.

[71]   William Morton Payne, *Dial*, November 1910. *Arnold Bennet: The Critical Heritage*, ed. James Hepburn (London, 1981), pp. 260–61.

[72]   *Atlantic Monthly*, May 1911. *Arnold Bennett: The Critical Heritage*, p. 245.

[73]   *Times Literary Supplement*, 15 September 1910. *Arnold Bennett: The Critical Heritage*, pp. 244–5.

absolutely into the inner consciousness of a human being'.[74] Intriguingly, however, the highbrow *Athenaeum* refused to consider the work as art except in the mind of its author, suggesting (somewhat in advance of Woolf) that realism was by this time unwieldy and outmoded as a form:

> Mr. Bennett revels in the commonplaces of life. Perhaps he would prefer to call himself sociological. His novel may claim to be that rather than psychological, for it is concerned rather with the play of a small number of commonplace characters on one another than with any complex *vie intime*. The psychology of Edwin Clayhanger is excellently rendered but it could, we think, have been suggested, by a master of art, in a quarter of the space.[75]

Since it had long possessed a reputation for publishing work at the cutting edge of literature and its critics were amongst the purest purists in the field,[76] the *Athenaeum*'s response to *Clayhanger* is significant. It suggests that while *Clayhanger* was thought of as 'art' by its author and by a significant number of middlebrow and trade journals, it was already being put in its place by the field's real symbolic capitalists. Jonathan Rose's recent work suggests, however, that most readers were conscious of Bennett's work as exemplifying a different position, and that their sense of Bennett as 'art' lasted some time. He cites the memoir of a second-hand bookseller who remembers that neither Huxley nor Bennett could sell in Camberwell in 1931, 'while Marie Corelli and Mrs. Henry Wood were among his strongest sellers as late as 1948'.[77] We could, of course, take this to mean that Huxley and Bennett had gone out of fashion, rather than that readers in a South London working-class district considered them too arty. But Rose doesn't seem to think so. He goes on to place Bennett as the ceiling even for the literate working class autodidact with a long history of interest in classic literature: 'There was not a trace of interest in modernist fiction at the Cymon and Duffryn Library [in the period 1927 to the early 1950s]. For these readers, the art of the novel culminated with Bennett, Galsworthy and Wells'.[78] He also demonstrates that in 1918, amongst working-class readers in Sheffield who were divided into three groups, Intellectuals (eight men, 14 women), Respectables (nine men, 12 women) and Underclass (seven men, six women), only three men and two women from the highest category – the 'Intellectuals' – recognised Bennett's name.[79]

---

[74]   James Douglas, *Star*, 17 September 1910. *Arnold Bennett: the Critical Heritage*, p. 247.
[75]   *Athenaeum*, 15 October 1910. *Arnold Bennett: The Critical Heritage*, p. 257.
[76]   Unsurprisingly, after the First World War it would go on to publish Aldous Huxley, T.S. Eliot and Katherine Mansfield, amongst others. Significantly, too, it was the *Athenaeum* that first published Woolf's first attack on Bennett, the essay 'Mr. Bennett and Mrs. Brown', on 1 December 1923.
[77]   Rose, p. 139.
[78]   Rose, p. 247.
[79]   Rose, p. 194.

Bennett, then, occupied a position in the field quite different from the position 'popular author' occupied by either Caine or Corelli. He was only inartistic or merely popular to the absolute elite. To the middlebrow and the serious autodidact his work was 'art'. To the less aspirational working classes he was out of their league altogether, one of the 'seekers after artistic effect' whom Barclay's daughter denounced as unable to speak for the herd with which her mother sympathised. The reasons for this position are, perhaps, obvious. Bennett had largely returned to nineteenth-century models for his 'art', a regressive step unlikely to impress the real purists. He did so, as we have seen, because for him realism represented a necessary disavowal of the popular romance form that he was elsewhere utilising. Realism was the straightest and clearest route to 'art'. He was not unaware of the direction being taken by the new generation of writers (unlike Caine, who loathed *Ulysses*) – indeed, as a critic he was enthusiastically engaged with it, admiring Joyce and Woolf and carrying on a friendly correspondence with Conrad for some years. But there are dispositional influences at work too, and these make it less likely that he could easily follow a Conradian model, despite their friendship.

The middle-class son of a brusque, self-educated Northern shopkeeper, Bennett defied his father's wishes when he abandoned law in favour of journalism. He had no independent income. His living was his pen. In his need for money he was certainly akin to the perpetually penniless Conrad. But he also had a vestige of the peculiarly English class insecurity denoted by his father's rise from the ranks in the socially anxious 1860s and 1870s. He was largely self-educated and, like Gissing's Nancy Lord, not yet in command of that 'audacious' relation to culture that characterises the true bourgeois. The portrayal of Edwin Clayhanger's determination to read all the classics and constant failure to stick to the resolve is indicative of Bennett's profound understanding of the nature of this insecurity.

I have chosen to concentrate on the Clayhanger trilogy for several reasons. First, because it was the second in this trilogy, *Hilda Lessways*, which Woolf chose to lampoon in 'Mr Bennett and Mrs Brown', the earliest form of the 'Character in Fiction' essay. Second, because it started life in 1910, the year in which Woolf thought human character had changed in ways which she later accused Bennett of missing completely, and was completed during the First World War, an event which has rightly been described as changing British literature – as well as British culture – forever. Third, because I believe it marks important departures from Bennett's previous serious novels, and holds some of the keys to Woolf's antagonism. I want to ask several questions here. Does this important set of novels miss the point? Does it ignore catastrophic social change? What is its relationship to realism, and to modernism?

The first volume, *Clayhanger*, follows the life of Edwin Clayhanger from boyhood through to his relationship with the New Woman Hilda. The second, *Hilda Lessways* (1911) is roughly the same story narrated from Hilda's point of view. The third, *These Twain* (1916), tracks them both after their marriage. The first volume's plot – typically of Bennett – revolves around the tension between patrilineal power and modernity's effects on class, gender and generation, and in fact the subject matter is, in essence, very similar to that of his first novel *A Man from the North*. Edwin the young hero wants to be an architect, to progress both socially and intellectually, but gets brow beaten into taking over his tyrannical father's printing business and staying put, experiencing a similar kind of social and professional dissatisfaction to Richard Larch. But *Clayhanger* takes important new steps in interrogating this position, steps which focus on and destabilise constructions of gender and form as well as of class.

Darius Clayhanger, Edwin's self-made father, despises the Board School education that he feels has feminised his son: 'To Darius it seemed that Edwin's education was like lying down in an orchard in lovely summer and having ripe fruit dropped into your mouth ... A cocky infant! A girl'.[80] One reviewer at least agreed with Darius. Writing in the *Bookman*, Lewis Melville felt the story's strength was the irascible old man and its emphasis on the girlish Edwin was a touch uncomfortable:

> Edwin is the commonplace incarnate, a weak, indeterminate, emotional, impressionable young man, uninteresting to the majority of his fellows, but never other than fascinating under the microscope of the author. So intimately is Edwin revealed that a sensitive reader may feel a little ashamed at the unveiling; and, thinking of the state of his own soul, shudder at this merciless dissection of another's.[81]

It was Melville who wrote of the novel's realism acting like a tonic on a public that did not know what was good for it. But for him, clearly, the novel's hero, a portrait of the common reader, is something of a problem, part of the weak, emotional, impressionable masses who buy cheap classics and are seduced by adverts. These masses are not men. Like Edwin they are struggling to become men. Darius has a class – and gender – purity of a sort that Edwin and the 'sensitive' reader, who do not understand that social realism is good for them, will never have. It is this liminality, this sense of the permeability of the boundaries of his identity, which makes Edwin so important as a Bennett hero. This is a new position, something which might have been prefigured by Richard Larch, but had never been seriously investigated by his creator until now.

There are obvious dispositional similarities between Bennett and his fictional hero which could make this portrait seem highly personal, even autobiographical. But Edwin is not Bennett. For one thing, the Bennetts were wealthier and more established than the Clayhangers. For another, as Robert Squillace observes: '*Clayhanger* ... is the story of the course his life did not take'.[82] Edwin feels trapped into staying in the Five Towns of the 1880s and 1890s, while Arnold Bennett, living in Paris in 1910, had affected a thorough escape. But those 20 or 30 years and those class divisions are visible as relational forces throughout the book. The curious instability of Edwin's

---

80 Arnold Bennett, *Clayhanger* (1910; London, 1976), p. 77. All subsequent references are to this edition and appear parenthetically in the text.
81 Melville, *Bookman*, Vol. 39, October 1910, p. 46.
82 Robert Squillace, *Modernism, Modernity and Arnold Bennett* (London, 1997), p. 112.

masculinity is, like Bennett's, profoundly modern as well as shaped by the 1870s, 1880s and 1890s. This is not autobiography, but it is very obviously empathy.

In this novel modernity's social effects rescue the characters as well as destabilising them; only his relationship with the 'New Woman' Hilda Lessways and her illegitimate son George prevent Edwin from repeating the pattern of patriarchal brutality laid down by his ancestors. This tension between courageous engagement with modern social forces and fear of losing one's identity is a reflection, perhaps, of Bennett's own tense political and professional position. In 1910 he was an avid Liberal but he lived in luxury in Paris and he found, on coming to Brighton to write *Clayhanger*, that he couldn't finish it there. Britain was in the grip of election fever, and Bennett's journal entries from this period mark both his desire to engage with the political situation and his equally strong desire to escape in order to concentrate on his work. 'I could spit in the face of arrogant and unmerciful Brighton sporting its damned Tory colours', he wrote. But a little later in the same entry he records that he had written 5,000 words in two days and begun to think that the class system as it stood 'would take a lot of demolishing, that I couldn't expect to overset it with a single manifesto, and a single election, or 50. So that even if the elections are lost, or are not won, I don't care'.[83]

The swing to self-interest did not last. Bennett found, in the end, that the effects of the political situation were simply too great and he retreated to Paris to finish the novel there. But the tension between the sense of a particular class identity (with its particular political consciousness) and the drive towards social and professional security is echoed in *Clayhanger*. Edwin feels increasingly confident in his class position and his masculinity as he settles into the printing business and learns to treat his father with superior scorn. The moment he steps outside the office and into the drawing room of a more confident bourgeois neighbour, however, he is at once de-stabilised. Amongst the established middle classes Edwin feels himself to be 'an ignoramus among a company of brilliant experts' (p. 158), and he blushes like a girl (p. 162). Significantly, it is here that he first meets the 'New Woman' Hilda Lessways who so unsettles him that, expecting to drown in the emotional sea of his own insecurity, he finds himself buoyed up instead by the recognition of their mutual liminality. Hilda is dark and sallow-skinned, quite unlike her fair hosts in every sense, and often described by them as 'odd'. When they meet 'Edwin felt the surprised relief of one who had plunged into the sea and discovers himself fairly buoyant on the threatening waves (p. 159). When they kiss for the first time he is changed in an instant from insecure emotional girlishness to manhood, but this manhood has come about through the acknowledgement that Hilda is stronger. 'That night he was a man. She, Hilda, with her independence and her mystery, had inspired him with a full pride of manhood. And he discovered that one of the chief attributes of a man is an immense tenderness' (p. 237).

---

[83] Arnold Bennett, entry for Tuesday, 11 January 1910. *The Journal of Arnold Bennett 1896–1910*, ed. Newman Flower (New York, 1932), p. 360.

This reversal of gender roles – an independent New Woman and a tender New Man, who are each given their own version of the story to tell – is Bennett's prescription for the future, his contribution to New Woman literature and part of his revisioning of fictional art. It was hardly the act of a 'daring' or rebellious position-taker. But like the New Woman novelists – both male and female – who, as Ardis has demonstrated, 'set out to correct the false idealization of women in both nineteenth-century English realism and French Naturalism',[84] to make it, in other words, more 'real', Bennett was making a sincere attempt to create a synthesis between the artistic, masculine solemnity of traditional forms and the demands of a new age.

If this synthesis was making a case for the correction of the idealisation of women, it was also demanding a correction of the vilification of lower-middle-class masculinity. We should not overlook the fact that Bennett himself was the victim of an overbearing Victorian self-made father. He was also a shy Northerner with a stammer and a regional accent trying to make it amongst London's literary elite, and a lone voice protesting that high earnings did not make his writing low art. It may be overstating the case to suggest that Bennett poured his own identity issues into his novel and exorcised them with realism, his own claim to artistry. But we cannot entirely discount this dispositional influence on his fiction's position in the literary field of the 1910s, just as we cannot discount Woolf's gender when we analyse her own position.

While it was as a group that Woolf dismissed the 'Edwardians' it was, after all, Bennett whom she singled out for his obsession with the surfaces of things, and there has to be a good reason for that. Woolf attacked Bennett, not popular novelists such as Barclay, because his works passed for 'art' amongst a dangerously large and growing sector of the population, and because he dared to claim the right to speak for it. And she attacked Bennett in particular, not Galsworthy or Wells, for equally important reasons. This personal attack is disguised as a compliment. 'Bennett is perhaps the worst culprit of the three', she wrote, 'insasmuch as he is by far the best workman. He can make a book so well constructed and solid in its craftsmanship that it is difficult for the most exacting of critics to see through what chink or crevice decay can creep in'.[85] Certainly, in attacking Bennett she was also attacking – had to attack – the male bastion that was 'literature' (and particularly, at this particular moment in time, realist literature). But we might also suggest that this singling out owed as much to the effect of the history of dispositions (Bennett's vulgar petit-bourgeois insistence on writing of a class and a history which the new purists deemed inappropriate subjects for Art) as to the history of the position 'realist literature' (his use of outmoded tools for the expression of modern life). The fact that he had blurred the boundaries between 'art' and 'the popular' by arguing that there was room for both is only part of what attracted Woolf's attention. The truth is that Bennett's finest serious novels came closer than

---

[84] Ann Ardis, *New Women, New Novels: Feminism and Early Modernism* (New Brunswick and London, 1990), p. 37.

[85] Virginia Woolf, 'Modern Fiction', *The Essays of Virginia Woolf, IV*, ed. Andrew McNeillie (London, 1994), p. 158.

those of any other financially successful Edwardian writer to endangering Woolf's literary challenge.

In essence, *Clayhanger* is about the root of those changes between 'masters and servants, husbands and wives, parents and children, religion, conduct, politics', which Woolf says happened in 1910. Bennett's novel deals with them all. It is not centred, though, on the comfortable middle classes like Woolf's and Forster's novels (**centred**, that is, on the stay-at-home wives, the artists, the men who do something in the city). Bennett, typically, focuses on the emergence in the late-nineteenth century of the lower-middle classes on whom these changes had the greatest effect (the tradesmen, once working class, who were dragged or who dragged themselves up, whose children were the first generation in the family to learn reading and writing at school, whose grandchildren would be the first to vote). Bennett's interest is in how history came to create this change in 'human character', and for whom, and how much.

Whether Woolf was right to seize on 1910 as the pivotal year for a change in character is probably immaterial; it was a memorable one on many counts. Edward VII died and there was a constitutional crisis over Lloyd George's 'People's Budget' which effectively brought to an end hereditary power in England. There were, in addition, the re-emerging spectre of Irish Home Rule, the Dreadnought competition with Germany, two elections, and a miner's strike. Bennett started writing *Clayhanger*, as I have noted, in the middle of the first of these elections. And despite his retreat to Paris, the backdrop to the novel is a picture of strikes, elections and the Home Rule question too vivid and integral to the plot to be coincidental. These two histories – that of the 1870s and that of 1910 – converge in *Clayhanger*. The novel is grounded in times of huge and lasting upheaval at the levels of both fiction and fact.

Old his tools might be, but in order to deal with the roots of a modern phenomenon Bennett recast them for a new use. Spurning the minute scientific observation of the older realists and the naturalists, and developing a practice that had emerged only occasionally in *The Old Wives' Tale*, this time Bennett chose a less rigid and sometimes unsettling narrative method that switches between narrated facts and an individual character's assessments of them, and not infrequently fails to provide any parity between the two. This occurs as a stylistic device within each individual novel, producing conflicting meanings and preventing the reader from being comfortably controlled by any notion of narrative point of view or historical truth. But it occurs even more dramatically at the structural level between novels. The narrating of the scenes between Edwin and Hilda in their respective novels is similar enough to be instantly recognisable, but different enough to be a subtle reminder that individuals remember differently, each according to his or her own nature – or social and cultural position.

When Edwin and Hilda first kiss, for example, from his point of view as narrated in *Clayhanger* 'All his past life sank away ... He had felt the virgin answer of her lips on his. She had told him everything, she had yielded up her mystery, in a second of time ... She was so unaffected, so simple, so heroic. He said to himself, with a floodtide of masculinity – "My God! She's mine"'.[86] Hilda's version of the episode in *Hilda Lessways* is, however, quite different. He 'kissed her like a fresh boy, like a schoolboy … she was calm, she was divinely calm'.[87] And far from being virginal and honest at this moment, she has kept from him the secret of her bigamous marriage to George Cannon and she is in fact pregnant. These first two novels make a genuine attempt to separate male and female consciousness. Edwin is ironically central in his own version. But he figures quite differently in Hilda's – she is for some time far more entranced by George than she is by Edwin. George appeals to the physical curiosity which, as a New Woman, she instinctively understands that dreamy Edwin will not satisfy.

If Bennett is blameworthy for figuring Hilda as incapable of self-expression except through her relationships with men, he is redeemed somewhat by the irony with which he treats those men, the honesty with which he depicts the emptiness at the centre of Hilda's life with her husbands. Hilda's version of the story is filled with material facts, not because Bennett did not know how to render female consciousness adequately (though he knew his limitations), but because Hilda's gender and class are structured – as all gender and class is structured – through her historical and cultural locations. The surface details are an ironic nod to realism, not a reproduction of its faults.

In the end, *Clayhanger* is a hybrid form, forcing together the old and the new, progress and stagnation, in a tense disharmony. One could certainly argue that the three-volume novel is an old form, dating back to the 'creativity' of the Victorian age. The novels are not always an easy or a thoroughly satisfying read. But this trilogy is not part of a traditional three-decker which spins out a continuous narrative, but more a kind of secular triptych in which the upheaval of social change has replaced the serenity of divine understanding traditionally achieved through narrative closure. These novels achieve no closure, merely an acknowledgement that the struggle goes on. The first volume ends with massive contradiction as Edwin 'braced himself to the exquisite burden of life' (p. 434). The second ends with Hilda's realisation 'that this that she was living through was life', that it contained 'Grief! Shame! Disillusion! Hardship! Peril! Catstrophe! Exile! Above all, exile!' but also a dawning 'consciousness of power' (p. 327). Edwin's final thought on their marriage at the end of the third volume is: "What a romance she has made of my life!" (p. 430). The words indicate the intimate relationship that exists between life and fiction, the impossibility of ever 'closing' life's mysteries satisfactorily, and the eternal misunderstanding between men and women. For Hilda's thoughts indicate that for her, Edwin's life is not romantic at all – it is utterly prosaic. While Edwin is thinking she is busy romanticising him, in fact what she is doing is noticing 'the whiteness of his shirt-front under his chin, and that reminded her of his mania for arranging his linen according to his own ideas, in his own drawer, and the absurd tidiness of his linen, and she wanted to laugh' (p. 430). In a sense, the three novels themselves disrupt history by refusing to obey the laws

---

86 Arnold Bennett, *Clayhanger* (1910; London, 1976), p. 235.
87 Arnold Bennett, *Hilda Lessways* (1911; London, 1976), p. 317.

of narrative progression. They double back on themselves, constantly reinvestigating and rewriting the past in an effort to understand its impact at the level of individual experience. Without that past, for Bennett there would be no engagement with the future, no possibility of progress for the class most displaced by the 'changes' taking place around 1910.

Bennett's work irritated Woolf, not just because he represented the kind of professional writer whom the purists abhorred and needed to distance themselves from, not just because the taint of the popular serial seeped through into his novels, but because he effectively articulated the concerns of a class which the new purists were trying wholesale to disavow, and because he did it with a deep, sympathetic humanism and with a genuine awareness that the old forms of realism were inadequate. In his serious novels, Bennett's dispositional influences meant that he attempted – and largely managed – to speak the unspeakable. He wrote as one who had been there. But his position as a professional middlebrow who might (frightening thought!) manage to popularise the new and revolutionary meant a necessary disavowal of his methods – and of literary professionalism generally – by the next generation of purists.

We need, though, to be cautious about drawing conclusions that might be in danger of reducing the literary field of the first part of the twentieth century to a simple binary opposition between popular middlebrow writers and highbrow literary purists, perhaps especially those whom we now call modernists. Rose's recent research on working and lower middle-class readers (and those who became writers) is invaluable as a resource. But in following John Carey's lead he makes assumptions about the relationship between high and middlebrow fiction and its readers, writers and critics that leaps a little too readily from empirical evidence to a summation of its social and symbolic effects. This is clearest in his claim that:

> In the first half of the twentieth century … two rival intelligentsia squared off against each other, competing for audiences and prestige. One was middle-class, university-educated and modernist, supported largely by patronage and private incomes; the other was based in the working and clerking classes, mainly Board School graduates and the self-educated, more classical in their tastes, but fearlessly engaged in popular journalism and the literary marketplace. One appealed to an elite audience; the other wrote best-sellers and feature films. One was inspired by Marx, Nietzsche and Freud, the other Carlyle, Dickens, and Ruskin. One read and wrote for the *New Age* and *New Statesman*, the other *T.P.'s Weekly* and *John O'London's*.[88]

One is driven to wonder into which of these two camps Rose would slot Bennett. Or Wells or Galsworthy, for that matter. I have concentrated on Bennett as an exemplary figure but in many ways he is not a special case. His career and the kinds of public debates which it sparked have simply served to highlight the period's discourses around popular and literary fiction and their relationships to gender and class. But

---

[88]   Rose, p. 430.

as I have demonstrated, many authors, including Watts-Dunton in the 1890s, wrote bestsellers *and* highbrow criticism. Watts-Dunton wrote for the *Athenaeum*. Bennett and Wells wrote for the *New Age*. Some authors combined a self-educated working or clerking class background with the writing of literary fiction (we need only think of Lawrence) or, conversely, an elite education with the writing of bestsellers (while both Bennett and Wells were certainly at least partly self-educated, Galsworthy went to Oxford).

The 'squaring off' described by Rose is also somewhat overstated; not all writers, even amongst those whom we might be able to slot into one category or the other, actually thought there was a war on. Lawrence read Bennett closely and even learned from him. Like Bennett, Galsworthy was a lifelong friend of Conrad. In a letter to Galsworthy praising a fable he had written, Conrad expresses his admiration in terms that indicate an honest belief both in the work's literary merit and in its author's understanding of the difference between literature and journalism: 'I revel in your grave, earnest slyness going deeper and deeper, leaving no nook unexplored and always managing somehow to achieve some bit of fine and beautiful expression. The direct, almost naive preciseness of [the hero's] meditation fit a mind capable of taking a serious departure from a newspaper par'.[89] This friendship, and the affectionate and respectful correspondence that is its legacy, serve as reminders that in their own time some of the literary elite whom we have tended to deify looked upon some of their best selling contemporaries as artists, not as enemies.

David Lodge has pointed out, too, that 'realism is a mode of writing derived from consciousness rather than the unconscious, the daylight rather than the night-time world, the ego rather than the id: that is why it is such an excellent mode for *depicting* repression'.[90] We might add here that the repression that most concerns Bennett in the *Clayhanger* trilogy is of several kinds. It is the repression by the aspirant middle classes of its own roots in the abyss. It is the repression of its sexuality, its relation to modernity's reformation of gender, its overwhelming sense of liminality and confusion. *Clayhanger*'s project was in large part to demonstrate that the forces of history had attempted to silence and dismiss an entire generation. The tools might have been old, but Bennett resharpened them, adding more experimental facets to his art in the recognition that a new and still-forming subject demanded new methods. His chosen subject was not the working-class poverty that provided the material for traditional realist texts, but a new underclass whose predicament was seldom written about without the scorn Gissing had heaped – and Forster was still heaping – on its head. In attacking Bennett's methods, Woolf was also disavowing his subject matter, attempting to claim a new high ground for art which owed as much to the old class-inflected taste wars as it did to the search for a new literary form.

---

[89]   Joseph Conrad, letter to John Galsworthy, 1 November 1910. *The Letters of Joseph Conrad*, 4, 1908–11, eds Frederick R. Karl and Laurence Davies (Cambridge, 1990), p. 384.
[90]   David Lodge, *The Modes of Modern Writing: Metaphor, Metonymy, and the Typology of Modern Literature* (London, 1977), p. 45.

Conclusion

The war between Bennett and Woolf has probably received more critical attention than it deserves. As I have attempted to show throughout this book, the relationships between art, the market, men, women, writers, publishers, readers and all the networks of literary dissemination in the late nineteenth and early twentieth centuries in England were far more complex than a long-running critical debate about literary form is able to express, even when this debate is so deeply embedded in gender politics. Form is intimately related to the relationships between these social phenomena. But it is only a part of what made them what they were. In order to begin to understand the relationships between gender and form, we need to understand the other relational forces with which they were surrounded, and to which they owe at least part of their symbolic positions. This is why a Bourdieuan model has, I think, proved fruitful. His work on gender, insisting as it does on reading patriarchy as a system of dominance – 'symbolic violence' – that gets its power from a process of naturalisation of what are in fact socially constructed oppositions ('"genders" as sexually characterized habitus')[1] might seem naïve to feminist critics who have long been aware of this fact. But considered as part of his larger project, his interest in systems of social relations, it points the way to a more complex reading of gender, one which enables a consideration of its embedding in culture, makes visible more of its hidden machinations, and perhaps explodes more of its myths. For literary historians there are a number of benefits to this approach.

Bourdieu's work on textuality is minimal. Indeed, his reading of Woolf's *To the Lighthouse*, while valuable, also on one level appears as something of an entrenchment of the gender myths he is trying to expose, in that it attributes perspicacity to a female character simply, it seems, because she was created by a canonical feminist author, and thus risks reading literature as some sort of truth. Fiction, as I have shown, is evidence of a sort. But the traces of symbolic violence which it displays cannot be decoded quite as straightforwardly as Bourdieu here implies. But then, textual analysis is not Bourdieu's concern. And as Toril Moi has pointed out, ultimately his value for literary historians lies elsewhere: 'What his analyses may help us to see … is the way in which certain texts enter into field-related intertextual relations with other texts'.[2] It is this system of intertextual – and indeed historical and sociological – relations with which I have been concerned in this book. Considering reading, writing, publishing and bookselling through a Bourdieuan lens, as practices just as imbued with social

---

[1]   Bourdieu, *Masculine Domination*, p. 3.
[2]   Moi, 'Appropriating Bourdieu', p. 296.

symbolism as – say – eating, or sport, or marriage rituals, has enabled me to step away somewhat from the enduring and ultimately empty idea of 'art' as a cosmological mystery which 'naturally' privileges white middle-class Western men.

A relational exploration of the literary field in England from 1880–1914 has demonstrated that books and the formation of taste in books are social signifiers loaded with symbolic capital; as a result, in my reading 'the text' has shrunk to what I consider its proper position as only part of what constitutes a book's meaning in culture. I demonstrated that male and female authors wrote as they did, and negotiated their markets as they did, because of deeply embedded, largely silent acts of 'symbolic violence' which privileged biological men over biological women, but also created gendered literary forms which changed their shape when under threat in order to maintain the *doxa* of masculine artistry. In the Public Library it was gendered mid-nineteenth-century discourses about public citizenship acting alongside that public's demand for novels that helped to formulate a male-dominated canon of classics and to encourage the link between reading and social identity. While patriarchal structures were also in place at the railway bookstall, their exertion of control was very different. It allowed travelling readers some license to relax into the myth of a tolerant bourgeois family framework that protected their interests and reputations even as it created new forms in order to give them what they wanted. As Lewis Melville commented in 1910, though, there was some kind of bourgeois consensus that 'while the public knows what it wants, it does not know what is good for it'.[3] The classics series, I have suggested, is situated in this anxious space between duty and desire, and it highlights the complexity of the reader's position in that period as s/he is simultaneously offered and denied access to the cultural capital attached to classic literature.

There are limits to what a Bourdieuan analysis can reveal, of course, which point to a need for more empirical work. We cannot, for example, know for sure how the buyer of a classics series felt about his/her purchases, or whether s/he even read them. Jonathan Rose has used working-class autobiographies to prove that 'for autodidacts, almost any one of the English classics could produce [a] kind of epiphany'.[4] But by the turn of the nineteenth/twentieth centuries a classic's symbolic value had long been recognised, and memoirists might be prone to a certain amount of self-aggrandisement. In addition, the classic itself is not something dropped from heaven in a pure, unmediated form; it is subject to fluctuations in taste and even textual verity, a fact which Rose's careful selection of extracts has (perhaps necessarily, but nonetheless unfortunately) obscured. Watts-Dunton's *Aylwin* was a classic according to OUP. So was George Borrow's work on gypsies. Charles Mackay, Marie Corelli's father, was a classic poet according to the editors of the Chandos Classics. Tolstoy was a classic fit for the lower classes only when he had been expurgated. Fielding was often banned altogether. Rose frequently mentions Dickens as an author who spoke to the working classes and uses this as an example of their capacity for innate taste

---

3   Lewis Melville, review of *Clayhanger*, *Bookman*, Vol. 39, October 1910, p. 45.
4   Rose, p. 406.

as though Dickens's status has always been a given, but to Q.D. Leavis he was the reading of the 'uneducated' alongside Marie Corelli and Edgar Wallace. To her, too, Charlotte Bronte was simply a Barclay or a Corelli from a better class and time.

It would, of course, be foolish to argue that all books are equal and deny that some are better than others. But we should attempt to understand how that qualitative judgement was formed and viewed during a book's lifetime, perhaps most particularly once it had gained its classic label. What we need to consider alongside readers' own responses as recommended by Rose is evidence – as much as we can gather – about the selection, production and ideology surrounding a book or a series of books. Only in this way can we begin to understand literature's relation to culture outside the myth of its purity, influence and endurance as 'art'.

There are many necessary omissions from this book. I have not, for example, considered the relationship between writers, publishers and literary agents except in passing. But agents were obviously a crucial part of the professionalisation of literature which I traced in Chapters 4 and 5, as well as a crucial part of how a work's symbolic value came to be understood in that agents both suggested changes to a text and made transparent its relation to the market. Nor have I considered the second-hand bookstalls from which so many readers acquired their books, or investigated in detail the actual contents of railway bookstalls which, as Stephen Colclough has recently suggested, displayed an important local as well as a national character.[5] All these things require another book, or several books.

What I have attempted here is a series of case studies that point to the need for more work on writing, publishing, distribution and reading practices which takes into account the nuances of the construction of a book's meaning as a cultural object in relation to other cultural objects in a field of production. Without these nuances, I have suggested, we are in danger of buying wholesale into the 'romantic vacuum' myth, which would be to assume that art and distinction are unchanging and beyond the forces of history of whatever sort. In fact, art and distinction change constantly – and they do so as a direct response to the forces in the field around them. Understanding these forces is crucial, perhaps especially as a way of understanding the emergence of a movement as politically and formally important as modernism.

Without the mass production of cheap classics which lessened their distinctive rarity, the empty space at the top of the canon might have invited a very different form of literary innovation. Without mass literacy and modern transport technologies there would in all likelihood have been no swing towards the easily accessible, fast-paced popular narrative associated with the lower middle classes that encouraged the development of its exact opposite. Victorian moral philanthropy created the Public Library, while Victorian moral panic insisted that it remain middlebrow and conservative, helping to ensure that narrative complexity, relative obscenity and

---

5   Stephen Colclough, 'Newspapers, Books and Periodicals, Advertisements, Handbills and Placards: The Creation of the English Railway Reader 1848–1880', paper given at the 10th annual SHARP conference, London, 11 July 2002.

shock value were likely to be an integral part of any new art form. The diversity and success of the mass publishing industry helped to encourage a new emphasis on limited editions, sponsorship and coterie publishing as the only radical places to go. Edwardian popular fiction's anxieties about gender, immigration and Empire came hard on the heels of the Victorian literary man's public involvement with issues of gender, class and race, and the Victorian literary woman's more complex and difficult relationship with those issues. Edwardian serious fiction, such as Bennett's, attempted to meld the flawed past and the uncertain present in order to explore the difficulties they had created for the new lower middle classes. Modernism's swing towards fascism can be seen as a next logical step – an art seeking to be free of social conscience and its mass appropriation, is an art advocating purification on all sorts of levels.

The struggles of women modernists to be recognised as critics as well as poets and novelists owe much to these traditions. Authors such as Caine and Corelli fought hard and fruitlessly to have their work accepted as art. As the author's professional position improved, the next generation – the Barclays and the Bennetts – admitted there was a distinct difference between the great and the merely popular, but announced that it did not matter for both had equal cultural validity. In a class-based society like Britain with a long history of attaching social significance to literary forms and tastes, these forces were bound to create an explosive response. Perhaps most important of all, in this period 'literary' or 'art' publishing was squeezed by market forces – forces inextricably connected with specific (usually lower class) readerships – as never before. This meant that the radical new literary movements of the early twentieth century inherited – and indeed intensified – deeply entrenched assumptions about the relationships between cultural competency, class and art. Without the widespread cultural knowledge circulating around publishing, distribution and literary form, literary modernism might have taken a very different political shape. To ignore this in favour of a text- or author-based hagiology is to write out of history the ideologies which – however uncomfortable we might find them –permeated and perhaps even drove the most sophisticated work of its time.

Bibliography

Primary Sources

Aesop's Fables (London: Routledge, 1886).

Aesop's Fables (London: Everyman, 1913).

A Hundred Years of Library Service (Winchester, 1952), Winchester Public Library, Department of Local Studies.

Alphabetical Catalogue of the Subscription Library, York, Instituted 1794, with the Rules of the Society and a List of Members (York: Thomas Wilson and Sons, 1842).

Annual Reports of the City of Leeds Public Free Library, 1870–1915, Leeds Public Library Records.

Annual Reports of the Literary and Philosophical Society of Newcastle-Upon-Tyne 1862–1903, Newcastle Literary and Philosophical Society Records.

Annual Reports of the Public Libraries Committee of the Town and County of the Town of Southampton 1888–1915, Southampton City Library Records.

Annual Reports of the Winchester Library and Museum Committee 1878–1910, Winchester City Library, Department of Local Studies.

The Athenaeum.

Austen, Jane, *Northanger Abbey* (1818; Oxford: Oxford World's Classics, 1990).

Author Files: John Aubrey's *Lives of the Poets*. Oxford University Press Archives.

Barclay, Florence, *The Rosary* (1909; London: Putnam and Co., 1948).

——, *Through the Postern Gate* (1914; London: Putnam and Co., 1944).

——, *The Broken Halo* (London: Putnam and Co., n.d.).

——, *The Mistress of Shenstone* (London: Putnam and Co., n.d.).

——, *The Following of the Star* (London: Putnam and Co., n.d.).

——, *In Hoc Vince*: *The Story of a Red Cross Flag* (London: Putnam and Co., 1915).

Bell, Lady, *At the Works: A Study of a Manufacturing Town* (1907; London: Virago, 1985).

Bennett, Arnold, *Books and Persons: Being Comments on a Past Epoch 1908–11* (London: Chatto and Windus, 1917).

——, *A Man From the North* (London: John Lane, 1898).

——, *The Old Wives' Tale* (1908; London: Everyman, 1944).

——, *Clayhanger* (1910; London: Eyre Methuen, 1976).

——, *Hilda Lessways* (1911; Harmondsworth: Penguin, 1975).

——, *These Twain* (1916; Harmondsworth: Penguin, 1975).

——, *The Card* (1911; London: Eyre Methuen, 1973).

——, *Letters of Arnold Bennett*, 2, 1889–1915 (Oxford: Oxford University Press, 1968).

——, *The Journal of Arnold Bennett 1896–1910*, ed. Newman Flower (New York: The Viking Press, 1932).

The Bookman.

Bowman, Anne, *The Common Things of Everyday Life: A Book of Home Wisdom for Mothers and Daughters* (London: Routledge, 1857).

Brittain, Vera, *Testament of Youth: An Autobiographical Study of the Years 1900–1925* (1933; London: Virago, 1999).

Buchan, John, *Prester John* (1910; London: Nelson 1925).

Caine, Sir Thomas Henry Hall, *Recollections of Dante Gabriel Rossetti* (London: Elliott Stock, 1882).

——, *The Bondman* (1890; London: Heinemann, 1921).

——, *The Bondman Play* (London: Daily Mail, 1906).

——, *The Manxman* (London: Heinemann, 1898).

——, *The Prodigal Son* (London: Heinemann, 1904).

——, *My Story* (London: Heinemann, 1908).

——, *The White Prophet*, vols 1 and 2 (London: Heinemann, 1909).

——, *The Woman Though Gavest Me* (London: Heinemann, 1913).

Cassell's Family Magazine.

Century Magazine.

Conrad, Joseph, *The Collected Letters of Joseph Conrad*, vol. 2, ed. Frederick R. Karl (Cambridge: Cambridge University Press, 1986).

——, *The Collected Letters of Joseph Conrad*, vol. 4, ed. Frederick R. Karl and Laurence Davies (Cambridge: Cambridge University Press, 1990).

The Contemporary Review.

Corelli, Marie, *The Mighty Atom* (London: Hutchinson, 1896).

——, *Temporal Power: A Study in Supremacy* (London: Methuen, 1902).

——, *Free Opinions Freely Expressed on Certain Phases of Modern Social Life and Conduct* (London: Archibald Constable, 1905).

Davenport Adams, W.H., *Woman's Work and Worth* (London: John Hogg, 1880).

Defoe, Daniel, *Robinson Crusoe* (London: Chandos Classics, 1878).

Dent, J.M., *The House of Dent 1888–1938* (London: J.M. Dent and Sons Ltd, 1938).

Dickens, Charles. *Dombey and Son* (1846–8; London: Penguin, 1985)

Du Maurier, George, *Trilby* (1894; London: Orion, 1994).

Early Material Relating to Free Libraries, York City Reference Library, Ref: YO72.4.

First General Report of the Public Library Committee 1893–4 (York). York City Reference Library, Ref: Y352.

Farr, Florence, *Modern Woman: Her Intentions* (London: Frank Palmer, 1910).

Fielding, Henry. *Tom Jones* (London: Routledge, 1867).

——, *Tom Jones* (London: Routledge, 1885, 1889 and 1896).

Foley, Alice, *A Bolton Childhood* (Manchester: Manchester University Extra-Mural Department and the Northwestern District of the Workers' Educational Association, 1973).

Ford, Ford Madox, *The Good Soldier* (1915; London: Norton, 1995).

The Fortnightly Review.

Forster, E.M., *Howards End* (1910; London: Penguin, 1989).

The Gentleman's Magazine.

Gissing, George, *New Grub Street* (1891; London: Eveleigh, Nash and Grayson, 1928).

——, *In The Year of Jubilee* (New York: D. Appleton and Co., 1895).

——, *Our Friend the Charlatan* (London: Chapman and Hall, 1901).

Glyn, Elinor, *Three Weeks*, 2nd edn (London: Duckworth, 1907).

Good Words.

Greenwood, Thomas, *Public Libraries: A History of the Movement and a Manual for the Organization and Management of Rate-Supported Libraries*, 4th ed. (London: Cassell, 1891).

The Hampshire Chronicle.

The Hampshire Independent.

Hansard Parliamentary Papers, 108, 3rd Series, January–February 1850.

Harrison, W. Ainsworth, *The Star-Chamber* (London: Routledge, 1861).

Harrison, Frederic, 'Charlotte Bronte's Place in Literature' (London: Edward Arnold, 1895).

Hughes, M.V., *A London Family 1870–1900* (Oxford: Oxford University Press, 1946).

Kelly's Directory of Hampshire 1903 (London: Kelly's Directories, 1903).

Jerome, Jerome K. (ed.), *My First Book* (London: Chatto and Windus, 1894).

Kimber, Sir Sidney, *Thirty-Eight Years of Public Life in Southampton* (London and Southampton: published privately, 1949).

Leeds City Council Libraries and Arts Committee Minute Books 1870–1914, Refs: SRQ 352.9LEE and SRQ 352.022 LS17, Leeds Public Library Records.

Leeds Public Libraries: Catalogue of the Central Lending Library 1894. Leeds Public Library Records.

Letterbooks of Henry Frowde, 1904–1914, Oxford University Press Archives.

The Library.

Library Association Minute Book, May 1892–February 1898, Library Association Archives.

Library Association Record, Vol. 1, Part 1, January–June 1899, Library Association Archives.

Library Association Yearbook, 1891. Library Association Archives.

The Library World.

London Metropolitan Archives, Refs: LMA 1297/Met 10/264; LMA 1297/Met 10/862.

Macmillan's Magazine.

Minute Books of the Whitechapel public library Commissioners 1892–1906, Tower Hamlets Local History Library and Archive.

The National Review.

The New Review.

The Newsbasket.

The Nineteenth Century

Pall Mall Magazine

The Passenger's Companion

The Publishers' Circular and Booksellers' Record.

The Quarterly Review.

The Railway Sheet and Official Gazette.

The Review of Reviews.

Ruskin, John, *Selected Writings*, ed. Philip Davis (1865; London: J.M. Dent, 1995).

Smiles, Samuel, *Self-help: with Illustrations of Conduct and Perseverance* (1859; London: John Murray, 1879).

——, *Character: A Book of Noble Characteristics* (1871; London: John Murray, 1905).

Smith, W. H., Archives. Letters 1908–1915; Refs: WHS 56/1–4;WHS 244/1–3; WHS 123/ 1–6.

The Spectator.

Sub-Committees Minute Book 1877–1897. Winchester Records Office, Ref: W/B5/22/2.

Sub-Committees Minute Book 1904–10. Winchester Records Office, Ref: W/B5/28/1.

The Times Index.

The Times.

Tit-Bits.

Transactions and Proceedings of the First Annual Meeting of the Library Association (Chiswick Press, 1879), Archives of the Library Association.

Watson, Robert Spence, *The History of the Literary and Philosophical Society of Newcastle-Upon-Tyne*, Vol. I , 1793–1896 (London: Walter Scott Ltd, 1897).

Watts-Dunton, Theodore, *Aylwin*, 15th edn (1898; London: Hurst and Blackett, 1899).

Wells, H.G., *Kipps: The Story of a Simple Soul* (London: Oldhams, 1905).

The Westminster Review.

Wood, Mrs Henry, *East Lynne* (1861; London: Everyman, 1994).

Woolf, Virginia, *The Essays of Virginia Woolf*, Vol. III, ed. Andrew McNeillie (London: Hogarth Press, 1988).

——, *The Essays of Virginia Woolf*, Vol. IV, ed. Andrew McNeillie (London: Hogarth Press, 1994).

Woman.

World's Classics Suggestions File, OUP Archives.

York City Council Minutes 1892–93, York City Reference Library, Ref: Y352.
The York Herald.

Secondary Sources

Books

Allen, Vivian, *Hall Caine: Portrait of a Victorian Romancer* (Sheffield Academic Press: 1997).
Altick, Richard D., *The English Common Reader: A Social History of the Mass Reading Public 1800–1900* (London and Chicago: University of Chicago Press, 1957).
Ardis, Ann, *New Women, New Novels: Feminism and Early Modernism* (New Brunswick and London: Rutgers University Press, 1990).
Barker, Nicolas, *The Oxford University Press and the Spread of Learning: An Illustrated History 1478–1978* (Oxford: Clarendon Press, 1978).
Batchelor, John, *The Edwardian Novelists* (London: Duckworth, 1982).
Bennett, Tony, *The Birth of the Museum: History, Theory, Politics* (London: Routledge, 1995).
Bigland, Eileen, *Marie Corelli: The Woman and the Legend* (London: Jarrolds, 1953).
Black, Alistair, *A New History of the English Public Library: Social and Intellectual Contexts 1850–1914* (Leicester: Leicester University Press, 1996).
Black, Jerry, *The History of the Jews Free School since 1732* (London: Tymsder Publishing, 1998).
Bland, Lucy, *Banishing the Beast: English Feminism and Sexual Morality 1885–1914* (Harmondsworth: Penguin, 1995).
Bourdieu, Pierre, *Outline of a Theory of Practice*, trans. by Richard Nice (Cambridge: Cambridge University Press, 1985).
——, *Distinction: A Social Critique of the Judgement of Taste* (1979; London: Routledge, 1992).
——, *The Field of Cultural Production: Essays on Art and Literature* (Cambridge: Polity Press, 1993).
——, *Masculine Domination*, trans. by Richard Nice (Cambridge: Polity Press, 2001).
Bowlby, Rachel, *Just Looking: Consumer Culture in Dreiser, Gissing and Zola* (London: Methuen, 1985).
Brake, Laurel, *Print in Transition 1850–1910: Studies in Media and Book History* (Basingstoke: Palgrave, 2001).
Brantlinger, Patrick, *The Reading Lesson: The Threat of Mass Literacy in Nineteenth-Century British Fiction* (Bloomington: Indiana University Press, 1998).
Bratton, Jackie, *New Readings in Theatre History* (Cambridge: Cambridge University Press, 2003).

Brooks, Peter, *The Melodramatic Imagination: Balzac, Henry James, Melodrama and the Mode of Excess* (New Haven and London: Yale University Press, 1976).

Carey, John, *The Intellectuals and the Masses: Pride and Prejudice among the Literary Intelligentsia, 1880–1939* (London: Faber and Faber, 1992).

Charney, Leo and Vanessa R. Schwartz (eds), *Cinema and the Invention of Modern Life* (Berkeley: University of California Press, 1995).

Chesney, Kellow, *The Victorian Underworld* (London: Purnell, 1970).

Cockburn, Claud, *Bestseller: The Books That Everyone Read 1900–1939* (London: Sidgwick and Jackson, 1972).

Collini, Stefan, *Public Moralists: Political Thought and Intellectual Life in Britain 1850–1930* (Oxford: Clarendon Press, 1991).

Daly, Nicholas, *Modernism, Romance and the* fin de siècle*: Popular Fiction and British Culture, 1880–1914* (Cambridge: Cambridge University Press, 1999).

Denning, Michael, *Mechanic Accents: Dime Novels and Working-Class Culture in America* (London: Verso, 1987).

DiBattista, Maria and Lucy McDiarmid (eds), *High and Low Moderns: Literature and Culture 1889–1939* (Oxford: Oxford University Press, 1996).

Drabble, Margaret, *Arnold Bennett: A Biography* (London: Weidenfeld and Nicolson, 1974).

Eagleton, Terry. *Literary Theory: an Introduction* (Minneapolis: University of Minnesota Press, 1983).

Eldridge Miller, Jane, *Rebel Women: Feminism, Modernism and the Edwardian Novel* (London: Virago, 1994).

Eliot, Simon, Some Patterns and Trends in British Publishing 1800–1919, *Occasional Papers of the Bibliographical Society*, 8 (London: The Bibliographical Society, 1994).

——, *A Measure of Popularity: Public Library Holdings of Twenty-Four Popular Authors, 1883–1912* (London: History of the Book On-Demand Series 2, 1992).

Ellmann, Richard, *Oscar Wilde* (London: Penguin, 1987).

Federico, Annette R., *Idol of Suburbia: Marie Corelli and Late-Victorian Literary Culture* (Charlottesville and London: University of Virginia Press, 2000).

Felski, Rita, *The Gender of Modernity* (Cambridge, MA: Harvard University Press, 1995).

Feltes, N.N., *Modes of Production of Victorian Novels* (Chicago: University of Chicago Press, 1986).

——, *Literary Capital and the Late Victorian Novel* (Madison, WN: University of Wisconsin Press, 1993).

Finkelstein, David and Alistair McCleery, *The Book History Reader* (London: Routledge, 2002).

Flint, Kate, *The Woman Reader 1837–1914* (Oxford: Clarendon Press, 1993).

Frisby, David, *Fragments of Modernity: Theories of Modernity in the work of Simmel, Kracauer and Benjamin* (Cambridge: Polity Press, 1985).

Gilmour, Robin, *The Victorian Period: The Intellectual and Cultural Context of English Literature 1830–1890* (London: Longmans, 1993).

Habermas, Jürgen, *The Structural Transformation of the Public Sphere: An Inquiry into a Category of Bourgeois Society*, trans. by Thomas Burger (Cambridge: Polity Press, 1989).

Haining, Peter (ed.), *The Penny Dreadful* (London: Victor Gollancz, 1975).

Harrison, Thomas, *1910: The Emancipation of Dissonance* (Berkeley: University of California Press, 1996).

Hansen, Miriam, *Babel and Babylon: Spectatorship in American Silent Film* (Cambridge, MA: Harvard University Press, 1991).

Hawthorn, Jeremy (ed.), *The British Working-Class Novel in the Twentieth Century* (London: Edward Arnold, 1984).

Hepburn, James (ed.), *Arnold Bennett: The Critical Heritage* (London: Routledge and Kegan Paul, 1981).

Hobsbawm, Eric J., *Industry and Empire* (Harmondsworth: Penguin, 1969).

——, *The Age of Empire 1875–1914* (London: Abacus, 1994).

Huyssen, Andreas, *After the Great Divide: Modernism, Mass Culture, Postmodernism* (Bloomington: Indian University Press, 1986).

Hynes, Samuel, *Edwardian Occasions: Essays on English Writing in the Early Twentieth Century* (London: Routledge and Kegan Paul, 1972).

——, *The Edwardian Turn of Mind: The First World War and English Culture* (Princeton, New Jersey: Princeton University Press, 1969).

James, Louis, *Fiction for the Working Man: 1830–50: A Study of the Literature Produced for the Working Classes in Early Victorian Urban England* (Harmondsworth: Penguin, 1974).

Jenkins, Richard, *Key Sociologists: Pierre Bourdieu* (London: Routledge, 1992).

Kaegbein, Paul, Bryan Luckham and Valeria Stelmach (eds), *Studies on Research and Reading in Libraries: Approaches and Results From Several Countries* (Munich and London: K.G. Saur, 1991).

Keating, Peter, *The Haunted Study: A Social History of the English Novel 1875–1914* (London: Secker and Warburg, 1989).

Kirby, Lynne, *Parallel Tracks: The Railroad and Silent Cinema* (Exeter: University of Exeter Press, 1997).

Leavis, Q.D., *Fiction and the Reading Public* (1932; London: Chatto and Windus, 1965).

Ledger, Sally, *The New Woman: Fiction and Feminism at the* fin-de-siècle (Manchester: Manchester University Press, 1997).

Lee, Alan J., *The Origins of the Popular Press 1855–1914* (London: Croom Helm, 1976).

Linsley, Robert, *Railways in Camera: Archive Photographs of the Great age of Steam from the Public Records Office 1860–1913* (Stroud: Alan Sutton Co. and the Public Records Office, 1996).

Lodge, David, *The Modes of Modern Writing: Metaphor, Metonymy, and the Typology of Modern Literature* (London: Edward Arnold, 1977).

McAleer, Joseph, *Popular Reading and Publishing in Britain 1914–1950* (Oxford: Clarendon Press, 1992).

McDonald, Peter D., *British Literary Culture and Publishing Practice 1880–1914* (Cambridge: Cambridge University Press, 1997).

Mitchell, Vic, *Ashford: From Steam to Eurostar* (Midhurst: Middleton Press, 1996).

Moi, Toril, *What is a Woman and Other Essays* (Oxford: Oxford University Press, 1999).

Moretti, Franco, *Atlas of the European Novel 1800–1900* (London: Verso, 1998).

Morris, R.J.B., *Parliament and the Public Libraries: A Survey of Legislative Activity Promoting the Municipal Library Service in England and Wales 1850–1976* (London: Mansell, 1977).

Mumby, Frank Arthur and Ian Norrie, *Publishing and Bookselling*, 5th edn (1930; London: Jonathan Cape, 1974).

Munford, W.A., *Penny Rate: Aspects of British Public Library History 1850–1950* (London: The Library Association, 1951).

Murison, W.J., *The Public Library: Its Origins, Purpose, and Significance as a Social Institution* (London: George C. Harrap and Co., 1955).

O'Day, Alan (ed.), *The Edwardian Age: Conflict and Stability* (London: Macmillan, 1979).

Parish, Charles, *The History of the Lit and Phil, Vol. II: 1896–1989* (Newcastle: The Literary and Philosophical Society, 1990).

Pykett, Lyn, *The 'Improper' Feminine: The Woman's Sensation Novel and the New Woman Writing* (London and New York: Routledge, 1992).

——, *Engendering Fictions: The English Novel in the Early Twentieth Century* (London: Edward Arnold, 1995).

Radway, Janice A., *A Feeling for Books: The Book-of-the-Month-Club, Literary Taste, and Middle-Class Desire* (Chapel Hill and London: University of North Carolina Press, 1997).

Rainey, Lawrence, *Institutions of Modernism: Literary Elites and Public Culture* (New Haven and London: Yale University Press, 1998).

Ransom, Teresa, *The Mysterious Miss Marie Corelli: Queen of Victorian Bestsellers* (Stroud: Sutton Publishing, 1999).

Rappaport, Erika Diane, *Shopping for Pleasure: Women in the Making of London's West End* (Princeton, NJ: Princeton University Press, 2000).

Rose, Jonathan, *The Intellectual Life of the British Working Classes* (New Haven and London: Yale University Press, 2001).

Rubin, Joan Shelley, *The Making of Middlebrow Culture* (Chapel Hill and London: University of North Carolina Press, 1992).

Schivelbusch, Wolfgang, *The Railway Journey: Trains and Travel in the Nineteenth Century* (New York: Urizen, 1979).

Simmel, Georg, *On Individuality and Social Forms: Selected Writings*, ed. by Donald L. Levine (Chicago: University of Chicago Press, 1971).

——, *The Conflict in Modern Culture and Other Essays*, trans. and ed. by K. Peter Etzkorn (New York: Teachers College Press, 1968).

Simmons, Jack, *The Victorian Railway* (London: Thames and Hudson, 1991).

Spaeth, Sigmund, *A History of Popular Music in America* (New York: Random House, 1948).

Squillace, Robert, *Modernism, Modernity, and Arnold Bennett* (London: Associated University Presses, 1997).

St John, John, *William Heinemann: A Century of Publishing* (London: Heinemann, 1990).

Sutcliffe, Peter, *The Oxford University Press: An Informal History* (Oxford: Oxford University Press, 1978).

Sutherland, John, *Victorian Novelists and Publishers* (London: The Athlone Press, 1976).

——, *Victorian Fiction: Writers, Publishers, Readers* (London: Macmillan, 1995).

The Life of Florence Barclay, by one of her daughters (London and New York: Putnam, 1921).

Thompson, Nicola Diane, *Reviewing Sex: Gender and the Reception of Victorian Novels* (London: Macmillan, 1996).

Thompson, F. M. L., *The Rise of Respectable Society: A Social History of Victorian Britain 1830–1900* (London: Fontana, 1988).

Trotter, David, *The English Novel in History 1895–1920* (London: Routledge, 1993).

Walkowitz, Judith R., *City of Dreadful Delight: Narratives of Sexual Danger in Late-Victorian London* (London: Virago, 1992).

Williams, Raymond, *The Long Revolution* (1961; London: Hogarth Press, 1992).

——, *The Politics of Modernism*, ed. by Tony Pinkney (London: Verso, 1989).

Wilson, Charles, *First With the News: The History of W. H. Smith 1792–1972* (London: Jonathan Cape, 1985).

Wolff, Hurt H. (ed.), *The Sociology of Georg Simmel* (New York: Free Press, 1950).

Articles and Chapters in Edited Collections

Ardis, Ann, 'E.M. Hull, Mass Market Romance and the New Woman Novel in the Early Twentieth Century', *Women's Writing*, 3 (1996): 289–99.

Bizup, Joseph, 'Architecture, Railroads, and Ruskin's Rhetoric of Bodily Form', *Prose Studies: History, Theory, Criticism*, 21 (April 1998): 74–94.

Daly, Nicholas, 'Railway Novels: Sensation Fiction and the Modernization of the Senses', *English Literary History*, 66 (Summer 1999): 461–87.

Fredeman, William E., 'Fundamental Brainwork: the Correspondence Between Dante Gabriel Rossetti and Thomas Hall Caine', *Journal of the Australasian Universities Language and Literature Association*, 52 (1979): 209–31.

Gilbert, Geoffrey. 'Intestinal Violence: Wyndham Lewis and the Critical Poetics of the Modernist Career', *Critical Quarterly*, 36 (Autumn 1994): 86–125.

Guillory, John, 'Bourdieu's Refusal', *Modern Language Quarterly*, 58 (December 1997): 367–98.

Hammond, Mary, 'Hall Caine and the Melodrama on Page, Stage and Screen, *Nineteenth Century Theatre and Film*, 31 (Summer 2004): 39–57.

Hansen, Miriam, 'Early Cinema: Whose Public Sphere?', in Thomas Elsaesser (ed.), *Early Cinema: Space, Frame, Narrative* (London: BFI, 1990).

Heidelberger, Michael, 'Force, Law and Experiment: The Evolution of Helmholtz's Philosophy of Science', in David Cahan (ed.), *Hermann von Helmholtz and the Foundations of Nineteenth-Century Science* (Berkeley: University of California Press, 1993).

Hiley, Nicholas, '"Can't You Find Me Something Nasty?": Circulating Libraries and Literary Censorship in Britain from the 1890s to the 1910s', in Michael Harris and Robin Meyers (eds), *Censorship and the Control of Print in England and France 1600–1910* (London: St Paul's Bibliographies, 1992).

Jameson, Frederic, 'Authentic Ressentiment: The "Experimental" Novels of Gissing', *Nineteenth Century Fiction*, 31 (September 1976): 127–49.

Kershner, R.B., 'Modernism's Mirror: The Sorrows of Marie Corelli', in Nikki Lee Manos and Meri-Jane Rochelson (eds), *Tranforming Genres: New Approaches to British Fiction of the 1890s* (New York: St Martin's Press, 1994).

Kowalczyk, Richard L., 'In Vanished Summertime: Marie Corelli and Popular Culture, *Journal of Popular Culture*, 7 (1974): 850–63.

Marcus, Laura, 'Oedipus Express: Trains, Trauma and Detective Fiction', *New Formations*, 41 (Autumn 2000): 173–88.

Rose, Jonathan, 'Rereading the English Common Reader: A Preface to a History of Audiences', *Journal of the History of Ideas*, 3 (1992): 47–70.

Films

Kiss in the Tunnel (UK, dir. G.A.Smith, 1899).
Kiss in the Tunnel (UK, Banforth and Co., 1899).

Unpublished Papers

Colclough, Stephen, 'Newspapers, Books and Periodicals, Advertisements, Handbills and Placards: The Creation of the English Railway Reader', 10th Annual Conference of the Society for the History of Authorship Reading and Publishing, London, 11 July 2002.

Skelton, Matthew, 'Re-presenting H.G. Wells: The Literary Agency of London and *Tono-Bungay*', 10th Annual Conference of the Society for the History of Authorship, Reading and Publishing, London, 10 July 2002.

Index

For Product Safety Concerns and Information please contact our EU representative GPSR@taylorandfrancis.com
Taylor & Francis Verlag GmbH, Kaufingerstraße 24, 80331 München, Germany

www.ingramcontent.com/pod-product-compliance
Ingram Content Group UK Ltd.
Pitfield, Milton Keynes, MK11 3LW, UK
UKHW020956180425
457613UK00019B/710

* 9 7 8 0 3 6 7 8 8 7 9 2 6 *